O9-BUA-482

SPECIAL FORCES IN ACTION

IRAQ • SYRIA • AFGHANISTAN • AFRICA • BALKANS

SPECIAL FORCES IN ACTION

IRAQ • SYRIA • AFGHANISTAN • AFRICA • BALKANS

ALEXANDER STILWELL

amber
BOOKS

First published in 2007

This updated edition printed in 2015

Published by
Amber Books Ltd
74–77 White Lion Street
London
N1 9PF
United Kingdom
www.amberbooks.co.uk
Appstore: itunes.com/apps/amberbooksltd
Facebook: www.facebook.com/amberbooks
Twitter: @amberbooks

© 2015 Amber Books Ltd

All rights reserved. With the exception of quoting brief passages for the purpose of review no part of this publication may be reproduced without prior written permission from the Publisher. The information in this book is true and complete to the best of our knowledge. All recommendations are made without any guarantee on the part of the author or publisher, who also disclaim any liability incurred in connection with the use of this data or specific details.

ISBN 978-1-78274-254-8

Project Editor: Michael Spilling
Designer: Brian Rust
Picture Research: Terry Forshaw

Printed and bound in China

CONTENTS

INTRODUCTION

This book is a history of special forces in action from 1990 to the time of writing. Owing to the nature of special operations, the more recent the history becomes the more obscure it is. It would be a cause for concern if this were not the case. Even medal citations for British special forces personnel do not provide details of the circumstances in which they were won. Having served in the British Territorial Army and having trained with special forces personnel, this author has no intention of exposing or compromising current or future operations.

Special forces as understood today are an elite cadre normally associated with particular services – be it army, navy or air force – in different national armed forces. Each unit has its own history, with some dating back to World War II, as is the case with the British Special Air Service or United States Rangers. Others have a more recent background, haveing been formed in the post-war period.

BRITISH SPECIAL OPERATIONS

The spirit of special operations or of irregular forces that use unorthodox military tactics extends far back into early military history and is to some extent bound up with guerrilla warfare. Although the term 'guerrilla', meaning 'small war' in Spanish, refers specifically to the activities of Spanish and

Facing page: British SAS soldiers deploy into the Borneo jungle from a Westland Whirlwind helicopter, 1963.

Portuguese irregulars against occupying French forces in the Peninsular War (1808–14), it could equally be applied to the hit-and-run tactics of Goths and Huns against the Roman Empire. The Duke of Wellington was able to benefit from Spanish and Portuguese guerrilla activity because the guerrillas had a similar aim to his own, namely the removal of the occupying power. This underlines the importance of the political element in guerrilla warfare. The British were to use 'irregular' methods in northern India in the middle of the nineteenth century, with British officers passing themselves off as local tribesmen in an attempt to monitor and subvert Russian influence in Afghanistan. This 'Great Game' was in advance of its time and would be played again in the same area with considerable success by another world power, the United States. In World War I, T.E. Lawrence (Lawrence of Arabia) would also harness the latent native genius against an occupying power, this time against the Turks in Arabia. Here, perhaps, we come closer to the genesis of modern special forces, in that Lawrence, himself a serving British officer, not only embodied many of the personal characteristics that make a special forces soldier stand apart from a regular soldier, but he also explicitly identified many of the essential characteristics of irregular warfare and irregular soldiers in his classic account of the Arab Revolt, *Seven Pillars of Wisdom*.

Forced to remain in his tent while recovering from an illness, Lawrence pondered on the aims of warfare, bringing to mind the teachings of such

7

T.E. Lawrence (Lawrence of Arabia) in Arab clothing. His reasoning for the use of highly mobile small forces would prove highly influential.

military luminaries as Sun Tzu and Clausewitz. The classic aim of war was, of course, the destruction of the enemy through the process of battle. Breaking up the logic of his thinking into 'algebraic', 'biological' and 'psychological' elements, Lawrence proceeded to cogitate on how he could break the traditional syndrome of large forces contending against each other in a trial of strength. Knowing the Arab forces at his disposal were not strong enough to take on the large Turkish army, he concluded that if the Arab forces made a virtue of their mobility they might be 'an influence, an idea, a thing intangible, invulnerable, without front or back, drifting about like a gas.' To neutralize such a small mobile force in such a vast area of territory, the Turkish Army would be forced to deploy

hundreds of thousands of men with no guarantee of ever finding their target, which could just melt away into the desert. The policy he articulated was to never engage with the enemy but only to damage his material assets, creating associated havoc. His force must always have the advantage of surprise and they must always have a high level of informational intelligence about the enemy:

> *'Our cards were speed and time, not hitting power … in Arabia range was more than force, space greater than the power of armies.'*

Although Lawrence taught the Arabs under his command how to use modern weapons and explosives, he did not otherwise attempt to imbue in them conventional military discipline. As he says in his book,

> *'The efficiency of our forces was the professional efficiency of the single man … Our ideal should be to make our battle a series of single combats, our ranks a happy alliance of agile commanders -in-chief.'*

Lawrence understood the Arab tribesmen he was with, spoke their language, harnessed their native wisdom and led from the front, performing feats of endurance worthy of the hardiest Bedouin. Although unable to fit into the traditional military mould, as exemplified by the British Army, he was able to formulate tactics that made the Arab Revolt a key part of a successful British strategy in Arabia, leading to the occupation of Damascus and capture of Jerusalem.

The effectiveness of the mobile force inspired by Lawrence could have been diminished if it were not for the imaginative approach taken by the British commander in Palestine, Field Marshal Allenby. By harnessing Lawrence's skills as a 'special forces commander', rather than treating him as a mad extrovert, as other British officers were inclined to do, Allenby effectively deployed 'special forces' as a key part of his military strategy.

Lawrence had brought irregular operations into the sphere of military strategy and they were ready to become an essential part of military operations.

The next steps in this direction were to be taken in World War II and it is no surprise to discover that Winston Churchill, a great admirer of Lawrence, actively promoted the formation of military special forces in the form of the Commandos or that he sent a founder member of the Special Air Service, Fitzroy Maclean, as his personal representative and Commander of the British Military Mission to the Partisans in German-occupied Yugoslavia.

Churchill also established Combined Operations Headquarters (COHQ), which was to coordinate planning for special operations between all three services.

BIRTH IN THE DESERT

One thing leads to another, and David Stirling, a member of the commando section of the British Brigade of Guards, asked permission to use a small elite force to carry out raids against Field Marshal Rommel's Afrika Korps in the north African desert. Stirling was not only drawing on his experience with the Commandos but was also inspired by the activities of the Long Range Desert Group, founded by Ralph Bagnold. These were hardy volunteers, many of them New Zealanders, who ranged out in Chevrolet trucks through the Libyan desert to carry out reconnaissance and disruptive activities. The principles were the same as those established by Lawrence, namely maintaining the initiative in pin-point attacks, aimed primarily at the enemy's material assets, followed by fast withdrawal into the emptiness of the desert before the enemy could muster effective resistance. Special operations personnel were not equipped to carry out conventional attritional battles. Each and every man exhibited at least some of the qualities of a T.E. Lawrence, particularly personal endurance and tenacity, initiative, resourcefulness and determination.

One problem with the Long Range Desert Group was the size of its patrols. These could too easily be spotted from the air and attacked like many another military column. This was one of the problems David Stirling pondered on when, laid up in hospital in circumstances uncannily reminiscent of Lawrence's feverish ruminations on war, he deliberated on the potential for raids similar in many respects to Commando or LRDG raids but pared down to small teams of men, each trained to a very high level of proficiency in particular skills. Again, the characteristic established by Lawrence of 'agile commanders-in-chief' would be a prerequisite. Through their sheer professionalism and personal qualities, a team of only four men could have an impact on the enemy of a force 10 times its size. Surprise and the ability to withdraw quickly once the mission was accomplished were also key to Stirling's thinking.

Unlike Lawrence's Bedouin, Stirling would be drawing on men from the British and Commonwealth armed forces, but the disparity was otherwise not so great. It is no accident that Wilfred Thesiger, who chose to spend much of his time

This photograph shows David Stirling (standing, left) and Don Steele, commander of A Squadron SAS, at Siwa, North Africa.

The Long Range Desert Group carried out several raids in North Africa, proving to be an important stage in the development of the Special Air Service.

with the Marsh Arabs and who crossed the Empty Quarter, served with Stirling's SAS in the Western Desert during World War II.

The British, Australians, New Zealanders and others in the Allied forces adapted extremely well to this kind of warfare. But apart from a force set up by Otto Skorzeny, the Germans showed little

interest in special operations during World War II, though the Italians proved to be proficient at underwater attacks against Royal Navy ships in port in the Mediterranean.

SETTING EUROPE ABLAZE

Winston Churchill not only inspired the formation of the Commandos, which were active military units capable of carrying out operations direct from Britain and British territories worldwide, he was also instrumental in setting up the Special Operations

many of them women recruited from the First Aid Nursing Yeomanry (FANY), were disguised in civilian uniform and thereby devoid of any protection under the Geneva Conventions. They were actively sought by the SS Intelligence Service, the *Sicherheitsdienst*, created by the infamous Reinhard Heydrich, and one of the most ruthless intelligence organisations ever created. They could expect no mercy if captured. As it turned out, many of them were tracked down or betrayed in the incestuous world of espionage, then interrogated, tortured and executed in concentration camps such as Natzweiler. SOE agents were some of the first British service personnel to discover the reality of the German concentration camp system, believed by many to be tasteless propaganda.

Apart from France, SOE agents operated under similarly dangerous conditions in Algeria, Czechoslovakia, Greece, Italy, Norway, the Netherlands and Yugoslavia.

THE CHINDITS AND MERRILL'S MARAUDERS

The most pressing requirement for the British to re-educate themselves in unconventional warfare was in the jungles of Burma. Having lost Singapore, one of the worst military defeats ever suffered by the British Army, and having been chased out of Burma by the Japanese, the British knew they would have to learn fast or face the threat of losing the Jewel in the Crown itself – India.

Fortunately the new British area commander, General Slim, was just the man for the job. The Americans also had a tough commander in the area, General 'Vinegar Joe' Stilwell. Neither of these men scared easily. As Slim and Stilwell set about re-educating their forces in jungle warfare, they could also call on the help of some gifted commanders in Orde Wingate and Frank Dow Merrill.

Wingate and Merrill began doing exactly what the Japanese would not have expected them to do: conducting deep-penetration operations into the jungle to disrupt Japanese operations. They used small forces that were resupplied by air, doing almost exactly what Lawrence had done many years earlier. Although not all the operations yielded results, they had a positive effect on morale at a

Executive (SOE), initially under a civilian, Sir Charles Hambro, and then under an Army officer, Major General Sir Colin Gubbins. The task of SOE was to foment resistance in occupied Europe, and the difference between their role and the activities of special forces such as the SAS was that this was often an indirect process. In other words SOE agents would provide a link between the British and local resistance units such as the French Resistance.

Their operations involved extreme danger and called for a special sort of courage. SOE agents,

US 2nd Ranger Battalion train on the Isle of Wight, England in preparation for their assault on the Pointe du Hoc on 6 June 1944.

time when the British and Americans were on the back foot. With the help of airborne troops, the Chindits and Merrill's Marauders would successfully cut the Mandalay–Myitkyina railway and General Slim followed up by pushing the Japanese out of Burma. Slim, like Allenby, had seen how useful special forces could be in enabling a general strategic advance. In the post-war period, British special

forces were reorganized, with the Commandos coming under the umbrella of the Royal Marines and the SAS continuing to exist as a Territorial Army regiment. In the opinion of David Stirling himself, this Territorial status was important to the individuality and independence of the regiment as it enabled an osmosis with civilian life and reduced the risk of the regiment becoming too ritualized in a military sense.

US RANGERS

The success of the Commandos inspired the United States Army to form a similar unit. Led initially by William Darby, this elite light infantry force was to coin the evocative name of Rangers.

The Rangers' name is derived from Rogers' Rangers, a group of colonial militia operating on behalf of the English in the mid-eighteenth century. Feared by their enemies, the French and Indians, and regarded with some suspicion by the English, these early rangers demonstrated precisely the kind of daring, initiative and endurance that is characteristic of special forces. The colonial rangers carried out long-range patrols across difficult country, often in severe weather conditions, and struck out at the enemy when least expected. In this game they became as adept as the Native Americans themselves.

Having trained with the British Commandos in Scotland, the US Rangers famously scaled the heights of Pointe du Hoc during the D-Day landings and carried out a series of other daring operations both in Europe and in the Pacific. After a period of disbandment at the end of World War II, the Rangers were restored for operations in Korea and subsequently served with distinction in Vietnam.

THE GREEN BERETS

Like the British Royal Marine Commandos, who are issued a green beret on successful completion of a gruelling training and test course, the US Army Special Forces also adopted a green beret as their insignia. The Special Operations Division was established under Colonel Aaron Bank in 1952 and a number of special forces groups were subsequently established in different locations. From 1990 it was known as US Army Special Forces Command (Airborne) and units from this Command played a significant role in Operation Enduring Freedom in Afghanistan, discussed later in this book.

OFFICE OF STRATEGIC SERVICES (OSS)

On 13 June 1942, Colonel 'Wild Bill' Donovan was placed in charge of the United States Office of Strategic Services which, like SOE, was responsible for a network of agents and for fomenting guerrilla activities in occupied countries, mainly in Europe but also in Southeast Asia. The FBI retained full control of operations in Latin America.

The OSS dropped small teams into Europe to organize resistance and were also prominent in the Burmese jungle, where they fomented resistance against the Japanese among Burmese tribesmen. The OSS proved to be the seed of modern US special forces and of the Central Intelligence Agency.

Although neither SOE nor the OSS still exist, their heritage is very much with us, both in the ongoing importance of fostering clandestine support among the local population, a matter which has been given greater priority particularly in the United States in recent years, and in their vital information gathering and pre-emptive work, still carried out by intelligence organisations such as MI6 in England and the CIA in the United States.

The special techniques and special kind of courage required of SOE and OSS agents living in occupied territory would also be demanded of special forces personnel. High-level language skills and other specialist attributes would also be demanded, setting this kind of soldier apart even from elite forces such as the British Royal Marine Commandos and US Rangers.

SAS IN BORNEO (1963–66)

The creation of the federation of Malaysia, consisting of Malaya proper, Sarawak and British North Borneo, was opposed by President Sukarno of Indonesia. The 1000 islands of Indonesia not being enough to monopolize his attention, Sukarno mounted insurgency operations in Borneo. The Clandestine Communist Organisation (CCO) was the centre of the insurgency and Britain was faced with interdicting insurgent patrols over an area about the size of mainland Britain. Once again, the policy of patiently fostering local support that had been so successful in Malaya began to bear fruit. Over an extended period, various Indonesian raids

THE MALAYAN SCOUTS

The British Army's experience in Burma was to prove very useful when faced with a communist insurgency in Malaya from 1948. Major Mike Calvert set up a separate unit based on the SAS Territorial organization in the UK in order to deal with the special challenges created by the Emergency. This unit was called the Malayan Scouts (SAS).

The Malayan Scouts began to send patrols deep into the jungle to both disrupt insurgent operations and create ties with the native population. This was achieved partly by providing medical support. The patrols were able to spend long periods in the jungle due to a system of re-supply by helicopter but even so, the extended operations took their toll on men and equipment. Apart from the communist enemy, the SAS units had to contend with Mother Nature. In the jungle,

sweat-soaked clothing would never dry and there were a multitude of other dangers and discomforts.

The number of insurgents captured or killed during the Emergency was not great but this was not the major purpose of British tactics. Rather than bludgeoning both friend and foe from both the ground and the air, the British contrived to gradually cut off the insurgents' life-support mechanism and to neutralize their influence on the local population. It was a long learning curve but the result was a success.

As with many successes, however, it has perhaps not received the prominence it deserves. The free federation of Malaysia emerged as a result of a carefully modulated strategy, depending largely for its military aspects on the role of special forces.

This 'hearts and minds' aspect of special forces operations, pioneered by the British, has achieved renewed prominence today.

British SAS soldiers, armed with a Sterling sub-machine gun and FN FAL automatic rifle, patrol a river in Borneo during the confrontation **(Konfrontasi)** *with Indonesia.*

were intercepted and Gurkha reinforcements helped to intercept a major Indonesian attack in 1963. Meanwhile, intensive training continued as SAS squadrons honed their jungle-warfare skills. The painstaking art of jungle patrolling was developed to such an extent that SAS losses were minimal in comparison with the toll they took upon the enemy.

US SPECIAL OPERATIONS IN VIETNAM

The Vietnam War was too protracted a conflict to discuss in detail here. Much criticism has gathered around US strategy and tactics in Vietnam, most

of it expressed with the wisdom of hindsight. Comparisons have rightly been drawn between the war in Vietnam and the Malayan Emergency as both conflicts involved insurgency operations in remote jungle areas.

Indeed, an attempt was made in Vietnam to repeat the successful resettlement strategy of the local population carried out by the British in Malaya but it became impossible in Vietnam to quarantine the local population from 'infection' by Viet Cong.

Although the Malayan Emergency was in fact a protracted guerrilla war, the Viet Cong insurgents in Vietnam had the backing of the North Vietnamese armed forces and of both the Soviet Union and China, all of which placed the Vietnam War on a different scale. US forces were also often hampered by poor generalship on the part of the South Vietnamese forces as well as poor coordination between US and South Vietnamese forces. Once the United States had failed to provide a viable alternative to communism for the local population, the war escalated, with the Americans resorting to area bombing and defoliants as a mark of their frustration.

United States special operations were carried out in Vietnam and in adjoining countries such as Laos and Cambodia right from the very beginning. This was part of a rational objective to undermine communist insurgent activity by empowering locally recruited armies and providing them with weapons and other equipment. Teams such as the 1st Observation Group were operational from 1956, and by 1961 the 5th Special Forces Group (Airborne) was controlling special operations activities in South Vietnam.

Maritime coastal operations were carried out by the US Navy SEALs. Early covert operations in Vietnam had largely been run by the Central Intelligence Agency (CIA) but due to increasing pressure from other commitments the CIA relinquished control of these to the US Army.

The Studies and Observation Group (SOG) was set up to control the activities of US Special Forces, US Navy SEALs and US Air Force special operations.

The discovery by agents of the Ho Chi Minh trail and the appreciation of its importance as the spinal cord for North Vietnamese operations lead to more intensive reconnaissance operations. Teams were inserted by helicopter to carry out forward observation and occasional target acquisition.

In order to provide assistance and extraction for US personnel or their allies, a Joint Personnel Recovery Center (JPRC) was launched in 1966. Short-Term Roadwatch and Target Acquisition Teams (STRATA) were also set up to provide intelligence from North Vietnam itself. These teams were retrieved and replaced at regular intervals in order to reduce the danger of being compromised by the North Vietnamese. Despite the precautions, however, the North Vietnamese and Viet Cong conducted effective counter-intelligence operations and captured hundreds of agents.

The operations conducted by SOG required the most extraordinary levels of bravery and agents could expect little mercy if they were captured. In order to reduce the chances of being interdicted during insertion by helicopter, teams were later dropped on the High Altitude Low Opening (HALO) principle, which greatly improved security.

As the political temperature changed, special forces were pulled out of Laos and Cambodia and, in due course, out of North Vietnam. The Studies and Observation Group (SOG) was finally stood down in March 1972, having lost about 300 personnel in operations in North and South Vietnam, Laos and Cambodia. Some special operations activities continued under different guises until the final pull-out of US forces from the region.

The reasons for the loss of South Vietnam are complex but there is no doubting the extraordinary valour of those US and South Vietnamese servicemen who took part in special operations activities in that difficult war.

A captain of 5th Special Forces Group in South Vietnam, 1965. He wears standard US Army jungle fatigues and carries a .30 M2 carbine.

Facing page: A US Special Forces Green Beret soldier wears the famous beret and temperate camouflage uniform. He is armed with an M16 assault rifle.

RAID ON ENTEBBE (3–4 JULY 1976)

Although much of the pioneering work for elite and special forces had been done by the British and Americans in World War II and immediately afterwards, they were not, of course, the only countries capable of carrying out special operations.

On 27 June 1976 the Palestinian Liberation Organisation (PLO) and Baader–Meinhof Gang collaborated in the hijack of an Air France Airbus (Flight AF139) en route from Tel Aviv via Athens to Paris. When the hijack was carried out at 12:10, the pilot managed to pressed a warning button to inform ground controllers. He was then re-routed by the terrorists to Benghazi for refuelling. The plane then took off for Entebbe in Uganda where the terrorists freed the French crew and the non-Jewish or non-Israeli passengers after disembarking into the old terminal building.

The French crew bravely insisted on staying with the Jewish hostages. Israel was given 48 hours to release 53 convicted PLO terrorists before the hijackers started executing hostages. In order to buy as much time as possible, the Israeli Government agreed to negotiate. The deadline was extended to 13:00 on Sunday 4 July.

Within their small window of opportunity, the Israeli Defence Force under Brigadier-General Dan Shomron put together a plan for a daring and powerful raid, aided by blueprints of Entebbe airport buildings provided by an Israeli construction firm and by descriptions of the terrorists provided by released passengers.

The troops that were to carry out the raid were drawn from the 35th Parachute Brigade and the Golani Infantry Brigade. They carried out a full rehearsal on 3 July, then at 16:00 four C-130 Hercules took off for Entebbe, escorted by Israeli Air Force Phantom jets and followed by two Boeing 707s, one of which was a communications centre and the other a hospital. The lead Hercules, carrying a black Mercedes and two IDF Land Rovers, landed at Entebbe at 23:01, with the rear ramp already down and the vehicle engines running.

US SPECIAL FORCES ORGANIZATION

1st Special Forces Group (Airborne)
US Base: Fort Lewis, Washington
Overseas: Okinawa, Japan (Pacific Command)

3rd Special Forces Group (Airborne)
US Base: Fort Bragg, NC
Overseas: European Command, Africa

5th Special Forces Group (Airborne)
US Base: Fort Campbell, Kentucky
(Central Command)

7th Special Forces Group (Airborne)
US Base: Fort Bragg, NC
Overseas: Puerto Rico (Southern Command)

10th Special Forces Group (Airborne)
US Base: Fort Carson, Colorado
Overseas: Stuttgart, Germany (European Command)

19th Special Forces Group (Airborne)
US Base: Salt Lake City, Utah (Pacific and Central Commands)

20th Special Forces Group (Airborne)
US Base: Birmingham, Alabama (Southern Command)

The Mercedes with its two Land Rover escorts was designed to look like an official Ugandan VIP entourage and they raced off the rear of the plane and towards the old terminal before the Hercules had even come to a halt. As they approached the building, the IDF in the vehicles engaged two Ugandan sentries before running to the entrance on foot. They shot another Ugandan guard and then killed a terrorist who had started to shoot the hostages. Two more terrorists were engaged, one of whom threw a grenade. In all, six terrorists were killed. Lieutenant Colonel Yoni Netanyahu was killed by a Ugandan sentry and three other members of the IDF were wounded. The IDF force immediately set about loading the hostages onto the waiting planes while other units destroyed 11

An Israeli Air Force (IAF) squadron leader is raised on the shoulders of the crowd after the return of the hostage rescue forces from Entebbe.

Ugandan Air Force MiG fighters on the airfield. The convoy of planes then took off to refuel at Nairobi before heading back to Israel.

The Entebbe raid was carried out at extremely short notice and its success was owed largely to an amalgamation of characteristics that define special operations and those involved with them. There was simply no time for caution.

Every person and unit that contributed to the operation, whether it was the commanders on the ground or the air force pilots, had to believe not only that the operation was possible but that they could definitely succeed.

It is also no surprise that many of the IDF participants came from the Golani Brigade. This is one of the most highly decorated units in the IDF and its members have a reputation for toughness and for taking up challenges that might make others think twice. Other special forces units involved in the raid were the Sayeret Mat'Kal (Unit 269) and Sayeret Tzanhanin.

RESCUE AT MOGADISHU
(18 OCTOBER 1977)

Members of the Red Army Faction, or Baader–Meinhof Gang, carried out another hijacking in 1977 in attempt to gain the release of imprisoned gang leaders. A Lufthansa Boeing 737 (Flight LH181) was hijacked over the Mediterranean by four terrorists and the plane re-routed to Rome for refuelling. It took off again and landed at Larnaca in Cyprus, where it was refuelled once more. When it flew on, various airports denied it permission to land but the pilot was eventually forced to bring it into Dubai due to lack of fuel. At Dubai the captain of the aircraft, Jurgen Schumann, succeeded in communicating the number of hijackers on board to the authorities. As a result, the terrorist leader, Zohair Youssef

Akache, threatened to kill him. When the plane flew on, it was again denied permission to land, and at Aden the runway was blocked with vehicles. Due to the shortage of fuel, the pilot brought the plane down on a sandstrip adjacent to the runway. Schumann was allowed out of the plane to check the landing gear and at this point he went across to the control tower. It is said that he advised the authorities of the positions of the explosives on the plane but was forced to return to the plane due to threats from the hijackers that they would blow it up if he did not come back.

Once Schumann had flown the plane out of Aden, he was taken out of the cockpit and taken to the main cabin. He was then shot in the head. The plane flew on to Mogadishu where it landed at about 3.30 on 17 October. Jurgen Schumann's body was thrown out on the tarmac.

At this time the German authorities were continuing negotiations with the terrorists, indicating that they would fly the requested terrorist prisoners out to Mogadishu for an exchange.

A team from Germany's GSG9 had, however, been following Flight LH181 from the outset, landing first at Cyprus and then at Dubai from where they flew on to Mogadishu.

Only 40 minutes before the deadline set by the hijackers for the handover of prisoners, at 02:05, a fire was lit by Somali troops on the runway in front of the plane. Two hijackers entered the cockpit to check what was going on. At the same time, radio contact was made by the authorities to discuss the hostage and prisoner exchange.

TWO DISTRACTIONS

During these moments, the German GSG9 had assembled underneath the fuselage and wings of the 737. Within seconds, they had mounted the wings and fuselage using rubber-covered ladders and wearing specially designed rubber boots.

At 02:07 the doors were blown and stun grenades thrown into the cabin. The GSG9 team burst in and engaged the terrorists, shouting at the passengers to keep their heads down. Although fatally wounded, Akache managed to throw two grenades into the cabin but the effect of the explosions was minimized by being shielded by

the seats. All but one of the hijackers was killed. The other was wounded and arrested. The German GSG9 had successfully accomplished one of the most difficult of all hostage rescues, involving the engagement of terrorists in a confined space, without causing fatalities among the hostages.

IRANIAN EMBASSY SIEGE, PRINCESS GATE, LONDON (30 APRIL–5 MAY 1980)

The Iranian Embassy at No. 16 Prince's Gate, London, was taken over by six heavily armed terrorists, purportedly representing the Democratic Revolutionary Movement for the Liberation of Arabistan, on Wednesday 30 April 1980.

Soldiers of the German GSG9 help hostages off the Boeing 737 after their successful assault on the plane at Mogadishu.

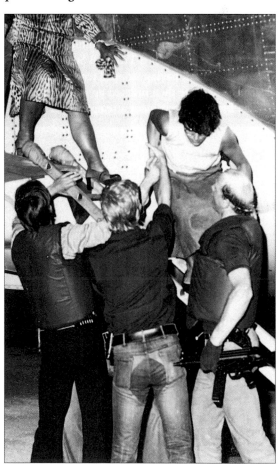

At about 23:30 the diplomatic protection squad policeman on duty, PC Trevor Lock, was taken by surprise and bundled into the building. Some embassy staff managed to escape in the first few moments. Two others were later released, making a total of 21 hostages in the building whom the terrorists threatened to kill if their demands were not met.

The Metropolitan Police immediately set up a negotiating base in the building next door and by Friday two more hostages were released in exchange for a media broadcast of the terrorists' demands. In Herefordshire, Lieutenant Colonel Michael Rose, Commanding Officer of 22 SAS, put the SAS Special Projects Team on immediate standby. After a rapid briefing, the team set off for London.

Lieutenant Colonel Rose himself travelled to London by helicopter, and, having liaised with the Metropolitan Police, carried out an initial reconnaissance. His personal assessment of the ground was to prove vital when planning the attack. The members of 6 Troop, B Squadron SAS (Special Projects), having stopped temporarily at Beaconsfield, were then ordered up to London.

The British Government attempted over the weekend to enlist the help of Arab ambassadors but to no avail. The terrorists became impatient and on Monday at about 13:30 they took the press secretary Abbas Lavasani into the main hall and executed him. His body was pushed out of the front door at about 17:00 and collected by a stretcher party, filmed on live television. At this point the Metropolitan Police formally handed over control of the operation to the British Army.

The Metropolitan Police had used a variety of methods to ascertain the exact location and movements of terrorists and hostages. Sound cover for drilling into walls to plant listening devices was arranged by asking the gas board to drill in a nearby street and then by lowering the flight paths of aircraft overhead. Detailed intelligence about the layout of the building was taken from escaped embassy staff or visitors who had been released.

As the world watched the blank face of the building in the aftermath of the murder of Abbas Lavasani, there appeared to be stalemate. By killing a hostage, the terrorists had thrown away the chance of a negotiated settlement which the Metropolitan Police had been genuinely striving for. The terrorists had also thrown away any flickering of support

MOLUCCAN TRAIN INCIDENT (23 MAY 1977)

Moluccan terrorists, calling for Dutch Government recognition for the independence of Molucca in Indonesia and the release of their convicted compatriots from Dutch prisons, took hostages in both a school and a train travelling between Assen and Groningen.

The circumstances called for a highly coordinated response from the Dutch authorities for if something went wrong at one crisis scene it would have implications for the other, the bottom line being the lives of the hostages.

Plans and rehearsals involving Royal Netherlands Marines were immediately instituted, including practice assaults on train mock-ups. Sophisticated monitoring equipment was employed to track the movement of the terrorists.

Negotiations had been ongoing between the Dutch Government and the terrorists but it was clear they were going nowhere. The order was given for an assault on 11 June.

At about 05:00 attacks went in on both the train and the school. Six Royal Netherlands Air Force Starfighters buzzed the train at high speed to create a distraction and noise whiteout while Marines and police moved in on the train. At the school, armoured personnel carriers attacked from all sides with roaring engines, one of them bursting through a wall. On the train, six terrorists were killed and unfortunately two hostages died in crossfire. At the school, all the terrorists were captured.

The terrorists had misjudged the Dutch authorities. They made the mistake of assuming that a nation with the liberal traditions of the Netherlands wouldn't have efficient armed forces or the will to protect the lives of its citizens. When the call came, Dutch security forces acted with decisive force.

from the hostages themselves. Before the murder, BBC sound recordist Sim Harris would have been happy for the terrorists to walk away, having made their point. After the murder, his attitude changed dramatically. He knew now that there was only one unit capable of getting him and his fellow hostages out alive. Little did he know that three four-man teams from the SAS were positioning themselves for an assault.

From the outset of the crisis, several well-oiled wheels had sprung into motion. One of these was the activation of a Police hostage negotiation team and the other was a meeting of the civil contingencies committee in Cabinet Office Briefing Room A, codenamed COBRA. It would be their decision to make the significant transfer of operational control from the Metropolitan Police to the British Army. This was underwritten by the Prime Minister, Margaret Thatcher.

THE SAS GO IN

As tension mounted both within and without the embassy, negotiators told the leader of the

A terrorist appears briefly at the door of the Iranian Embassy in Prince's Gate, London. He would soon face the SAS.

terrorists that a coach was on its way to take him and his compatriots to Heathrow. Meanwhile Red and Blue Teams, B Squadron SAS, moved to their start positions.

As the television cameras played on the blank face of Prince's Gate, there was a huge explosion. Two black-clad figures appeared on the balcony of the building next to 16 Prince's Gate and immediately began to climb over to the Embassy balcony. They laid a frame charge against the large window and moved back quickly. Almost instantly there followed a huge explosion and cloud of dust, then within a second or two the armed figures reappeared and climbed through the wrecked Embassy window.

At the same time members of Red Team SAS abseiled from the roof of the building down to the second floor balcony. Another group descended by ladder and via a roof to the third floor. Others

SAS soldiers appear in black uniform and respirators at the Iranian Embassy. Filmed live, the daylight special forces attack caused a sensation.

entered the top floor via a skylight. Blue Team was responsible for the basement, ground and first floors. The SAS men were armed with Heckler & Koch MP5 sub-machine guns and Browning 'Hi Power' 9mm (0.35in) automatic pistols. They forced their way in using frame charges and hatchets. One of the men was caught in the abseil rope and was eventually cut down and released by his colleagues.

Around the building, there were back-up teams of SAS with pistols and also snipers ready to provide covering fire or to intercept any escaping hostages. Inside the building, despite the shattering effect of the explosions and the effects of stun grenades and CS gas, the terrorist leader Oan was ready to shoot an SAS soldier as he came through the window and would have done so if he had not been floored by PC Lock. The SAS soldier shouted at the PC to get clear and then shot the terrorist.

A terrorist called Shai headed for the room where the hostages were held and was joined by terrorists Feisal, Ali and Makki. Feisal began shooting at the hostages with a machine pistol and another terrorist shot at them with his pistol. An embassy press attaché, Al-Akbar Samadzadeh, was killed and Ahmed Dadgar was hit in the chest. Dr Ali Afrouz was hit twice in the legs.

An SAS trooper entered the room and shot one of the terrorists with a Browning pistol. The other terrorist joined the hostages on the floor. Other troopers entered and started bundling the hostages out of the door but one spotted Makki who was shot and found to be holding a grenade. Further down the stairs, Feisal, also holding a grenade, was identified and shot.

Once all the rooms had been cleared, the soldiers formed a chain and manhandled the hostages and one terrorist out of the building. Outside, they were all forced to the ground and rapidly handcuffed before each one was positively identified. The one remaining terrorist was arrested, lucky to be alive. There has been some discussion about the number of terrorists killed in the operation and whether the SAS response was 'proportionate', as it should be under international law for a military engagement. The answer seems to be that the terrorists had already killed one hostage in cold blood and attempted to kill more once the raid was underway. They were armed, dangerous and unpredictable. For their own safety and for the safety of the hostages, the SAS acted with extreme scepticism.

The British Government and the Metropolitan Police had gone out of its way to try to find a peaceful solution to the hostage crisis but once a murder had been committed a button labelled 'justice' was pressed. From this point on the terrorists and the hostages experienced the maximum efficiency of a military unit created in World War II and honed to a high level of operational efficiency through live operations all round the world and through constant training to be the sharp point of the British military dagger. In some respects, at the Iranian Embassy siege a whole country was held hostage. Terrorists had simply walked in and effectively put a gun to the head of the British people and their diplomatic guests. A British police constable was also held hostage. The symbols of law and order were challenged and nobody seemed to be able to do anything about it. It was in the midst of this power vacuum that those black-clad figures with hoods and respirators suddenly entered the world stage. The SAS were known to be operating in Northern Ireland and elsewhere and there had been much speculation about their activities. Other special operations groups had performed dramatically and successfully at Entebbe, Mogadishu and in Holland. Now was the opportunity for the masters to show their hand. They did not fail. They dared and they won.

The Iranian Embassy siege may have been a watershed. A certain type of terrorist activity had been proven to be futile against the determination of free societies not be held hostage and by the professionalism of their armed forces. Terrorism, however, did not cease. It went deeper underground and linked with deeply rooted causes and highly organized networks. The poison of terrorism, denied the light of day by ever more efficient security systems across the world, became more concentrated. When it burst out again onto the world stage it was to be on a scale never seen before and which would look like the prelude to Armageddon.

OPERATION URGENT FURY: GRENADA 1983

The island of Grenada is part of the Lesser Antilles in the Caribbean Sea and lies about 160km (100 miles) north of Venezuela. The island is 34km (21 miles) long and 19km (12 miles) wide with a surface area of 344 square km (133 square miles). It is a volcanic island with a high mountain ridge covered in forest which culminates in Mount St Catherine at 840m (2757 feet). The nearby Southern Grenadines is a group of islands which are a dependency of

Grenada and several of them are uninhabited. The capital of Grenada is St George's, on the south-west coast and with a substantial natural harbour.

Grenada was first discovered by Christopher Columbus in 1498. In the early 1670s it became a French colony and it was captured by the British in 1762. It remained a British crown colony until it became independent in 1974, remaining within the Commonwealth. The island remains a constitutional monarchy and the British monarch is represented by a governor-general as the nominal head of state.

In 1979 a coup resulted in a left-wing government under Maurice Bishop, Marxist leader of the New Jewel Movement (NJM). He formed the People's Revolutionary Government (PRG) and was backed by Cuba.

Grenada was turned into a militarized state under the thumb of the Cuban-backed People's Revolutionary Armed Forces (PRAF). Looming in the background was the colossus of the Soviet Union, which was supplying a range of equipment including armoured vehicles.

In 1982 a team of 27 Cuban military specialists arrived to provide advice on a range of communications, logistics and engineering projects.

On 19 October 1983 there was another coup led by Bernard Coard. A Revolutionary Military Council (RMC) then took over.

Not only the United States but also the Organization of East Caribbean States (OECS) became increasingly concerned about these developments. According to US intelligence, Soviet and Cuban

An SAS trooper wearing an SF10 respirator, black uniform and high-grip boots. He is armed with a Heckler & Koch MP5 sub-machine gun.

involvement was increasing, and there was also a potential threat to US, British and other nationals on the island.

The OECS requested US military support in a combined invasion of Grenada that would involve not only taking on Grenadan revolutionary forces but also the substantial number of Cuban forces and advisers on the island.

THE AMERICANS INVADE

The invasion of Grenada was a significant moment in the Reagan administration as it was effectively to be a prelude to the swan-song of the world's other superpower, the Soviet Union.

The operations came under overall command of US Commander-in-Chief Atlantic, Admiral Wesley L. McDonald, while Joint Task Force 120, the major naval and amphibious force, was under the command of Vice-Admiral Joseph Metcalf. This task force included an earlier battle group, Amphibious Squadron Four and 22nd Marine Amphibious Unit, the last two designated as Task Force 124.

Major General Richard Scholtes would command Task Force 123 which comprised the special operations element. This included 1st Special Forces Operational Detachment–Delta (SFOD–D), SEAL Team 6, 160th Special Operations Aviation Regiment (SOAR), 1st and 2nd Battalions 75th Ranger Regiment. The USAF 1st Special Operations Wing was also deployed. Task designation included capture of the governor's residence by US Navy SEALs, capture of Pearls Airport by US Marines and the capture of Port Salinas airfield by the Rangers. The Rangers left Barbados in the early hours of 25 October and parachuted in. The planes were met with anti-aircraft fire which was mostly silenced by AC-130 gunships. The 24th Marine Amphibious Unit attacked Pearls Airport at 05:00.

As they landed, the Rangers came under fire from the 600-strong Cuban contingent at Port Salines, including six armoured personnel carriers. After a fierce gun battle, the Rangers took control. On the night of 23-24 October, 12 members of US SEAL Team 6 and four Air Force Combat Central Team members were tasked with a reconnaissance mission to Salinas airfield and to plant direction-finding radar beacons for the Rangers parachute drop.

Support for the mission was provided by two USAF Special Operations Squadron MC-130E aircraft and USS *Clifton Sprague*, a guided-missile frigate.

The SEAL and USAF team carried out a night jump into the sea, with two Zodiac inflatable boats, about 40km (25 miles) from Port Salinas. As there was apparently a shortage of suitable maps at the time, the special forces team would need to recce a suitable landing site before bringing the boats in and camouflaging them. Once ashore, the SEALs were to make and maintain contact with incoming Ranger force and link up with them once they were landed.

MISSION ABORT

The weather was difficult for the air drop and the men were carrying heavy combat loads. For a variety of reasons, which may have included excess weight or some form of entanglement, four of the team were tragically drowned.

Having tried and failed to locate their teammates, the remainder of the team continued with the mission but soon ran into the path of a Grenadan patrol boat. They cut the engines of the Zodiacs and waited for the boat to pass but unfortunately the outboard motors on the Zodiacs could not be re-started. The team had little choice other than to rendezvous with another US Navy vessel, USS *Caron,* and pull out. The insertion was attempted a second time the following night (24–25 October), this time launching from a US Navy vessel. As they approached land, the Zodiacs were swamped in the surf and vital pieces of equipment lost. The mission was again aborted.

RADIO FREE GRENADA TRANSMITTING STATION

SEAL Team 6 were also tasked to capture and hold the RFG transmitting station pending the arrival of relief forces from the Rangers.

On the night of 24–25 October the SEALs were landed by UH-60 Black Hawk helicopters of 160th SOAR adjacent to the transmitting station which was located on the west coast of Grenada not far from St George. The number of enemy forces in the area was not known. Once the SEALs were

in place they assaulted the transmitter building and neutralized the guards. By 06:30 they were in control of the transmitting station. The SEALs also ambushed a Grenadan military truck, killing five soldiers.

A Grenadan officer, however, organized a counter-attack, backed up by a BTR-60 armoured personnel carrier with a turret-mounted machine gun, and an 82mm (3.2in) mortar. The Grenadans then assaulted the building with 20 men.

As the SEALs had no heavy fire support and aerial support was not available, they began to take casualties. After at least an hour they took the decision to destroy the building and transmitter and carry out an escape and evasion (E and E) towards the sea. A fierce gun battle ensued as the SEALs vacated the area, taking their wounded comrades with them. They managed to reach the beach and then swim out to a rendezvous with USS *Caron*.

ASSAULT ON THE GOVERNOR-GENERAL'S MANSION

The governor-general's mansion was also in the St George area. SEAL Team 6 were put down by two

The Radio Free Grenada station north of St George's. SEAL Team 6 carried out an attack on the station during Operation Urgent Fury.

UH-60 Black Hawk helicopters at 06:15, under heavy fire.

The security personnel ran away when the SEALs were inserted and the team took up firing positions for the expected counter-attack. A SEAL sniper was posted in a top floor window with a G3 SG-1 sniper rifle and shot at least 20 members of the People's Republican Army as they manoeuvred to attack.

When the attack came it included a BTR-60 armoured personnel carrier. The initial attack was repulsed but the position was serious. Fortunately for the SEALs, Admiral Metcalfe decided on his own initiative to send in two USMC AH-1 Cobra helicopter gunships to provide the SEALs with aerial fire support.

One AH-1 Cobra was hit by ground fire and had to carry out an emergency landing. As the other Cobra attempted to provide covering fire, it was also shot down and crashed into the harbour.

Soldiers of 1st Battalion 75th Rangers attend a briefing for a night patrol during Operation Urgent Fury.

Emboldened by these events, the PRA attempted a second assault but this time the US aerial response was an AC-130 gunship which flew in and destroyed the PRA BTR-60 and kept the enemy ground forces at bay. A-7 attack aircraft were sent in from USS *Independence* to destroy the PRA anti-aircraft positions. The SEAL team held out within the building until relieved by US Marines ground forces on 26 October.

The Governor's mansion was not of itself a particularly important strategic target for US forces. Once the major forces had landed, they would have taken the area in due course. Politically, however, the attack on the mansion had some significance. The Head of State of Grenada, despite the various coups, was in fact still Her Majesty Queen Elizabeth II. The United States had omitted to inform the British Government until the last minute that they were about to invade

sovereign territory. The legality of the operation and US relations with a close ally were placed in considerable doubt. It is said, however, that the Governor-General Paul Scoons had written a letter formally inviting the United States to intervene. As he was the representative of the Queen, it was important that both the Governor General and his letter were secured. On the other hand, if the Americans had liaised with the British earlier, they might have been able to provide the US forces with some accurate maps.

PEARLS AIRFIELD

SEAL Team 4 were tasked to carry out a recce of the beachhead adjacent to Pearls Airfield in preparation for the amphibious assault of 22nd Marine Amphibious Unit.

The SEAL team was embarked on USS *Fort Snelling* (LSD-30), a dock landing ship. Once within range, SeaFox special operations craft were dropped carrying the SEAL teams as well as their Zodiac inflatable boats. Enemy patrol craft were identified by radar but the SeaFox Teams managed to avoid them. Once within range the SEALs recce'd the beach visually with night-vision goggles to discover that the beach was being prepared by substantial numbers of Grenadan troops to resist an amphibious assault. Swimmers were sent in to confirm the status of the beach. Fortuitously a change for the worse in the weather caused the Grenadan soldiers to seek cover, and they departed. This provided an opportunity for the SEALs to bring in their Zodiac craft. After a quick and detailed reconnaissance, the SEALs were able to confirm that the beach surface would not sustain an amphibious assault and that an aerial option should be considered. The team then exfiltrated, managing to survive being fired on by a Grenadan anti-aircraft position.

ASSAULT ON RICHMOND HILL PRISON

Five Black Hawk Helicopters arrived at Richmond Hill Prison with soldiers of Delta Force and a company of Rangers. Unfortunately for the insertion team, the prison which had been cleverly positioned and designed to prevent the occupants from getting out was equally difficult to get into. It was set on a sharp ridgeline with thick jungle all around. To make things worse, Fort Frederick with its well-armed garrison and anti-aircraft guns was only 300m (330yd) distant.

THE GIBRALTAR INCIDENT

A controversial incident involving the IRA and SAS occurred in Gibraltar on 6 March 1988. Provisional IRA members Dan McCann, Sean Savage and Mairead Farrell had been tracked to Gibraltar where they planned to detonate a bomb adjacent to the Governor's palace, in front of which there was a regular changing of the guard ceremony.

The IRA team, basing themselves in Spain, drove the car into Gibraltar, parked it near the main square and then began to walk back towards the airport and the Spanish frontier. They were tailed by four SAS soldiers dressed in civilian clothes and carrying the British issue L9A1 Browning Hi Power pistol. It was assumed that the car that had been left may have had a bomb in it and that the terrorists may have been armed and carrying detonation devices.

Savage began to walk back into town and was followed by two SAS men. At this point a police siren was heard, which alerted the IRA members. Dan McCann is said to have turned round and looked directly at one of the SAS soldiers. He is also said to have moved his hand as if reaching for a weapon or the detonator, as conjectured by the security forces. One of the SAS men fired at McCann, upon which Mairead Farrell is said to have reached for a bag. She was shot by the same soldier, and the other soldier also fired at both IRA members. When he heard the sound of firing, Sean Savage turned round. One of the SAS soldiers called out to him to stop and he is said to have moved his hand towards one of his pockets. The two SAS soldiers then fired at him.

As it transpired, none of the IRA terrorists was armed and neither did any of them carry a detonator. The car left by the IRA members in Gibraltar did not contain a bomb, though later a car belonging to the terrorists was found in Marbella with explosive materials inside it.

Although the intention of the IRA team to plant a bomb in Gibraltar in order to kill or maim about 100 people was not disputed, a major controversy blew up around the rules of engagement adopted by the SAS in the incident.

Especially in view of the fact that the IRA members proved to be unarmed, it was deemed by many unnecessary to have killed them. The response of the British Government was that the terrorists were assumed, on the available intelligence, to be armed and dangerous and that the soldiers on the spot had no way of knowing otherwise.

SAS soldiers are trained for incidents of maximum danger where a hair's breadth of time could mean the difference between life and death. Their lightning reactions and use of lethal force is part and parcel of the kind of operations they are trained for. If the IRA members had been tailed by policemen, the result may have been different, but the controversy surrounding the death of an innocent man in the wake of the 7 July 2005 bombings in London suggest that even this is not certain.

Not surprisingly, as soon as the Fort Frederick garrison saw the helicopters, they opened up and began to hit their targets. Casualties on board began to mount and one of the helicopter pilots was killed. After the co-pilot tried to head for safety, the helicopter was hit again and crashed. Another Black Hawk put down a Delta team to protect the wounded men in the crashed helicopter and received backup from an AC-130 Spectre gunship.

Members of Delta Force made a successful assault on Fort Rupert and neutralized the force there. The force was also quickly extracted by 160th SOAR and taken back to USS *Guam*, a helicopter carrier.

SAS IN NORTHERN IRELAND (1969–94)

The SAS, along with the rest of the British Army, was involved throughout the 1970s and 1980s in a long and bloody campaign in Northern Ireland. The SAS was ideally suited to covert operations and anti-insurgency work and members of the Irish Republican Army (IRA) developed a particular hatred for them. British officers associated with the SAS, such as Robert Nairac (Grenadier Guards; 14th Intelligence Company) and Herbert Westmacott (Grenadier Guards) were killed by the IRA during the troubles. For their part, the SAS succeeded in pre-empting several terrorist strikes by the IRA, including an attack by the East Tyrone Brigade on the RUC barracks at Loughall when the IRA drove a JCB armed with a bomb through a perimeter fence round the barracks and began to fire on the building. About 20 SAS soldiers, concealed in the area, then opened fire and all of the IRA members were killed.

SAS IN THE FALKLANDS WAR (APRIL–JUNE 1982)

Despite their successes in various small wars since World War II, it has been suggested that the SAS were not initially regarded as an essential item on the crowded Task Force that was to set sail for the Falklands after the Argentine invasion. If this was the case, it may have been because the planners thought of the operation as an infantry affair and that they had enough by way of elite forces in the Royal Marine Commandos and the Parachute Regiment. They could call on excellent infantry in the shape of 2nd Battalion Scots Guards and 1st Battalion Welsh Guards, the Duke of Edinburgh's Own Gurkha Rifles and the light armour of the Blues and Royals, not to mention the specialist skills of the Royal Artillery, Royal Electrical and Mechanical Engineers and the Army Aviation Corps.

Every bit of space on the transport ships needed to be accounted and argued for, especially in view of the fact that the United Kingdom at that time was set up for a major slogging match in Europe with the Soviet Union and not for long-range amphibious operations reminiscent of the days when the sun did not set on the British Empire.

The SAS were set up to deal with insurgents, whereas the Falklands was about ousting a full-scale army. Clearly, if this was the mindset, the planners had forgotten the circumstances in which the SAS regiment was created; the German Afrika Korps under Rommel were no insurgents.

As it was, the SAS soon found themselves involved in a crucial curtain-raiser to the Falklands War – the recapture of South Georgia. If this operation were to fail, it could have incalculable effects on British morale, both civilian and military, and might even have implications for the political and diplomatic battle that was being slogged out behind the scenes. The spectre of Suez hung over the ice caps of South Georgia.

The SAS unit was to be landed on South Georgia to provide vital reconnaissance before a main landing was made by members of 42 Commando. When a team from D Squadron SAS was put ashore, however, the weather conditions were so atrocious that they could do little more than wait for conditions to improve. As it became apparent that this was not going to happen and the danger of exposure became a reality, an operation was mounted to recover them by helicopter. In the appalling conditions, two helicopters were lost and the team were lucky to get back to the ship in the remaining helicopter.

Later, after a successful attack on an Argentine submarine, the SAS were put ashore again, secured their locations and 42 Commando landed. The Argentine garrison saw the writing on the wall and surrendered. Prior to the main landings at San Carlos on the Falkland Islands, the SAS mounted a diversionary attack on the Argentine garrison at Darwin, near Goose Green. Although carried out by only 60 men, the attack was designed to seem like a major infantry assault, with the SAS soldiers laying down a heavy barrage of automatic fire.

On 14 May, the SAS mounted a successful attack on Argentine aircraft at a base on Pebble

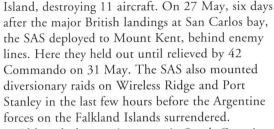

An SAS trooper equipped for service in the Falklands War (1982). He is armed with an M16 automatic rifle.

Island, destroying 11 aircraft. On 27 May, six days after the major British landings at San Carlos bay, the SAS deployed to Mount Kent, behind enemy lines. Here they held out until relieved by 42 Commando on 31 May. The SAS also mounted diversionary raids on Wireless Ridge and Port Stanley in the last few hours before the Argentine forces on the Falkland Islands surrendered.

Although the opening scene in South Georgia had been a close call, as the Falklands campaign unfolded the professionalism of the SAS in carrying out operations such as reconnaissance, destruction of high-value enemy assets and diversionary operations became apparent. Lessons would be learned and equipment improved but the disproportionate effect of small teams of special forces would not be lost on the planners of military operations in the future.

OPERATION JUST CAUSE: PANAMA 1989

In 1989 the United States carried out an invasion of Panama in order to depose the then political and military leader in that country, General Manuel Noriega. The operation involved a substantial special forces deployment.

Panama forms the isthmus that connects North and South America. Its western border is with Colombia and its eastern border with Costa Rica. The country with its associated islands covers 75,517 square km (29,157 square miles). Panama also separates the Caribbean Sea and Atlantic and the Pacific Ocean. The Panama Canal, which connects the two oceans, is about 60km (40 miles) long and shares with the Suez Canal the status of one of the most important strategic waterways in the planet. Between 1914 and 1979 the Panama Canal was controlled by the United States, which built it. It then passed to joint US/Panamanian ownership and is now run by the Panama Canal Commission.

Due to its border with Colombia, Panama is an important conduit for narco-traffickers taking their wares from South to North America. For this and for its strategic importance, which included its importance as a base for US Southern Command (SOUTHCOM), what goes on in Panama is a matter of intense interest to the US Government.

Manuel Noriega was commander of the Panamanian Defence Force from 1983. He backed the presidency of General Omar Torrijos Herrera and was the real power in Panama. Noriega was connected with drug trafficking and, although he had liaised with US agencies such as the CIA in the past, his attitude to the United States had become increasingly hostile.

Due to the strategic importance of Panama, Noriega's increasingly unpredictable and hostile behaviour became a matter of intense concern and plans for an invasion were put in place.

SPECIAL FORCES OPERATIONS

The Joint Special Operations Task Force (JSOTF) was tasked with key components of the wider invasion, including the capture of Noriega himself. Task Unit Papa (TU Papa) incorporated three SEAL platoons and associated command and control and mortar elements.

The operation was launched on 19 December at 19:30 in raiding craft which came within range of the beach near Paitilla airport. Combat swimmers were sent ashore to recce the beach and once the all-clear had been given the remainder of the team came in.

The SEAL teams and their support moved up to the runway where they expected the imminent arrival of Noriega himself and they planned to ambush his plane as it taxied.

One of the teams approached a hangar known to house Noriega's private jet, which would be his most likely form of getaway. At this point the Panamanian guards spotted the unit and a firefight ensued in which the SEALs were wounded. As the other teams moved in to support, the Panamanian Defence Force were gradually moved back.

Eventually the SEALs were relieved by a Ranger force. With four dead and eight wounded, it had proved a costly operation but one that ultimately achieved its objectives. One of the problems during the operation was that there was no communication between the ground team and the AC-130H gunship circling above and which would have been able to provide critical fire support.

OPERATION ACID GAMBIT

The poor relationship between the United States and Panama was not only reflected in the threat to US strategic interests but also came to be focused on a single US citizen working in Panama called Kurt Muse. Having served in the US armed forces, Muse had returned to Panama to run a communications business and his disenchantment with the political developments in the country led him to publish leaflets and carry out broadcasts against the government.

Muse was eventually arrested and ended up in the notorious Modelo prison, whose occupants were regularly tortured and murdered.

Muse's plight was known in the United States and a plan was conceived to rescue him. Aware of the importance Muse represented to the Americans, Noriega turned the prison into a military fortress and used Muse as a hostage. A guard was placed outside Muse's door with instructions to kill him if there were any attempt at a rescue.

In order to get Muse out alive, SFOD–D (Delta) would need to get in and out on a hair trigger. They would have to insert a team by helicopter, neutralize large numbers of armed guards and reach Muse's cell before the guard standing outside Muse's cell could open the door and shoot him.

Knowing that shock and awe and sheer speed were of the essence, the US special forces built a mock-up of the Modelo prison at Eglin Air Force Base in Florida. Aerial support would be provided by the redoubtable 160th SOAR flying MH-6 'Little Birds' and UH-60 Black Hawk Helicopters. An AC-130 gunship of 1st Special Operations Wing would also be on standby.

Unknown to the Panamanian prison detachment, on 19 December Delta snipers in plain clothes walked by and around the prison, making a final assessment of the defensive positions and best lines of attack. There was a range of hills above the prison and it was probably these very same snipers who took up positions on the 20 December and adjusted their sights. By 00:40 the assault team was airborne. By 00.45 AH-6 'Little Birds' were approaching the prison compound and strafing likely Panamanian sniper positions. They then fired rockets at the headquarters building which caused the local garrison to emerge and carry out defensive measures. At this point one of the AH-6 helicopters was shot down.

At much higher altitude, two AC-130 gunships were circling in a 'top hat' formation, which meant that they were circling at different altitudes and with a different radius. This provided a potential for devastating firepower, though this would be limited to some degree by the presence of friendly forces on the ground. The AC-130s had designated targets which would provide a distraction from the hostage rescue operation. Meanwhile the snipers located in the hills above selected their targets and squeezed their triggers. Several Panamanian prison guards went down.

Fortunately for Muse, the intensity of the attack was such that all the guards were focused on defending the building. Soon there was a shout outside the door from an American voice telling him to stand clear from the door. The door was then blown open and a Delta soldier appeared carrying an MP-5 and holding a bullet-proof vest and Kevlar helmet for Muse. They moved out of the building and headed straight to an AH-6 'Little Bird' helicopter

on the roof. Muse and six Delta operators mounted the aircraft while a fierce battle took place in the streets below. As the helicopter gained height, it was hit by gunfire from the ground and began to go down. The skilled pilot managed to get it outside the prison compound area but could do little more than skim along the street outside. When the pilot tried to get the helicopter airborne, it was hit again by ground fire and crashed on its side.

Although some of the Delta soldiers were hurt, they managed to move away from the helicopter with Muse and set up a defensive position. Muse was armed with a pistol. A US helicopter gunship appeared and helped to defend the position until relief ground forces arrived with armoured personnel carriers that took Muse and the Delta team to safety.

The sheer determination, courage and endurance shown by Kurt Muse and his rescuers resulted in a successful rescue. Delta force had found and rescued a soulmate.

A US Navy SEAL undergoes anti-terrorist, ship-boarding training in the mid 1990s.

Operation Desert Shield (Defence of Saudi Arabia)
Operation Desert Storm (Air Assault on Iraq)
Operation Desert Sabre (Ground Assault on Iraq)
Operation Granby (British code for operations in
   first Gulf War)

THE FIRST GULF WAR

If military planners in Britain had needed reminding at the beginning of the Falklands War of the utility of special forces, it was certainly not lost on those who drew up the Orbat for operations in the Gulf in 1990, following the invasion of Kuwait by Iraq.

Almost the entire SAS regiment was deployed to the Gulf, including A, B and D squadrons as well as elements of R Squadron reserve. The Royal Marines Special Boat Squadron (SBS) was also deployed as were other specialized units, including special operations elements of the Royal Air Force.

The change in significance for UK special forces was also underlined in the command structure of British forces in the Gulf. Although the overall commander of British forces was Air Chief Marshal Sir Patrick Hine, the General Officer Commanding British land forces was General Peter de la Billière, an SAS officer through and through. De la Billière had served with the SAS in Malaya, Oman, Aden and Borneo and he was Director of the SAS group during the Northern Ireland troubles, the Iranian Embassy siege and the Falklands War. De la Billière had lived through the development of the SAS in the post-World War II period, seeing it become perhaps the leading counter-insurgency and

Facing page: This photograph shows a US Navy SEAL during training on board a US Navy aircraft carrier during the Gulf War, 1991.

counter-terrorist military unit in the world. Now he and the SAS were effectively coming home. The SAS had been created in the North African desert during World War II and desert operations should be second nature.

BY 'ALL NECESSARY MEANS'

The Allied deployment into the Gulf region and Saudi Arabia was carried out with great efficiency and speed, substantially helped by the fact that the operation had the full backing of the United Nations, which ruled that the Iraqis should be removed from Kuwait by 'all necessary means'. The immediate priority was the defence of Saudi Arabia, lest the emboldened Iraqi forces should decide to rampage into the Kingdom and seize control of most of the world's oil reserves. Once defence in depth had been achieved in Saudi Arabia through Operation Desert Shield, and with all necessary forces assembled, the next step would be to go on the offensive.

As far as special forces were concerned, at the outset of the war it was thought they might be used in a hostage-rescue operation. Saddam Hussein had cynically paraded British nationals on television and there was a fear that they might be used as human shields. In due course, however, the hostages were released and such an operation proved unnecessary. The Iraqis, however, had another very useful distraction up their sleeves in the form of their modified versions of the S-1 Scud tactical ballistic missile (TBM) which was transported on an eight-wheel MAZ-543 transporter-erector-launcher (TEL) truck and was thus easily moved around the vast expanses of the Iraqi desert. The maximum range of the Iraqi al-Hussein missile was thought to be about 650km (404 miles) and the al-Hijarah had a range of up to 900km (560 miles), which gave the Baáthist regime plenty of scope to target both Saudi Arabia and Israel.

In the event, although the Scud missile system had been used to great effect by Iraq in its war against Iran (1980–88), the direct damage caused by Scuds during the Gulf War was relatively modest. The real effect of the Scuds lay in their potential to be armed with either chemical or nuclear warheads,

their disproportionate psychological impact as a terror weapon (similar to the effect of the German V2 rocket in World War II) and the political implications of their targeting.

Although held together by the glue of UN resolutions and fears of what Saddam Hussein might do next, the Allied coalition could easily be prised apart if Israel were to become involved. If this happened, the Arab members of the coalition would most likely leave and Saddam Hussein would be in a better position to make his war part of the wider Arab cause.

THE SCUD PROBLEM

As daily reports were filed by the world's media on Scud missile attacks on Israel and elsewhere, the Allies gave urgent priority to drawing the Scud sting. One solution was to set up a missile defence system capable of shooting them down. The MIM-104 Patriot Surface to Air Missile (SAM) was deployed in Saudi Arabia and it began to score some successes against Scuds. In view of the enormous speeds involved, this was a considerable achievement but the Patriot system did not prove to be impregnable. A Scud missile hit a US Army barracks at Dhofar, killing 28 people, and some continued to get through to Israel. It has been suggested that part of the problem was a fault in the Patriot timing system that was later corrected. It was clear, however, that an essential part of the solution to the Scud problem was locating the missiles and destroying them. Aerial assets had been assigned to the task, but locating the Scud launchers continued to be an issue.

There was no better qualified person than General de la Billière to suggest how mobile Scud launchers might be tracked down to be either destroyed from the ground or from the air. It seems that de la Billière lost no time in persuading the commander of US forces, General Norman Schwarzkopf, that special forces would be ideally suited to the task. As Israel became more and more restless, political pressure built up to do anything and everything to diminish the Scud threat. It is thought that British special forces were already behind enemy lines, carrying out unspecified disruptive missions, before the focus was switched

US SPECIAL FORCES DEPLOY

The United States also deployed a large special forces contingent under US Special Operations Command (USSOCOM).

US Army special forces
Delta
1st Special Forces Group
5th Special Forces Group
160th Special Operations Aviation Regiment (SOAR)
82nd Airborne Division
101st Airborne Division

US Navy special forces commanded by Naval Special War Group One (SPECWARGRU)
SEAL teams 1, 2, 3, 4, 5, 8
SEAL Delivery Vehicle Teams (SDV) 1, 2
Special Boat Units (SPECBOATU) 11, 12, 13, 20
US Air Force special forces under 1st Special Operations Wing (1 SOW)
8th Special Operations Squadron (SOS): MC-130E Combat Talon
9th SOS: HC-130H Combat Shadow Tankers
16th SOS: AC-130H Spectre gunships
20th SOS: MH-53J Pave Low helicopters
55th SOS: MH-60 Pave Low helicopters

to the Scud launchers. After that, there was little time for anything else. The operations against the Scuds soon became a major component of Allied operations, with almost the entire array of military special operations groups and substantial aerial assets devoted to the task.

Not surprisingly, the Iraqi armed forces were as aware as the Allies of the importance of the Scud launchers and it did not take the presence of an SAS commander in theatre for them to predict that the Allies would be using all available means to hunt them down.

Considerable efforts were made by the Iraqi armed forces to maximize the manoeuvrability and concealability of the Scuds, using both natural cover in the form of wadis and gullies, as well as specially built shelters on the sides of roads and existing man-made cover such as bridges and tunnels. Since the most dangerous moment for the Scud launch team was immediately after the launch, great efforts were made to pare this window of time down to a minimum, with an average of about 30 minutes spent on site. This gave very little time for aerial observers to intercept. In addition, the Iraqis also employed decoys to confuse the searchers still further.

Although Allied aircraft had been given designated particular 'kill boxes' in the likely launch areas, with the operational aim to strike the launchers after release of missiles, their onboard sensors often proved to be unable to distinguish the launchers from other vehicles or general background 'noise'.

Once US special forces had been ordered into Iraq to join the British in the Scud hunt, they were allocated separate areas of operations in Western Iraq, an area encompassing in total about 29,000 square km (11,200 square miles). The US area of operations, known as 'Scud Boulevard', was located to the north-west of the main Baghdad to Amman highway.

The area designated for SAS operations, nicknamed 'Scud Alley', extended south from Highway 10 to the Saudi Arabian border. General Norman Schwarzkopf's contention, delivered in the early days of the Gulf War, that small teams of men could not hope to cover such

General Sir Peter de la Billière. As commander of British land forces in the Gulf, he made maximum use of special forces in the battle against the Scuds.

a vast area of territory seemed to be correct. What effect could teams of eight men have in an area of about 75,000 square km (29,000 square miles), roughly the area of Scotland?

HUNTING THE LAUNCHERS

The answer is that, whereas Scotland is rugged, mountainous and wooded, most of western Iraq is as flat as the proverbial pancake. Although the Scud teams were highly efficient in using available cover, what they could not disguise was the large fireball that would glow across the desert when a missile

S-1 Scud B missiles. Although the missiles were not very accurate, there was concern that Iraq would arm them with biological or chemical warheads.

was fired. In a totally flat area such as the Iraqi desert, such a 'signature' could be seen from many miles away and any mobile teams on the ground would instantly set about working out the nearest possible position of the launcher and the likely direction of onward travel. Taking into account the speed of the launch vehicle, the nature of the ground, the direction of nearby highways and roads and likely sites for concealment, the team would be ale to narrow down their search area considerably. The Western desert is at an elevation of about 490m (1600ft) above sea level. The Al-Hajarah

or southern desert consists of a rocky surface interspersed with occasional wadis, depressions and ridges. There is very little vegetation. During the day, the sky is normally clear and the desert becomes extremely hot. At night, again with clear skies, the heat quickly evaporates and is replaced by often intense cold. In the Iraqi winter, which runs from about the end of October, rain, sleet and even snow can make life miserable for anyone unfortunate enough to be caught outside.

Although advantageous in some respects, as its sheer size constituted in itself a form of protection, the hard and unforgiving desert was not an easy place in which to find cover. Just as a British or American unit might find it easy to spot the signature of a Scud launch in such a moonscape, so could a unit of soldiers be all too easily spotted by the Iraqis.

Both US and UK special operations personnel were trained in desert warfare, but this was a different style of desert to the one that many were expecting. There were no rolling dunes here to provide cover. No soft sand in which to easily dig a lying-up position and observation post, formed from sand bags and duly covered with camouflage nets for concealment from both the ground and the air.

It comes as little surprise to discover, therefore, that no sooner had one patrol from B Squadron SAS, namely Bravo One Zero, been dropped by Chinook helicopter in the southern part of the British sector that, after a rapid reconnoitre, they are thought to have decided that the risks were too great. 'Who Dares Wins' is one thing but it should also be remembered that any fool can get himself killed. Having requested that the helicopter crew remain on station during the initial recce, Bravo One Zero asked to be extracted.

WHEELS OR FEET

Some SAS units had elected to bring their own transport with them in the form of modified Land Rover Defenders, known as 'Dinkies' or 'Pinkies'. Fast and heavily armed transport of this kind had obvious advantages. The unit would be able to cover a much wider area at greater speed and would be likely to be on location soon after one of the elusive Scud launchers had betrayed its presence by firing a missile. It would also provide the team with considerable firepower to either engage the enemy or get out of trouble. Last but not least, a vehicle could carry the substantial amount of equipment used by an eight-man SAS team, avoiding the need for an exhausting march on foot and possible loss of operational efficiency.

The disadvantages of a vehicle behind enemy lines were also obvious. This was territory in which powerful enemy forces could appear at any moment and a vehicle would be much easier for them to pinpoint than a unit on foot. The whole concept of concealment could be easily compromised, especially in such harsh and open territory. The Iraqi desert was such, however, that fast movement in a vehicle was probably the better option.

From its earliest years in the North African desert, the SAS had made good use of a fast, light all-terrain vehicle exemplified by the Willys Jeep. The SAS somehow managed to cram as much equipment and firepower on to a military Jeep as was normally found on a vehicle twice its size. The British successor to the Jeep, the Land Rover, became a legend in its own right. With substantially more space and power, the short-wheel-base Land Rover Defender was ideally suited to fast and relatively inconspicuous operations with small

Wreckage caused by a Scud attack in Tel Aviv, Israel in 1991. Scuds became a priority target for special forces.

British SAS soldiers pose during the Gulf War in 1991. There is a close similarity with the Long Range Desert Group soldiers of World War II.

teams. It was adapted to special forces use and could carry two Browning machine guns.

Notwithstanding all the advantages provided by this rugged vehicle, as well as the backup of considerable firepower, Bravo Two Zero elected to go without transport. According to details released by some of its members, after Bravo Two Zero was set down by a Chinook helicopter the soldiers were shocked to discover how little cover was available. It also became clear that, despite being weighed down by heavy bergens and belt kit, they did not have sufficient clothing to endure the harsh winter conditions of the desert. Unfortunately for Bravo Two Zero, their only hope of rescue was via Chinook helicopter as they had no option of a fast escape by Land Rover.

Whereas Bravo One Zero had quickly appraised the ground as unsuitable for an eight-man unit without vehicles, once Bravo Two Zero had come

to the same conclusion their only transport had already departed and they had no way of finding cover or extracting themselves other than by using their own feet.

To maximize the discomfiture of the Bravo Two Zero team, they had been dropped within only a few hundred metres of a major Iraqi anti-aircraft position. In view of the lack of cover, they would be extremely exposed during daylight hours, especially if their tracks were spotted. The last straw was that, when they tried to establish radio contact with their base in order to be moved to a safer location, they could not get through. Later they would discover they had the wrong radio frequencies.

Like the fiasco at Arnhem at the end of World War II, Bravo Two Zero found themselves compromised amongst large numbers of enemy and with no radio communications. It was a disaster which only one of them would survive without death or capture.

Despite initial qualms about its insertion, Bravo One Zero, made up of soldiers from A Squadron SAS, re-entered Iraq as a convoy consisting of

Land Rovers, a Mercedes UniMog support vehicle and some all-terrain motorcycles. The vehicles were armed with 12.7mm (.50 cal) Browning machine guns as well as Milan or TOW anti-tank missile launchers. There was an assortment of light weapons, including the 7.62mm (0.3in) General Purpose Machine Gun (GPMG), 40mm (1.57in) Mk19 grenade launcher and personal weapons such as the M16 rifle.

The patrol of vehicles travelled at night, having crossed the Iraqi border, and the vehicles were camouflaged in wadis or other available cover during the day.

There are some accounts that Bravo One Zero carried out a successful assault on an Iraqi radar position that was responsible for guiding Scud missiles to their target. The site had apparently already been hit by Allied aircraft but was still able to function and was in the process of being repaired.

As it was a large team with a full backup of supplies, Bravo One Zero would have been able to mount a powerful attack on such an installation. Accounts suggest that the target was rendered inoperable in the attack and that the SAS team then withdrew unscathed.

Despite the much larger size of Bravo One Zero, it had managed to achieve an attack that met the criteria of special forces missions, namely a fast attack and withdrawal, with minimal contact with enemy forces in carrying out the primary aim, which was the disablement of the asset. This is in contrast to the plight of Bravo Two Zero, which found itself in a position dangerously close to the enemy, and unable to extricate itself quickly due to the amount of equipment it had to carry.

Special forces such as the SAS, along with other units with covert responsibilities such as forward target observers, and also aircrew, receive advanced training in escape and evasion (E and E) but a basic principle of such training is not to engage enemy forces.

Special forces are trained to carry heavy equipment over their backs in specialized Bergens over long distances. They are prepared for this in lengthy endurance exercises in areas such as the Brecon Beacons in the UK. But no one is naive

enough to assume that even these exceptionally fit soldiers can carry out a firefight with over 25kg (55lb) carried on their backs.

Bravo Two Zero found themselves placed in a position that all special forces are trained to avoid and one in which even the world's most highly trained soldiers can be overcome by sheer numbers of third-rate infantry. That Bravo Two

An artist's impression of an SAS soldier in the 1991 Gulf War. He is armed with the L1A1 7.62 (0.3in) self-loading rifle.

Zero managed to extract themselves from their initial engagement with Iraqi forces is a testament to their fitness and skill. Almost every time an SAS man turned to fire at the pursuing enemy, his shot found a target, and this would have been enough to keep them at bay.

Surprisingly, in view of the more open attitude of the US authorities to sensitive military information when compared to the British, there is considerably more information available on British ground counter-Scud operations than American.

The 1st Special Forces Operational Detachment – Delta (1st SFOD–D), commonly known as Delta Force, is one of the most secretive units in the US military, even by usual special forces standards. The unit was originally based on the SAS, as its founder, Colonel Charles Beckwith, had spent some time with the British unit.

DELTA FORCE

The selection process for Delta Force is even more exclusive than that of the SAS. Rather than wait for volunteers to come forward, Delta recruiters proactively examine military records from various units, including the Rangers, and then send a letter of invitation to start the selection process. The selected candidate is, of course, under no pressure to proceed. From this stage on, it will require all of his personal determination to get through the grinding Delta selection process. This starts with a tough physical test to weed out any potentially unfit candidates. Those that are unqualified for parachute drops then go on a paratroop course. There follows

The SAS Bravo Two Zero team. Their mission was bedevilled with bad luck but also demonstrated the extraordinary qualities of the SAS soldier.

The badge of 1st Special Forces Operational Detachment Delta. The unit has highly secretive recruitment and operational procedures.

February and it is said there was an engagement with a Scud launcher and other Iraqi vehicles on 7 February. F-15E aircraft were called in by the Delta soldiers and it is thought that a Scud launcher may have been destroyed, in addition to other damage. On another occasion, there were accounts that Iraqi helicopters were attacked and destroyed by F-15s after the fighters had been called in by a helicopter of 160th Special Operations Aviation Regiment (SOAR). If this was the case, the likely scenario is that the SOAR helicopter was in the process of either inserting or extracting the special forces unit when they were intercepted by Iraqi airborne units. This ability to call in air strikes was, of course, crucial to the success of the special operations units

a 'warm-up' phase of intensive physical training that includes runs, swimming exercises and forced marches with heavy weights.

Major selection takes place at Camp Dawson in the Appalachian Mountains where the applicants are put through a further gruelling series of marches and other endurance exercises which thoroughly test their physical and mental abilities. After a month of this, the selectors are pretty sure that they have whittled the group down to a cadre of exceptional performers.

Like the SAS, Delta is organized on a squadron basis, namely A, B, C and D squadrons, each comprising 25 soldiers. The squadrons are subdivided into troops and these are divided in turn into four- or six-man teams. As with the SAS and other special forces organizations, there are a number of specialists within each unit, covering, for example, high altitude low opening (HALO) parachuting, mountaineering, scuba diving and so on.

Members of the Joint Special Operations Task Force (JSOTF) began to deploy into Iraq from early

Delta Force soldiers undergo fast-rope training. This is a widely used technique for rapid insertion of special forces.

and it proved fatal for the SAS Bravo Two Zero patrol that their radio communications with base were down.

THE NIGHT STALKERS

The US 160th Special Operations Aviation Regiment (Airborne), otherwise known as the Night Stalkers, is the dedicated US Army aviation regiment for infiltration, exfiltration and support of special operations soldiers. They are specialists in night flying and have the difficult task of being sometimes the most visible and audible indication of the presence of a special operations unit. Their tenacity in standing by units on the ground would place them in extremely hazardous predicaments, not least when extracting troops under fire, as they did over Mogadishu, as discussed later in this book. Based at King Khalid International Airport for the course of the Gulf War, the 160th was equipped in theatre with MH-47E and MH-47D Chinook and MH-60K, MH-60L and MH-60L Direct Action Penetrator (DAP) Black Hawk helicopters. The Chinook MH-47E and D versions are specially equipped for special operations missions, with Fast Rope Insertion Extraction System (FRIES) for rapid insertion or extraction of personnel, an armament system that includes two M-134 Miniguns and one M-60D machine gun, weather avoidance/search radar (MH-47D), aerial refuelling probe and other non-standard features.

The MH-60K Black Hawk is a tailored special operations helicopter with aerial refuelling (AR), aircraft survivability equipment (ASE) and advanced navigation systems including multi-mode radar. The MH-60L is again tailored to special operations, but with fewer advanced features than the K version. The MH-60L Direct Action Penetrator (DAP) is specifically devised for attack missions, including either direct action (DA) or troop assault missions. In DA role it is equipped with precision guided munitions.

These helicopters were used in the infiltration and exfiltration of units as well as occasional direct

action patrols against designated targets. The Night Stalkers had the ability to fly missions with night vision goggles.

It is possible that, apart from engaging with the Scuds, Delta force were also tasked with locating any stocks of chemical, biological or even nuclear weapons.

A US Navy SEAL team emerges from the water during training, the lead SEAL armed with an M16A2 with attached grenade launcher.

SPECIAL BOAT SERVICE

Apart from the SAS and Delta force units in the area, there was also a detachment of Royal Marine Special Boat Service (SBS) personnel who were tasked with destroying the electronic communications network between Baghdad and the Iraqi forward and mobile units, such as the Scud launchers. The Special Boat Service has the same roots as the SAS, having been formed in 1941 as a diver unit to carry out reconnaissance or sabotage missions against enemy installations. The Royal Navy formed a similar unit in 1942 called the Experimental Submarine Flotilla and in 1946 the Special Boat Service became part of the Royal

The badge of 160th Special Operations Aviation Regiment (Airborne). This regiment exposed itself to extreme danger during insertion and extraction.

Marines and in turn the School of Combined Operations.

The SBS specialized in water-borne insertions, either by submarine or boat, and would then become highly effective land operators, sabotaging or destroying either coastal installations or enemy assets further inland. They saw action in the Korean War, landing from submarines to destroy railways and other installations, and they are also said to have provided specialist advice during the Vietnam War. The SBS were deployed to Kuwait in 1961, when Iraq threatened to invade, and they were back on station again in 1991.

A team of 36 SBS operators were infiltrated into Iraqi territory in two RAF CH-47D Chinook helicopters. The level of danger can be construed from the fact that the unit was dropped only about 95km (60 miles) south of Baghdad. This meant that

the RAF pilots had to fly at extremely low altitude in order to keep under the Iraqi radar envelope and to avoid detection by anti-aircraft units. The risk was, of course, that the helicopters could be detected by the sound of their engines or that they would be visible to the human eye at such close proximity to the capital.

The Iraqis had a substantial array of anti-aircraft and other military installations in the area and there were also regular patrols. It goes without saying that all Iraqi units were on maximum alert. Unusually for a special operations mission of this type, the helicopters remained on station while the operation was carried out, greatly increasing the risk of detection. The MH-47 Chinook is over 30m (98ft) long and over 5.5m (18ft) high and therefore difficult to conceal in flat, open terrain. But the risk of remaining on station has to be weighed against the risk of the helicopters being detected as they fly out again.

The SBS group was divided into separate teams, one tasked with locating the fibre-optic cables under the ground, digging them up and planting explosives, while the other team provided all round defence for the both the explosives team and the helicopters. The protection team are thought to have been armed with a powerful array of weaponry, including the highly effective L7A2 General Purpose Machine Gun (GPMG), which can put down 850 rounds per minute at a range of up to 1500m (1640yd). Other weapons probably included anti-tank weapons such as MILAN, grenade launchers and mortars.

Having located the underground cables, the team then dug down and planted fused explosives before returning to the helicopter, followed by the protection team. In order to ensure the disruption to the cable network was effective, the team must have had to dig a considerable trench and to place a large quantity of explosives, all of which could have taken up to an hour and a half to achieve.

With the teams re-embarked, the helicopters then lifted off and headed back at low altitude towards the Saudi Arabian border. The glow from a powerful explosion in the vicinity of Baghdad would have been an indication to Allied forces that the mission was successful.

BRITISH AIR ASSETS

The Royal Air Force special forces dedicated flights are No. 47 Squadron, currently operating Hercules C1/C3 aircraft, and No. 7 Squadron, operating CH-47 Chinook HC2s. At the time of the Gulf War, however, No. 7 Squadron was still operating the Chinook HC1, along with No. 18 Squadron.

No. 7 Squadron pilots are trained in the use of night vision goggles and the squadron motto: *Per diem, per noctem* ('By day, by night') is appropriate to what they do. The Squadron is trained to fly at very low level and such skills were employed in inserting SAS troops behind enemy lines and in carrying out the SBS raid against Iraqi cable communications.

No. 47 Squadron provides long distance transportation and insertion of special forces and elite troops and is currently equipped with an adapted version of the C-130 Hercules, fitted with terrain-following radar. This enables the aircraft to fly at extremely low altitude, at night and in adverse weather conditions.

No. 8 Flight of the British Army Air Corps is based at Hereford and there are no prizes for guessing which special operations regiment it supports. The Army Air Corps is currently equipped with the Apache AH Mk 1, the Lynx AH Mk 7, the Gazelle AH Mk1 and the Eurocopter Squirrel.

The Army Air Corps Apache helicopter is a variant of the Boeing AH-64 Apache Longbow, assembled by Westland and incorporating a number of differences. The British variant is powered by Rolls-Royce RTM-322 engines, has a BAE Systems Helicopter Integrated Defensive Aid System (HIDAS) and it is armed with CRV7 rockets and the Brimstone missile.

Despite the well publicized misfortune surrounding Bravo Two Zero, the overall SAS and Delta force operations against the Scuds were a success. In their armed convoys, the SAS were able

Map showing the main SAS operational areas in 'Scud Alley' during the 1991 Gulf War.

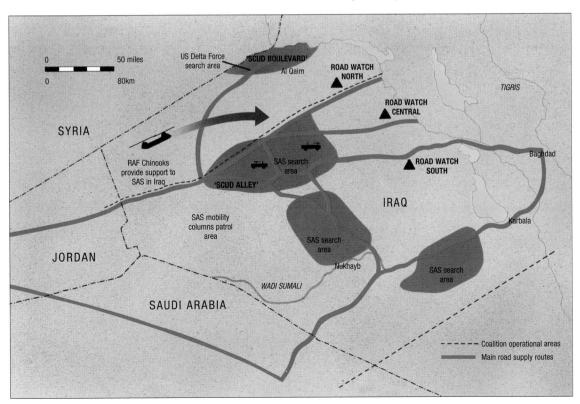

to target launchers with the portable medium-range anti-tank missile, known as MILAN. This missile has a range of about 2km (2190yd) and is said to have a 94 per cent hit probability. The effect of these precision raids was that the Scud launchers were driven further back towards Baghdad and thus constituted far less of a threat to Israel.

The SAS not only operated boldly by day and night, but also solved resupply problems by deploying a convoy of four-ton trucks in a hidden location where the reconnaissance and attack units

SAS soldiers mounted on British Army trail bikes, which offered mobility for reconnaissance around the convoy of Land Rovers and Mercedes Unimogs.

could return for resupply. It should be said that such tactics owed much to Allied air dominance in theatre.

Having deployed behind enemy lines before the US special operations forces, the SAS were able to provide their allies with plenty of useful advice with regard to such matters as weather conditions and the state of the ground. The US forces, for their part, integrated the British special operations units into their sophisticated communications network, which may have helped to obviate communications problems such as those experienced by Bravo Two Zero.

Other US elite forces in the Gulf included the US Rangers. Company B and 1st Platoon,

Company A, 1st Battalion 75th Ranger Regiment carried out a number of raids, some of which were behind enemy lines. A major assault was carried out on an Iraqi communications centre near the Jordanian border.

US AIR UNITS

Special operations teams on the ground benefited from the expertise of Air Force Special Operations Command (AFSOC), which included the 160th Special Operations Aviation Regiment, mentioned already. AFSOC had been established as recently as 22 May 1990, though its roots extended back to World War II.

AFSOC units in theatre included 1st Special Operations Wing (SOW), 71st Special Operations Squadron of 919th Special Operations Group (SOG), 1720th Special Tactics Group (STGP), 20th Special Operations Wing (SOW), 193rd Special Operations Group and, of course, 3rd Battalion of 160th Special Operations Aviation Regiment (SOAR).

The 1st Special Operations Wing was equipped with AC-130s, HC-130s, MC-130s, MH-53s and MH-60s. The 193rd SOG had EC-130s, the 919th SOG had AC-130s and the 71st SOS had HH-3s. The 39th SOW was equipped with HC-130s, MC-130s and M-53s.

AFSOC deployed combat controllers who were sometimes allocated to ground special forces units in order to provide invaluable expertise in directing coalition aircraft on to targets such as Scud launchers and in maintaining optimum communications throughout the mission.

The AC-130 is an armed version of the C-130 Hercules and is equipped with powerful side-firing weaponry, including a 105mm (4.1in) howitzer, 40mm (1.56in) Bofors cannon and a GAU-12/U Equalizer Gatling gun, though the specific armament depends on the variant.

The HC-130 is equipped for tactical air refuelling, airdrops of either personnel or equipment and search and rescue. Latest versions are equipped for night vision goggle (NVG) missions, which requires special on-board lighting.

The MC-130 Combat Talon and variants (MC-130E Combat Talon 1 and MC-130H Combat Talon II) are designed for infiltration and exfiltration of special operations personnel and equipment in covert combat conditions. The aircraft is fitted with high specification terrain-following navigation equipment which allows it to fly at low level. A powerful array of electronic warfare devices enable it to neutralize enemy radar and anti-aircraft threats, while the aircraft can also provide refuelling for special operations helicopters in flight.

The MH-53 Pave Low helicopter is specifically designed for covert penetration into enemy territory, with particular regard to the infiltration and exfiltration of special operations forces. It is equipped with advanced terrain-following radar that includes a projected map display, enabling the pilots and navigators to read ground contours and to pinpoint obstacles. Other technological assets include an infrared sensor, Doppler navigation system and inertia global positioning system.

Armour plating provides some protection from both ground and aerial threats. It is armed with at least three 7.62mm (0.3in) or 12.7mm (.50 cal) machine guns. At least one of these can be mounted at the tail ramp which is lowered for offensive or defensive fire. The loading ramp can also be used for dropping equipment and personnel.

The EC-130 is a variant of the HC-130 Hercules and is specifically configured for psychological operations (PSYOP) and other broadcast and communications missions. These included disruption of Iraqi communications during the Gulf War.

EQUIPMENT SHORTAGES

Despite the considerable technological assets at their disposal, US special forces on the ground were initially lacking GPS equipment that would have enabled them to carry out a ground attack on Iraqi radar installations as a prelude to the major bombing missions that opened the war. They also needed a longer time frame in order to adequately reconnoitre the ground and to make their approach under cover of darkness. In addition, Iraqi forces had moved some of their radar assets further back from the border. The special forces mission was therefore changed to become an aerial attack involving initially MH-53 Pave Low helicopters.

The AC-130 gunship could provide devastating fire support from its side-firing armament which includes an 105mm (4.1in) howitzer.

Then another hitch was encountered: the MH-53 Pave Low was only armed with machine guns that were unlikely to be powerful enough to obliterate the radar installations. A joint mission was therefore devised involving US Army AH-64 Apache helicopters.

The AH-64 Apache is the primary attack helicopter of the US Army and its armament includes Hydra 70 rockets and AGM-114 Hellfire missiles. The Hellfire in use was a laser-guided weapon that travels at just under 1600km (1000 miles) per hour.
The Apache is equipped to operate at night by use of an integrated display sight system. It also deploys Target Acquisition Designation Sight, Pilot Night Vision System (TADS/PNVS), a ground navigation system and a global positioning system (GPS).

THE FIRST STRIKE OF THE WAR
The MH-53 Pave Low helicopters of 20 SOS were to attack intermediate Iraqi mobile radar sites between the Saudi border and the main target. The Apaches would save their missiles (the Hellfires cost $42,000 apiece) for attacks on the main sites.
US Air Force Airborne special operations units therefore had the responsibility of opening up the entire Desert Storm campaign. Their destruction of the radar sites would effectively blind the Iraqi defences, allowing the aerial armada to pour through undetected. In view of the importance of the operation it would be perfectly rational to surmise that fail-safe backup alternatives had been put in place.

This, however, was not the case. As so often in special operations planning, failure was simply not an option. Despite flying at ground-hugging level in the dead of night over enemy territory with any number of Iraqi mobile radar-detection and anti-aircraft units in the area and as part of a joint

USAF and US Army team that had only recently been put together, with little time to rehearse, the USAF commander of the operation gave General Schwarzkopf a 100 per cent guarantee of success.

At 02:12 on 16 January 1991, the task force crossed the Iraqi border. If there was a point at which the first Gulf War began, this was it. The crews of the MH-53 Pave Low helicopters were equipped with night vision goggles (NVGs) and otherwise were flying on instruments. At times, they were flying at a height of only 15m (50ft) above ground level and were following the ground contours so closely that they dipped in and out of wadis. In order to obviate any chance of early warning, they even circumvented Bedouin camps, which the Iraqis sometimes used as cover.

A hypothetical attack by British special forces on a Scud unit. In reality greater use of ground cover and camouflage would be used by both sides.

As the MH-53 Pave Lows approached the target area, they dropped glowing sticks on the desert floor so that the Apache helicopters behind them could get their bearings. Once the Apaches were over the target area, things began to happen very quickly. An Iraqi sentry tried to run back towards a bunker but a Hellfire missile got there first. Both radar bunkers were then hit by a series of rockets and completely destroyed.

Despite the euphoria of success, on the return journey the Iraqi defences had truly woken up. One MH-53 Pave Low helicopter found itself being tracked by two SA-7 ground-to-air missiles. These missiles are programmed to lock on to the heat source from helicopters or other low-flying aircraft and the Pave Low crew fired flares in order to confuse the missiles while also ducking and diving to throw them off. It was a close call but the evasive tactics worked. The immediate follow up to the mission was that hundreds of Allied aircraft

ATTACKING A SCUD SITE
Key
1   SAS Land Rovers launch MILAN missiles at the site.
2   Mobile Scud launchers and command and control vehicles are the priority targets.
3   Iraqi BMP and BRDM armoured vehicles attempt to respond to the SAS attack.
4   After launching their missiles, the SAS evades any pursuers.
5   Any remaining targets of worth are destroyed by air attack.

flew into Iraq undetected to begin the major aerial assault of Desert Storm which has become so famous.

SEARCH AND RESCUE

AFSOC aircraft were subsequently on standby to carry out Combat Search and Rescue (CSAR) operations for downed pilots. One such mission was carried out by two MH-53 Pave Low helicopters in the immediate vicinity of a major Iraqi air base. The aircraft remained on station for up to 30 minutes in an attempt to locate the downed pilot via his radio beacon but they were either in the wrong area or the pilot had already been intercepted by Iraqi forces.

On 22 January, 39 SOW flew another CSAR mission only to find that the Iraqis were waiting for them. Having captured the downed pilots, the Iraqis waited for the MH-53 Pave Lows to get into the area and communicate with the aircrew's radio beacon, now in Iraqi hands. The minute the CSAR crew did so, anti-aircraft batteries opened up all around and the rescue team beat a hasty retreat. Had the

Facing page: An MH-53J Pave Low IIIE helicopter of 58th Special Operations Wing, 551st Special Operations Squadron.

pilots not already been captured, it is almost certain that they would have been rescued.

The rescue missions flown by MH-53 Pave Lows were not all flown by night. Despite the extreme vulnerability of the aircraft should it be spotted from the ground (even the concentrated fire of personal weapons could seriously damage the helicopter), in order to rescue downed pilots before the enemy reached them it was sometimes necessary to fly by day.

One such daylight rescue mission was flown by an MH-53 with aerial support from two F-15 fighters and two A-10 'tank busters'. The F-15

A Land Rover 110 converted for special forces use. The vehicle is mounted with a MILAN anti-tank weapon. Smoke grenades are fitted on the front fender.

Eagle was one of the most successful aircraft used in Desert Storm, with an aerial combat record of 34 Iraqi MiGs, Sukhois, Mirage F1s and helicopters. It was also allocated to nocturnal Scud-hunting and attacks on Iraqi tanks, artillery and other assets.

The A-10 Thunderbolt is designed for close air support of ground forces. Its characteristic straight wings allow it a high level of manoeuvrability at low speeds and at low altitude and, in view of the likelihood of ground fire, it is protected by 400kg (900lb) of titanium armour. The aircraft is designed to remain flying with half a wing blown off.

The A-10 is armed with a GAU-8/A Avenger Gatling gun that can fire 3900 rounds per minute of 30mm (1.18in) armour-piercing shells. These are capable of defeating tanks and other armoured vehicles. It also carries the Maverick air-to-ground missile, cluster bombs and rocket pods. During the Gulf War, A-10 Thunderbolts are said to have destroyed 1000 Iraqi tanks, 2000 other military

vehicles and 1200 artillery pieces. In this case, although the MH-53 Pave Low helicopter could not communicate with the pilot and eventually returned to base, the A-10 Thunderbolt sighted the downed pilot and two MH-53 Pave Lows were immediately dispatched. Due to other mission parameters at the time, this second CSAR mission was accompanied by no less than 12 F-16 fighters, four A-10s and two F-15s.

The rescue helicopters flew straight over a large convoy of Iraqi military vehicles, at about 3m (10ft) off the ground, and, as they approached the pilot, the MH-53 made voice contact. Almost simultaneously they noticed an Iraqi vehicle speeding towards the pilot and the A-10 Thunderbolt was called in. The vehicle was quickly

British SAS soldiers in a Land Rover 110 armed with a MILAN anti-tank weapon, during Operation Desert Storm.

US Navy SEALs and French commandos prepare for a joint training exercise on the oiler USNS Joshua Humphreys.

destroyed. The pilot was nearby and one helicopter landed, with two crew members going out to retrieve the pilot, with one providing cover. The helicopter then headed back to base.

Another downed pilot was picked up in Iraqi territory by a CH-47 of 3rd Battalion 160 SOAR on 17 February.

SETTING A BENCHMARK

The 1991 Gulf War created a new benchmark in the use of special forces and the change in attitude is probably best illustrated by the sharp learning curve of the US Commander-in-Chief, General Norman Schwarzkopf. For perfectly understandable reasons, Schwarzkopf had been sceptical about the viability of small teams of men in an area as vast as the western Iraqi desert but, with the increasing success of SAS operations, the pressure to resolve the Scud threat to Israel and the arrival of US ground special forces in theatre, Schwarzkopf's attitude was

transformed. He became aware that the targeted attacks by highly trained men were in actual fact extremely effective in controlling the Scud threat and that the liaison with special operations aerial assets, whether from the US Air Force, US Army, Royal Air Force or Army Air Corps, was working extremely well.

Special forces were not just a useful sideshow, a fly buzzing around the head of the enemy, but rather, as General Allenby had discovered in his campaign against the Ottoman Turks in 1917, a major strategic asset.

Schwarzkopf stated in a letter to the overall commander of British forces in the Gulf, Air Vice Marshal Sir Patrick Hine, that the SAS had succeeded 'in totally denying the central corridor of western Iraq to Scud units'. The combination of the SAS and US special operations forces was such as to cause 'the enemy to be convinced that they were facing forces in Western Iraq that were more than tenfold the size of those they were actually facing. As a result, large number of enemy forces that might otherwise have been deployed in the eastern theatre were tied down in Western Iraq.'

Operation Restore Hope (Supporting United Nations
operations in Somalia)
Operation Octave Fusion (Rescuing Jessica Buchanan
and other hostages)

SOMALIA

Somalia is a coastal nation in east Africa that
borders the Indian Ocean and the Gulf of Aden.
Its immediate inland neighbours are Djibouti,
Ethiopia and Kenya. In the colonial period it was
run by the British, though Italy took over the
southern region of the country.

During World War II, the Italians invaded
British Somaliland but the British drove them
out and also took control of the Italian territory
until 1950, when the Italian part became a UN
protectorate. In 1960 the United Republic of
Somalia was created out of both the British and
Italian territories.

After a period of some unrest and economic
difficulty, Major General Mohamed Siad Barre took
over in 1969, following the assassination of the
previous president. The country became the Somali
Democratic Republic, with strong links with the
Soviet Union.

Through the 1980s, unrest grew and warring
factions began to make claims of independence.
An insurgent group in the north declared itself
the Somaliland Republic. In Mogadishu, different
factions supported either Mohamed Ali Mahdi or
Mohamed Farah Aideed (Somali National Alliance)
as president. The ensuing civil war combined with

*Facing page: Protesters take to the streets of
Mogadishu in support of the national government
following violence in the Somali capital in 1993.*

a drought led to the death of about 300,000 people
in 1992.

In 1991 the UN Secretary General had sent an
envoy to gain agreement for UN involvement and
for humanitarian relief operations to be established.
In 1992 the United Nations Operation in Somalia
(UNOSOM) was established. Such was the ongoing
strife among the factions, however, that the
humanitarian convoys came under attack from local
warlords and their followers. It became very difficult
for non-governmental organizations (NGOs) and
the UN to deliver the aid and relief that the local
people so desperately needed.

In September 1992 a UN security force of about
500 Pakistani troops arrived in Somalia and in
November 1992 the United States took the lead in
organizing a humanitarian protection force.

US MILITARY INVOLVEMENT

Members of the US 5th Special Forces Group
(Airborne) were involved at an early stage in
protecting relief flights carrying humanitarian
supplies. They also carried out covert reconnaissance
of airfields and other assets that might be useful for
a future US force deployment.

On 3 December 1992, UN Security Council
Resolution 794 authorized the use of 'all necessary
means to establish as soon as possible a secure
environment for humanitarian relief operations in
Somalia'.

A Unified Task Force (UNITAF) was authorized under US direction and comprised both US and associated UN troops from 23 nations. The first elements of the new force deployed on 9 December 1992 and their mission, Operation Restore Hope, was to establish throughout Somalia a secure environment for humanitarian assistance. These means had been established under Chapter VII of the new UN Charter and the United States provided the necessary organizational and logistical infrastructure.

Supported by Humvees, soldiers from 9th Psychological Operations Battalion (PSYOPS) patrol down a street in Kismayo, Somalia.

About 1500 US Marines and US Navy SEALs arrived on 9 December and they were joined by 2nd Brigade 10th Mountain Division, comprising about 10,000 soldiers and including an aviation brigade and artillery. In total there were about 38,000 troops from the various contributing nations under UNITAF command.

EARLY PROGRESS

By February 1993, substantial progress had been made in confiscating arms, establishing security for humanitarian supplies and distribution centres and gaining agreement among warlords to cooperate with relief efforts. The country was divided into nine relief sectors and infantry battalions were

assigned to each one of them. Although several political parties agreed to attend a conference for national reconciliation in March, the fierce rivalry between the faction of General Mohamed Farah Aideed and Ali Mahdi remained. UNITAF was not authorized to actively interfere with either faction, only to protect humanitarian relief work.

In January, Special Operations Command Central established Joint Special Operations Forces – Somalia (JSOFOR) in Mogadishu to provide command and control of all special operations throughout Somalia. Teams of special operations personnel deployed to the nine relief sectors to liaise with the military units there and to conduct psychological (PSYOPS) and Civil Affairs (CA) missions. Operational Detachment A (ODA) from 5th Special Forces Group (Airborne) placed teams of about 12 special forces soldiers in each region, including the Canadian and Australian controlled regions of Beledweyne and Baidoa.

There were encouraging signs that a certain degree of normality was returning to Somalia, policed by the various military forces and despite the simmering tensions between the various factions. From the military perspective, Operation Restore Hope was proving to be a success. Even though UN Chapter VII resolutions had authorized use of force, the mere presence of well equipped and highly trained military forces was proving to be a deterrent to those who would wish to interfere with the peaceful relief efforts. UNITAF, however, was not set up as a long-term mission and arrangements were underway to transfer power back to UNOSOM.

In view of the underlying threats from factions and the fact that they were likely to burst into the open once the UNITAF mission was closed, UNOSOM II was also set up on the basis of Chapter VII of the UN Charter, authorizing the use of force. Although the US presence in the country was scaled down to a tactical reaction force at the disposal of the new UN commander, Lt Gen Bir, as well as logistics and other support, a brigade of the 10th Mountain Division remained in the country. Despite having signed up to an Agreement of the First Session of the Conference of National Reconciliation in Somalia on 27 March 1993,

THE HUMVEE (HMMWV)

The M998 Truck High Mobility Multipurpose Wheeled Vehicle (HMMWV), commonly known as the Humvee, was first produced in 1985 to fulfil a US Army specification to replace the M151 Jeep and other light reconnaissance and associated vehicles. It is produced in a very large number of variants that include ambulances, TOW missile carriers and cargo troop carriers.

Its width and high ground clearance are said to give it exceptional cross-terrain mobility while carrying a substantial payload.

While it is said to fulfil the above roles satisfactorily, the weaknesses of the Humvee were revealed in Somalia where it was shown to be vulnerable to small arms fire, let alone anti-tank weapons such as an RPG. Once their request for armoured vehicles had been refused, Task Force Ranger were forced to rely on armoured personnel carriers from the Malaysian and Pakistani contingents.

Although up-armoured versions of the Humvee have been produced, the increase in urban conflict has led to calls for a more secure armoured vehicle that can provide light reconnaissance while also affording protection against small arms and other attacks. Such vehicles would include the Force Protection Cougar 4x4 and 6x6 vehicles recently ordered by both the US and UK armed forces

which included a commitment to disarmament, General Aideed's faction were clearly unwilling to hand over their weapons. The underlying tensions soon flared up into violence. Members of Aideed's faction went on to the offensive against Pakistani UN soldiers, killing 25 of them and wounding 54, while 10 remained unaccounted for. Security Council Resolution 837, passed the next day, authorized UN agencies to arrest those responsible for the attacks and to bring them to trial.

CROSSING THE MOGADISHU LINE

The UN forces now crossed what was to become known as the 'Mogadishu Line', namely the transition from a mostly peacekeeping to a peace enforcement and offensive military role. Pakistani

Paratroopers from the US 101st Airborne patrol in a Black Hawk helicopter. Helicopters were to prove vulnerable to attacks from rocket-propelled grenades.

and Italian armed units were sent out to actively destroy weapons, and US Air Force C-130 Hercules and AC-130 gunships carried out air strikes against weapons storage dumps in Mogadishu and on the Aideed faction's broadcasting installations. On 17 June a warrant was issued for the arrest of General Aideed. The die was cast.

On 12 July, when US helicopter gunships carried out an attack on another of Aideed's installations, a Somali mob murdered four western journalists who were reporting at the scene. A unit known as Task Force 3-25 Aviation was put together to carry out air patrols to intercept and capture Aideed

the moment he was spotted. The Aideed faction responded by killing four US military policemen. It was now abundantly clear that the stakes were very high indeed. In view of the fact that Aideed's forces possessed anti-tank rockets, anti-aircraft guns, mortars and light artillery, the threat needed to be faced with the best possible forces available.

TASK FORCE RANGER

A Joint Special Operations Task Force, codenamed Task Force Ranger, was deployed to Somalia from 22 August 1993. Its mission was to capture General Aideed and his lieutenants and to hand them over to UNOSOM II forces for questioning. Task Force Ranger was under direct US command and was not tied into, although it closely collaborated with, either the Quick Reaction Force (QRF) or UNOSOM II command structures.

Task Force Ranger consisted of: 75th Ranger Regiment, 1st Special Forces Operational Detachment – Delta (Airborne), US Navy SEALs, 160th Special Operations Aviation Regiment (Airborne) and US Air Force special tactics personnel.

Task Force Ranger conducted missions in Mogadishu to track leaders of the Aideed faction and on 21 September they captured one of his lieutenants. Not surprisingly, Aideed's faction reacted with more violence. The US Rangers and Delta Force were not easy targets so they took out their venom on UN personnel and vehicles. Pakistani and US soldiers of the Quick Reaction Force were attacked at a roadblock on 8 September with rocket-propelled grenades (RPGs) and small arms. Even more ominous was an attack accompanied by a large crowd of civilians. Another attack was carried out by Aideed's Somali National Alliance (SNA) on the airfield used by Task Force Ranger and on 25 September a US Black Hawk helicopter was shot down, killing three soldiers.

In view of the escalation in violence, the commander of Task Force Ranger, General Montgomery, requested armoured support from the US authorities but his request was not heeded at the time, probably because it was thought it would create a greater psychological barrier between the armed units and the local population.

THE LAST RAID
It has been said that a Somali agent working for the US Central Intelligence Agency (CIA) reported that several important members of the Aideed faction were planning to meet near the Olympic Hotel in the Black Sea slum district of Mogadishu on 3 October at 15:00.

Elements of the Task Force were soon ready to move in a pre-arranged formation. The perimeter and assault force left the base aboard 14 helicopters and the ground convoy left at the same time. There were about 75 Rangers and 40 Delta Force soldiers

deployed. When the helicopters reached the target area, groups of Rangers used fast-rope techniques to reach the ground and set about sealing off the area, blocking approach and exit roads.

Delta Force soldiers then approached the target aboard AH-6J 'Little Bird' helicopters piloted by 160th SOAR. They burst into the building and arrested 24 members of the SNA. Having rounded them up, they escorted them out of the building towards the convoy of waiting vehicles.

Everything was going smoothly and according to plan. Then RPG rounds started to come in on

Mohammed Farah Aideed, leader of the Somali National Alliance, became a primary target for US Task Force Ranger.

The AH-6J Little Bird helicopter, with its small dimensions, was ideal for inserting and extracting special forces teams in urban environments.

the vehicle convoy, destroying a five-ton truck and an HMMWV multi-terrain vehicle. Soon afterwards, as the ground force were about to load the detainees onto the vehicles, an MH-60 Black Hawk that had been circling overhead was hit by an RPG round. It crashed a couple of blocks away, northeast of the target area.

The perimeter security force had already come under sporadic fire from the ground and they had also suffered a casualty who had tragically missed the rope when descending and fallen to the ground below. Amidst the sporadic fire, an ever-larger crowd was now gathering, including a substantial number of women and children.

When the MH-60 crashed, a six-man Ranger squad rushed towards the scene on foot while a 15-man combat search and rescue team (CSAR), consisting of Rangers and Delta Force soldiers, flew in by MH-60 Black Hawk helicopter and fast-roped down to the wreckage.

Two crew members of the downed MH-60 were rescued by an AH-6J Little Bird helicopter. While two members of the CSAR team were still on the rope, their MH-60 Black Hawk was also hit by an

RPG round, but the pilot contrived to keep the helicopter airborne and it limped back towards base.

The CSAR team had arrived at the site just in time, for the SNA had also been rushing towards the spot, baying for blood. When they arrived, they continued to fire on the rescue team with RPGs and small arms. Although the vehicle ground force had tried to head towards the crash site, in the confusion and under heavy fire they lost their way. They lost two five-ton trucks and suffered numerous casualties.

The perimeter force, however, did reach the crash site on foot, though they took casualties on the way, and started to lay down suppressive fire.

A SECOND BLACK HAWK DOWN

Another MH-60, hovering over the first crash site, was now also hit by an RPG and plummeted to the ground south of the first crash site.

Although a Delta and Ranger Quick Reaction Force left the airport base area in a ground convoy in an attempt to reach the second crash site, this time the SNA, accompanied by a mob, got there first. Despite limited airborne rescue elements in the area, one MH-60 helicopter managed to drop two Delta Force soldiers about 90m (100yd) from the second crash site.

The MH-60 was almost immediately hit by an RPG but managed to get back to HQ before making a forced landing. The two Delta Force soldiers then set about defending the second crash site. Although these were some of the most highly trained men in the US Army, their options were drastically limited when faced by a mob of civilians. In due course the SNA and its mob overwhelmed the two defending soldiers and killed them along with everyone else in the helicopter, apart from the pilot, whom they took prisoner.

The US Quick Reaction Force, consisting of a company of the 2nd Battalion, 4th Infantry, 10th Mountain Division, also headed towards the second crash site but was pinned down by SNA ground fire. The 10th Mountain Division eventually had to withdraw back to the base at the airport.

Due to the difficulty of reaching the first crash site, where about 90 Rangers and Delta Force soldiers were still holding out, the Task Force

AH-6J LITTLE BIRD

Known as the Little Bird, the AH-6J has been developed specifically for special forces. Its major advantage is its small size, which allows it to deliver up to six men, sitting three-aside on bench-like structures along each side of the fuselage, into urban or other restricted spaces that larger helicopters could not reach. Its appealingly diminutive appearance masks a formidable array of weaponry that can include a mixture of M-60 machine guns or M134 miniguns; two 12.7mm (.50 cal) machine gun pods; two 70mm (2.75in) Hydra 70 rocket pods, two TOW missile pods or two Hellfire rails.

The helicopter is fitted with a GPS/inertial navigational system and forward-looking infra-red (FLIR), allowing it to fly in adverse conditions and at night, in accordance with the requirements of its main operators, 160th SOAR.

Ranger commander called on the assistance of the only units in the area who had tanks and armoured fighting vehicles, namely the Pakistani and Malaysian UN contingents.

In view of the complexity of the Mogadishu streets and the confusion caused by small arms and RPG fire, it required several hours of planning to bring the Pakistanis and Malaysians into the planning loop and to coordinate operations.

Eventually, over 60 vehicles from the UN contingents plus the 10th Mountain Division moved from the New Port Facility, just under 1.6km (1 mile) southeast of the first crash site. The rescue force consisted of four Pakistani tanks, 24 Malaysian armoured personnel carriers (APCs), two light infantry companies of 10th Mountain Division and 50 members of Task Force Ranger. The rescue force was accompanied overhead by AH-1 Cobra helicopters, UH-60 Black Hawks and OH-58A Kiowa observation helicopters.

Once the rescue convoy had reached National Street, it headed east towards the crash sites. The force split into two: column one heading for the first crash site and column two to the second. Some Malaysian vehicles from column two got lost in the streets and the soldiers had to leave their vehicles and take refuge in a building.

After a journey of about two and a half hours, the first column got within about 500m (546yd) of the estimated location of the first crash and the troops dismounted in order to fight their way forward.

The second column reached the second crash site only to find a burnt-out helicopter and bloodstains. By approximately 01:55, the 10th Mountain Division had fought its way through to the first crash site and helped with the rescue work, while maintaining all-round defence against ongoing attacks from the enemy. Overhead, AH-6 and AH-1 attack helicopters helped to deter the enemy, sometimes with rockets. The casualties from crash site one were loaded onto the APCs and the column prepared to move out towards the Pakistani headquarters, located in the football stadium, about 1200m (1320yd) northeast of their location. The 10th Mountain Division and Rangers travelled on foot, using the armoured vehicles for cover, and after an arduous battle against marauding SNA militia, they finally arrived at the base at 06:30.

The Task Force Ranger casualties on 3–4 October were 16 dead and 12 wounded. The 10th Mountain Division had two dead and 22 wounded; the Malaysian contingent had two dead and seven wounded and the Pakistani contingent had two wounded. Somali casualties were estimated at over 1000.

Two 70mm (2.75in) Folding Fin Aerial Rockets (FFARs), fired from an AH-1 Cobra gunship, streak towards their target.

ARMOUR ARRIVES

As a direct result of the experiences of Task Force Ranger, US armour was immediately despatched to the country, comprising 24th Infantry Division (Mechanized), with Bradley Fighting Vehicles and M1 Abrams tanks. AC-130 gunships were also sent out along with reinforcements for the 10th Mountain Division, a Marine Expeditionary Unit and special operations reinforcements.

Although the United Nations decided to renew the mandate for UNOSOM II even in the face of ongoing difficulties and lack of progress, the United States did not intend, despite its armour reinforcements, to maintain a presence in the country. The US set a date of 31 March 1994 for the withdrawal of its combat troops and most of their supporting agencies. US withdrawal clearly had serious implications for the continuing survival

Somali civilians inspect the wreckage of a US Army Black Hawk helicopter which was shot down over Mogadishu by a rocket-propelled grenade (RPG).

of UNOSOM II as a viable peacekeeping operation, in view of the fact that it could only call on under 20,000 troops to cover the whole country. Belgium, France and Sweden had withdrawn their contingents and, having seen what had happened to Task Force Ranger, no other country was willing to put forward its troops for similar treatment. The mandate of UNOSOM II was altered to reflect the new reality. They would no longer use coercive force to confiscate weapons or bring warlords to book but would only use force in self-defence.

Much would depend on the cooperation of the competing factions but, as it was now becoming clear, such cooperation was not forthcoming.

THE 10TH MOUNTAIN DIVISION

This division was formed in 1943, though it was related to units formed earlier, such as the 87th Mountain Infantry Regiment, formed in 1941. The division saw distinguished service in Italy towards the end of World War II, where it used its Alpine skills to good effect in securing high ground. By 1958, however, the unit had been deactivated and it was to remain dormant until 1984 when the 10th Light Infantry was based at Fort Drum, New York. As if to make up for lost time, the 10th Mountain Division has seen a wide range of deployments from Desert Shield and Desert Storm in 1990, through Operation Restore Hope in Somalia to Haiti and Bosnia and, more recently, in Afghanistan and Iraq.

Almost inevitably, with the US troops out of the country, far from coming together to resolve their differences, the Somali factions set about each other in an orgy of fighting. The humanitarian operation all but ground to a halt in and around Mogadishu. The UN Secretary-General's patience was running out and was only a matter of time until the UN pulled the plug on Somalia. The final extension of the mandate for UNOSOM II was to 31 March 1995.

LESSONS FROM TASK FORCE RANGER

The experiences of Task Force Ranger reflected in microcosm the experience of the wider UN peacekeeping mission in Somalia. Peacekeeping contingents, who were also mandated for peace enforcement, had arrived in Somalia to protect the majority of the Somali people from their own nationals who were raiding relief convoys and otherwise interfering with the relief effort. Despite the humanitarian disaster taking place around them, the rival factions could not bring themselves to cease their endless rivalry and competition for power and the relief agencies needed security forces to protect them while they went about their work. The use of force by peacekeeping and associated forces in Somalia was in the first instance benevolent and restrained. In the wake of the successful campaign

to oust Saddam Hussein's forces from Kuwait, US President Bush sr. thought US forces could contribute to establishing security in Somalia so that the relief effort could continue.

He did not, however, envisage a long-term commitment. The UN interventions in the form of UNOSOM I and UNOSOM II had the same objective with regard to the relief effort but they were also part of a wider UN objective to re-establish viable government and law and order in Somalia.

In the short term, the first objective was a success. The warlords were deterred by the presence of highly trained armed troops and the various international relief agencies were able to make some progress. Although a terrible humanitarian disaster had already occurred, the relief agencies prevented it from getting worse and saved millions of lives.

What remained unresolved, however, was the underlying antagonism of the factions, such as the SNA, towards each other and towards the UN and US security forces. Although the local population may not have been particularly well disposed towards the factions, they were ambivalent and later hostile to the foreign security forces.

Provoked by the confiscation of their weapons, the factions in turn succeeded in provoking the UN and US forces to react with increasing violence. It was difficult for the security forces to distinguish the insurgents from the local population and the insurgents made full use of their ability to lose themselves in the crowd or to turn the crowd against the foreign occupiers.

Once General Aideed had become identified as the main perpetrator of attacks against the security forces, the US political and military authorities focused on capturing him, as if this on its own were the key to resolving the crisis. Aideed became a hate figure for the Americans, much in the same mould as Saddam Hussein or Colonel Gaddafi. It is perhaps human nature to demonize a particular individual and to invest such an individual with full responsibility for the threats emanating from a particular country or region. As the Americans were to discover once they had defeated Saddam Hussein in Iraq in 2003, this was a dangerous illusion.

The hunt for Aideed was a distraction from

the wider imperatives of the UN and associated US presence in Somalia, which was to provide security for the humanitarian relief effort and an environment in which the local factions could reconcile their differences and begin to establish grounds for peace and rebuilding. This was also, however, to prove to be a chimera. The local factions did not share the high ideals of the UN: they only wanted to grab power for themselves by whatever means.

The hunt for Aideed also helped to define the gulf between the local Somali population and the security forces who came out in force to seize faction members. These snatches, performed by Delta commandos and US Rangers with aerial support from 160th SOAR, were textbook operations and largely successful. They were performed with such regularity, however, that it did not take long for the SNA to work out crude but effective tactics to counter them. Although a rocket-propelled grenade is theoretically designed to be used against a tank, a Black Hawk helicopter also makes a substantial target, and a comparatively easy one to hit if it is hovering over a particular location. Relatively thin-skinned vehicles such as HMWWVs or five-ton trucks are also easy targets for an RPG – and the local insurgents had plenty of RPGs.

The US soldiers that formed part of Task Force Ranger were present in the country on a humanitarian basis to protect the people of Somalia but unfortunately the people of Somalia had been turned against them by insurgents. Although the initial snatch operation on 3 October was carried out correctly and successfully, it soon turned into something else – a battle with the insurgent and local Somali population of Mogadishu.

The local people also had the advantage of knowing all the alleyways and back entrances of their town like the backs of their hands and it

A soldier of 2nd Brigade 10th Mountain Division provides cover while a Canadian Forces Air Command C-130 Hercules takes off in Mogadishu, 1993.

is no surprise that both the US and Malaysian contingents literally got lost during the course of the battle. A key special forces principle is not to engage with superior numbers of enemy forces. Special forces soldiers are highly trained and will be superior to their regular counterparts in most military skills but, even so, one man cannot fight an army. Sheer numbers will eventually overwhelm even the best soldier.

At the second crash site, two members of Delta Force attempted to defend the crash site but, with

Somali militia relax around a heavily-armed vehicle. Their considerable resources of weapons were soon turned on US and UN forces.

limited ammunition, they would have been selecting targets among a mob that included the very people they had been sent out to Somalia to protect. While wrestling with this conundrum and striving to defend the wounded members of their own team, they were killed.

The title of the book and film that cover the events in Mogadishu, *Black Hawk Down*, should perhaps have been written in the plural. Black Hawks were falling from the sky as they had no defence against well aimed RPGs, or any similar ordnance for that matter, fired from a concealed site or from amidst a crowd.

The only other option was travel by road, which in soft-skin vehicles was akin to suicide once the

insurgents had the crowd under their control. With a vast supply of weaponry available to them, every Somali could become a hero in the fight against the common foreign enemy who were arresting their fellow nationals.

Some commentators have observed that if Task Force Ranger had been better equipped it would have suffered fewer casualties. Weapons with a wider spread of fire have been mentioned as well as the use of AC-130 gunships, which, with their titanium armour, would have been immune to RPG rounds. Their Gatling guns would have made short work of enemy insurgents. And the ground troops should also have been provided with armoured vehicles.

Some of these comments are indeed correct. If the troops were to travel on the ground, given the hostility of the insurgents and the local population they would have indeed been wise to use armoured transport. The AC-130s may have provided a deterrent but they could not of course deliver ground troops. The other side of the coin, however,

A US UH-60 Blackhawk helicopter during a joint exercise in Africa. The Black Hawk proved vulnerable to ground fire during urban operations.

is that aircraft such as the AC-130 and A-10 tank buster were designed for major engagements with military forces, not to mow down crowds of civilians. And the soldiers on the ground would have been equally loath to use such powerful area weapons against civilians.

Armoured vehicles had indeed been requested for Task Force Ranger and the speed with which they were delivered after the events of 3 October reveals the wisdom behind the initial request, which was refused.

While it had become clear that Task Force Ranger had been set up on the basis of an offensive operation against General Aideed and his followers, the US forces whose mission it was to capture him were equipped with vehicles that were unable to resist the most basic infantry weapons or even small arms. A direct hit from an RPG could completely destroy an HMMWV, which was a major component of the transport for Task Force Ranger.

ACHILLES HEEL

The experiences of Task Force Ranger revealed a gap in US Army training and operations doctrine which was highlighted all the more against the backdrop of the successful campaign in Iraq in 1991.

In Iraq the US had shown how it could use overwhelming technological superiority to defeat a substantial and well armed foe with the minimum of its own casualties. In Somalia, the technological superiority was almost an irrelevance.

The fact is in Somalia and with particular reference to the operations of Task Force Ranger, the US Army found itself doing what armies throughout history have sought to avoid, namely fighting in urban terrain. Fighting in built-up areas is difficult enough when the enemy is in uniform and part of an organized force but fighting an insurgent army in an urban environment where the civilian population is fully present and liable to be co-opted by the insurgents is even more difficult still.

US forces would continue to project themselves around the world and large-scale ground battles had still to be fought against major armies, such as in the invasion of Iraq in 2003. The enemy, however, was not organized as a state that had accepted defeat; it developed into a hydra that grew heads as many times as they were lopped off. Insurgency and asymmetric warfare remained a long-term component of the clearing-up operation and if success was not achieved all the gains of the initial victory would be lost.

The US field manual for operations in urban terrain was re-written in the wake of Mogadishu and similar urban challenges where the US military Goliath found itself at the mercy of the insurgent David.

Much work was carried out in improving equipment, with the development of urban camouflage clothing, specialized elbow and knee pads to facilitate movement in the hard urban environment and specialized boots, designed for greater grip and resistance to the abrasion from asphalt and other hard surfaces. Lighter body armour was introduced to allow for greater ease of movement.

In a built-up environment, explosions and weapon noises are magnified while buildings can impede both electronic and visual communications. Research was therefore undertaken into developing ear protection devices that could electronically distinguish between unwanted loud noise, such as weapons fire or explosions, while still allowing the wearer to hear voices or radio messages.

For both US and British forces, it became imperative to purchase armoured vehicles that were resistant to mines and other threats in order to replace soft-skinned vehicles such as the Humvee and Land Rover. The issue of helicopters also remained to be resolved. Relatively lightly armoured helicopters simply could not afford to hover for long periods in potentially hostile urban areas.

More importantly, tactics would need to change. Much would depend on accurate information gathered through covert means, including close cooperation with intelligence agencies. Snatch squads would need to operate in such a way that they could move in and depart without being compromised by either organized or impromptu resistance.

Although Task Force Ranger was focused on the hunt for a particular faction leader, it was only a part of a wider operation, Operation Restore Hope, designed to give the people of Somalia a chance and a future.

A month after the arrival of the US Marines in Somalia in 1993 a young man from England, Sean Devereux, was shot in the back by one of the faction members. Sean Devereux was a Salesian teacher working for UNICEF and who had been outspoken in protesting against the abuses suffered by the Somali people. He tried to stop their food and other supplies from being stolen. He died for his pains.

Facing Page: US Marines carry out a routine patrol through the Bakara Market, Mogadishu, searching for arms and munitions.

MAERSK ALABAMA HIJACKING AND RESCUE OF CAPTAIN PHILLIPS

The MV *Maersk Alabama* container ship was bound for the port of Mombasa, Kenya, in April 2009. Despite advice from NATO to sail at least 600 nautical miles (1100km) off the coast of Somalia due to the pirate risk, the *Maersk Alabama* was sailing 240 nautical miles (440km/280 miles) southeast of the Somali port of Eyl when it was attacked by four pirates in a speedboat. The pirates managed to board the ship despite evasive action by the crew, including sharp turns, flares and fire-hosing.

Fourteen members of the crew locked themselves in the engine room while the captain of the ship, Phillips, and two other crew members remained on the bridge. The crew in the engine room took control of the ship, rendering the bridge controls useless. When the pirates went down to investigate, the chief engineer took the pirate ring-leader hostage. The crew then attempted to exchange the pirate for the captain, but the pirates kept hold of

US Navy SEALs jump from a C-130 Hercules transport aircraft during a High Altitude Low Opening (HALO) training exercise.

Captain Phillips. When he tried to escort them to a lifeboat, they forced him in and took him with them as a hostage.

The guided missile destroyer USS *Bainbridge* and the frigate USS *Halyburton* were despatched to the Gulf of Aden to shadow the lifeboat. They were later joined by the amphibious assault ship USS *Boxer*. The *Bainbridge* carried a Scan-Eagle reconnaissance drone as well as rigid hull inflatable boats while the Halyburton carried two SH-60B helicopters. A P-3 Orion surveillance aircraft was also deployed to the area.

Negotiators aboard USS *Bainbridge* established communications with the pirates but on Saturday 11 April the pirates lost patience and opened fire on the *Halyburton*. As the wind picked up, the captain of the USS *Bainbridge* persuaded the pirates to attach a towline.

SEAL TEAM 6 DEPLOY

On Friday 10 April elite snipers from US Naval Special Warfare Development Group (DEVGRU) or SEAL Team 6 boarded an air force C-17 Globemaster transport at Training Support Center, Virginia and flew direct to the Gulf of Aden. At

A US Navy team tows the lifeboat from the **Maersk Alabama** *where Captain Phillips was held following the successful rescue mission.*

dawn on Saturday 11 April they jumped out of the back of the C-17, performing a High Altitude Low Opening (HALO) jump to avoid detection. Landing in the sea near the USS *Halyburton*, the SEALs then transferred to USS *Bainbridge*.

Meanwhile, zodiacs went out from the ship so that negotiators could talk to the pirates. Eventually, the pirate leader was persuaded to come on board USS *Bainbridge* to discuss the ransom demands. When Phillips felt ill, the pirates called for a doctor. A zodiac came over with some food and also a bright yellow shirt and blue trousers for Phillips to put on. Neither Phillips nor the pirates guessed the real purpose of the bright yellow shirt. It was an identifier for the SEAL snipers so that they could easily spot Captain Phillips and keep him out of the line of fire.

Amid the ebb and flow of tensions in the negotiations with the pirates, on Sunday 12 April the SEALs covertly took up positions on the fantail of USS *Bainbridge*, lowered the bipods on their Mk 12 Special Purpose Rifles and began to scan the life boat through their Leupold Var-X Mil-dot riflescopes. Each sniper had to select a target

through the small windows of the lifeboat about 30 metres (100 feet) astern of the ship. They knew that they would have to kill all three pirates simultaneously if Captain Phillips was to survive.

The three pirates on the lifeboat were becoming more and more agitated, arguing among themselves. They had tied up Captain Phillips and threatened him repeatedly. When one of the pirates was seen to point an AK-47 assault rifle at Captain Phillips' back, Captain Castellano of USS *Bainbridge* gave permission for the snipers to fire. Two of the pirates poked their heads out of the back of the lifeboat while one could be seen through the window. Once each sniper had acquired their target, the SEALs, judging the rise and fall of the ship's deck and the movement of the lifeboat, squeezed their triggers. In an instant all three pirates were dead. One of the Navy SEALs climbed down the tow-rope to check if Captain Phillips was unharmed. Then the SEALs brought him out of the lifeboat, put him on their Zodiac and took him to the safety of the ship.

OPERATION OCTAVE FUSION, 2012

Jessica Buchanan, a US national, and Paul Thisted, who was Danish, had been working for the Danish Demining Corp, an organization that clears landmines and other explosives, when they were kidnapped on 25 October 2011. The kidnapping

was organized by members of three local gangs, the Sa'ad, Suleiman and Ayr, from southern Somalia, in an area between Galkayo and Mogadishu.

Following their successful raid on the house of Osama bin Laden in May 2011, it was no surprise that the President of the United States should call on the services of SEAL Team 6 for a rescue mission that could not only save the lives of two hostages but also maintain the reputation of the United States.

The main motive for the kidnapping was to extract ransom money from the US and Danish governments. However, the terrorists refused an initial ransom offer of US$1.5 million from the US Government, in the expectation that they could extract more.

Jessica Buchanan was suffering from a severe infection that threatened to damage her kidneys and could therefore be fatal. Negotiators tried to send her essential medical supplies but these were refused by the terrorists. They were using her illness as a bargaining chip, knowing that it would force the US Government to raise the stakes.

With the urgency of Jessica's condition, the case was ratcheted quickly up to top priority in the US system, with the Department of Justice passing the case to the Department of Defense. The Federal Bureau of Investigation (FBI) stepped up its ongoing surveillance in the Horn of Africa region, co-ordinating active searches from their Nairobi office.

At the top secret Joint Special Operations Command (JSOC) base at Camp Lemonnier, once a French Foreign Legion base in Djibouti, 300 special operations personnel organized unmanned drone surveillance of the area.

Having been briefed that there would be a full blackout of the moon in two days' time, President Barack Obama ordered Secretary of Defense Leon Panetta to give the necessary clearance to the commander of SEAL Team 6. Once special forces have been activated, it indicates that all attempts at mediation and negotiation have failed and that the only option is now an operation of extreme prejudice.

Facing page: A US special forces soldier uses night vision equipment while carrying out a mission.

A Lockheed C-130 Hercules took off from Djibouti on the night of 25 January 2012 with 24 members of SEAL Team 6 on board. The plane maintained a stand-off position from the drop zone so as to minimize the risk of the terrorists hearing the plane's engines. The SEALs jumped at high altitude to perform a High Altitude High Opening jump, opening their RAM-air parachutes and gliding silently in a group towards the landing zone, relying on their personal electronic navigation systems for direction in the pitch dark.

The SEALs performed a three-stage landing, going past the target, turning 90 degrees, flying the base leg and then turning 90 degrees again to make the final approach. Their boots hit the ground silently amid the low scrub and acacia trees of the region.

Having stowed their 'chutes, the SEALs then moved silently towards the target area. They were each equipped with infra-red night-vision devices so they could see clearly around them and each other, despite the pitch black of the night. The SEALs carried an array of weaponry, each weapon selected for 100 per cent accuracy and reliability. Although SEALs are allowed a certain degree of personal choice in weaponry, likely weapons would have included the Heckler & Koch MP-7 submachine gun, the H&K MP5 machine pistol, the H&K 416 assault rifle and the compact Sig Sauer P226 Navy pistol.

Despite their formidable weapons, the SEALs knew better than to underestimate the capabilities of their enemies. It is likely that all-weather drone reconnaissance had already revealed to them that the 26 terrorists would be armed with Kalashnikov AK-47 assault rifles along with heavy machine guns and rocket-propelled grenades. It was imperative for the safety of the hostages and their own safety that the SEALs hit them so hard and with such surprise that they would not have time to respond.

RESCUE LAUNCHED

Fortunately for the SEALs, dogs were held in low regard by the local people and there were no guard dogs in the enemy camp. Another stroke of luck was that that day, the terrorists had eaten a heavy meal of roasted goat accompanied by the drug *khat*, the after effects of which were soporific. As Jessica

US Navy SEALs practice a mock insertion using a rigid hull inflatable boat (RIB) during a capabilities exercise.

Buchanan got up painfully in the middle of the night to answer the call of nature, all of the guards around her remained fast asleep.

As the SEALs approached, the first thing they noticed through their night-vision devices was Jessica Buchanan moving around in the cold dark air before returning to her mat. There were no fires or guards, as they had expected.

As she lay back on her mat, cold, exhausted and as ever fighting the pain of her illness, Jessica remembered the warmth of her family and wondered if she would ever see them again. She noticed some noises and imagined it was insects fluttering around. Then one of the guards suddenly sprang up holding his weapon, peering uselessly into the dark. It was the last thing he did.

All hell broke loose. Pre-selecting their targets, the SEALs opened fire and those guards who were able to overcome the shock of noise were too slow to react. Jessica herself was overcome by the noise and could barely make out what was being said to her when a masked man knelt down next to her

and said with an American accent, 'We are the US Military'. Next she was being carried away from the camp. The soldier asked her if she had all her belongings and went back twice to the camp to fetch first her shoes and then her medical bag.

Paul Thisted was also brought out and next they were moving quickly towards the rescue helicopters. Jessica flung herself on board and, as the helicopter lifted away and the SEALs exchanged small arms fire with the terrorists, she realised she had been freed and was now safe.

THE CAPTURE OF IKRIMA, 2013

On 5 October 2013, SEAL Team 6 carried out an attack on a house in Barawe, Somalia occupied by Abdulkadir Mohamed Abdulkadir and insurgents from the group al-Shabaab. Barawe is on the cost of Somalia, about 217 kilometres (135 miles) south of Mogadishu.

Abdulkadir Mohamed Abdulkadir, also known as Ikrima, and the al-Shabaab insurgents were known to have plotted attacks on parliament buildings and the UN headquarters in Nairobi. On 21 September 2013 they attacked a shopping mall in Nairobi. These plans were sanctioned by al-Qaeda to which al-Shabaab had pledged allegiance. The US

Government decided on a daring plan not just to attack the al-Shabaab house, but to capture Ikrima and take him back for interrogation.

The operation was well suited to the SEALs' expertise in covert maritime assault operations. Their rigid hull inflatable boat (RIB) was dropped off well out at sea along with support boats, and the 20 SEAL operators tasked for the assault headed in towards the shore under cover of darkness.

At about 02:00, having negotiated the dangerous rocks standing offshore from the beach, the SEALs landed on the beach, while the reserve boats stood out to sea, ready to provide help if necessary.

The SEALs manoeuvred up the wide, flat beach and regrouped under cover of the sandbank in front of the town before passing like ghosts through the sandy streets towards their objective. As they moved into the compound

US Navy SEALs carry out a training exercise armed with a Colt M4 Carbine fitted with a silencer (left) and FN SCAR-H battle rifle (right).

of the al-Shabaab house, a guard came out onto a balcony smoking a cigarette before turning nonchalantly back and heading inside. Before the SEALs could breathe a sigh of relief, the guard, who had pretended not to see them, re-emerged firing an AK-47 assault rifle.

Their cover blown, the SEALs split into their pre-arranged groups: one to carry out the assault and the other to provide covering fire. The training took over as they carried out their routine of room clearance, but they were under intense fire from the al-Shabaab fighters inside the building. The battle raged intensely for minutes until further al-Shabaab reinforcements began to arrive. The SEALs realised that they would soon be overwhelmed by sheer numbers and began a fighting withdrawal.

Soon they were back in their boat and heading out to sea towards their rendezvous. Although the mission had not been fully accomplished, they had come within a few feet of capturing al-Shabaab's most senior commander and given notice to the terrorists that they had no place to hide.

THE BALKANS

The Balkans region has a long, complex and often violent history. Ground between the millstones of east and west, with Christian and Muslim influences swirling in volatile eddies, it is hardly surprising that from here came the spark that ignited World War I. In World War II, the British agent Fitzroy Maclean was parachuted in to help coordination and supply of the partisans in Yugoslavia who were fighting the German invaders. Several German divisions were fully occupied in fighting their enemies in the rugged, wooded countryside.

After the war, Marshal Tito exerted a very individual style of control over Yugoslavia, maintaining an air of independence from his Soviet masters. When he died in 1980 it was to prove a turning point for the region. By 1992 Slovenia, Croatia, Macedonia and Bosnia had all been recognized as independent states while Serbia and Montenegro declared themselves the Federal Republic of Yugoslavia (FRY). Slobodan Milosevic, who had taken control of the League of Communists of Serbia in 1986, wanted to bring together the various Serb elements into a greater Serb republic and was prepared to use the Yugoslav National Army (JNA) to realize his dream. When Slovenia opted to secede from FRY's unwelcome embrace, Milosevic used force to bring it into line,

Facing page: A Bosnian special forces soldier returns fire in Sarajevo. Having targeted civilians, Bosnian Serb snipers were later indicted for war crimes.

while there was further heavy fighting in Croatia in the latter half of 1991 when the JNA intervened to support the Krajina Serbs.

As a result of the continued fighting, the UN declared an arms embargo against all the republics of the former Yugoslavia. Since Serbia had inherited the bulk of the former Yugoslav Army and its weapons supplies, the effect of this was to limit the ability of the other republics to defend themselves against Serbian incursions.

Bosnia-Herzegovina declared independence in 1992 and Bosnian Serb forces immediately then set about occupying territory. Soon the Bosnian Serbs had taken over 65 per cent of the country and were carrying out a policy of ethnic cleansing.

From February 1992, a UN Protection Force (UNPROFOR), primarily based in Croatia, had its mandate extended to Bosnia-Herzegovina. By August 1992, UNPROFOR had been mandated under Chapter VII of the UN Charter to ensure by 'all means necessary' that humanitarian aid should get through to its destination.

The war in the region was to carry on agonizingly, with a stream of atrocities and with the UN striving to maintain its impartiality so that it should not be seen to be another participant in the conflict. Eventually the Dayton Peace Accord was ratified on 15 December 1995.

INTERNATIONAL CRIMINAL TRIBUNAL FOR THE FORMER YUGOSLAVIA

During the course of the vicious conflict, a large number of atrocities were committed and in the

Radovan Karadzic, who was indicted for war crimes by the International Criminal Tribunal for the Former Yugoslavia (ICTY).

wake of the war a criminal tribunal was set up in The Hague to bring the criminals to book. Established in 1993 by Resolution 827 of the UN Security Council, the court set about bringing to account a number of individuals suspected of committing war crimes and who had escaped trial by local courts in the former Yugoslavia. A major aim of the court, therefore, was to counter the

climate of impunity that had followed the horrors of the war and to give the victims of these crimes a chance to seek totally impartial justice.

By early 2006 over 160 individuals had been indicted, 43 of whom had been found guilty and six of whom had died in custody, either through natural causes or by suicide. The most prominent indictee was the President of Serbia, Slobodan Milosevic, who had died of a heart attack in his cell. Other prominent indictees were Radovan Karadzic, former President of Republika Srpska, and Ratko Mladic, former Bosnian Serb army commander. Karadzic was wanted for genocide, crimes against humanity and violations of the laws and customs of war, and both men were still at large at the time of writing.

Not surprisingly, many of the indictees, secure within their communities or among their supporters, not only did not respond to the summons to appear before the tribunal but went into hiding or actively resisted arrest.

SPECIAL FORCES ASSIGNMENT

In view of the notoriety of the indictees and their apparent contempt for human life, it was clear that it would take more than an ordinary police operation to bring them to trial. The operations would involve extreme danger for those concerned, and they would almost invariably be dealing with armed men, some of whom could call on armed bodyguards to protect them. On 13 March 1997 a sealed indictment and secret arrest warrant were issued for Simo Drljaca and Milan Kovacevic.

Simo Drljaca had been in command of the civil and secret police in the Prijedor area once the Serbs had taken control. He then set about organizing a number of camps in the area, including Omarska, Keraterm and Trnoploje, where non-Serbs were said to have been beaten up, tortured and murdered. As police chief at the time, Drljaca was also allegedly responsible for the 1995 disappearance of a Catholic priest, Father Tomislav Matanovic, and his parents. This was all part of a continued Serb programme of ethnic cleansing, and the evidence of some of the captives indicate that those taken to the camps were beaten with chains or metal hoses and were deprived of food and water. Some of the detainees are even said to have never reached the camps but were instead murdered where they were found.

Simo Drljaca also ran his own crime ring and demanded kickbacks from local businesses by way of protection money. After the end of the war and the signing of the Dayton Agreement, Drljaca continued to be obstructive and is alleged to have continued to run his own private rackets. As other indictees were brought before the International Criminal Tribunal for the Former Yugoslavia (ICTY), and some of them convicted, the evidence began to mount against Drljaca. Survivors of the camps also had plenty to say about his activities.

The second warrant was for Dr Milan Kovacevic, deputy mayor of Prijedor and responsible for delivering Muslim prisoners to the Omarska concentration camp.

Kovacevic, who was an anaesthetist, was also director of Prijedor hospital and it was alleged that at least some of the aid that was meant for the hospital found its way into his pocket. This included part of a 350,000 Deutschmark donation from the UN High Commission for Refugees (UNHCR) to the hospital. It was alleged that fuel donated to the hospital was being sold in the streets of Prijedor.

Non-Serbs were said to enter the hospital with some trepidation, fearing the treatment they might receive, not least from an anaesthetist who ran a concentration camp. It was not only the patients, however, who had reason to be fearful. The organization Physicians for Human Rights and the UN Commission of Experts testified that a number of non-Serb doctors had 'disappeared' from the hospital and were believed to have been sent to Kovacevic's Omarska concentration camp.

SFOR

Following the conclusion of the Dayton Agreement, a NATO-led stabilization force (SFOR) was established in Bosnia-Herzegovina. This was designed to deter further hostilities and to provide support for peace consolidation and rebuilding of both the physical and political infrastructure. The SFOR mandate also extended to persons indicted for war crimes. SFOR personnel were authorized

to detain any Persons Indicted for War Crimes (PIFWCs) during the course of their duties. Their role in this work was all the more important due to the fact that, although many of the indictments were made public, the local authorities did nothing to bring the indictees to justice. Sealed indictments were therefore issued.

The phrase 'normal course of its duties' is somewhat ambivalent as this would cover carefully planned operations by the SAS and other special forces to bring the indictees to book. The areas of responsibility for SFOR were divided among different contributing nations, including the United Kingdom, the United States and France. The headquarters of the British sector under the

General H. Shelton from US Army Special Forces Command arrives at Sarajevo Airport.

SFOR mandate was Banja Luka, which was about 113km (70 miles) from Prijedor, where both the notorious Simo Drljaca and Milan Kovacevic lived.

SAS OPERATIONS

The attitudes towards the indictees were somewhat different in the different areas, with the British taking the most proactive approach.

In July 1997 a team was inserted by a Chinook helicopter from the RAF into a remote area of Bosnia-Herzegovina. The SAS had plenty of experience of tailing dangerous suspects, partly gained from their lengthy periods of operations in Northern Ireland. Techniques for roadblocks and other forms of ambush had been practised and carried out for real.

The experience of the American forces in Somalia had shown that picking up suspects could

Facing page: A child stands in front of a ruined Mosque in Ahmici in Bosnia.

British SAS soldiers and a Royal Navy Harrier pilot await extraction from a wood near Gorazde by a French helicopter during the war in Bosnia.

be fraught with danger if the local community were to become embroiled. Although the techniques practised in Somalia had been efficient and correct in many respects, there was no accounting for the reaction of an unpredictable mob.

Similarly, although both Kovacevic and Drljaca were by all accounts monsters, they could be accompanied by bodyguards and other Serb extremists who would have relished the opportunity to engage in a firefight with the security forces. And despite the fact that SFOR's British forces effectively controlled the area, the suspects were embedded deep enough in their own communities to be able to put up resistance or disappear if troops were to appear.

In order to capture Milan Kovacevic, therefore, the snatch team posed as locals in order to gain

A well camouflaged Dutch special forces sniper keeps watch from a hide in Bosnia-Herzegovina, September 1995.

access to the hospital at Prijedor. Once inside the hospital, the team confronted Kovacevic, who surrendered. He was then taken out of the hospital and driven rapidly away. There was not much scope for Kovacevic to resist within the confines of the hospital but the same could not be said for Simo Drljaca.

Drljaca's history revealed that he could be completely ruthless and, as a former head of police, he would undoubtedly have a network of equally ruthless and well armed supporters. The point of the surveillance work that preceded the arrests was to provide an accurate picture of the suspect's movements and any moments of opportunity that would minimize the risk to the snatch squad.

It was observed that Drljaca occasionally went fishing with his son and brother-in-law, unaccompanied by cronies or bodyguards. A small team mounted a watch on Drljaca from nearby woods. On 10 July he was fishing with his son and brother-in-law on the banks of Lake Gradina. The son and brother-in-law were in the midst of making breakfast next to a caravan when an assault team came down the road in three cars and a van. The soldiers got out of the vehicle. While four of them floored Drljaca's son and brother-in-law, the other six grabbed Drljaca himself.

A struggle is said to have ensured during which Drljaca broke free, wielding a gun. He is said by SFOR sources to have fired and wounded one of the soldiers, whereupon the soldiers opened fire on him and killed him. There is evidence to suggest that Drljaca was shot in the side and back while running towards his boat. The fact that he was shot in the side may indicate that he was turning to fire at his pursuers when he was shot.

It is clear from records of other arrests carried out on behalf of SFOR that the intention was to detain the suspect and not to physically harm him.

THE DUTCH MOVE IN

The next arrest operation involving British forces took place five months later. In this case the indictee was Vlatko Kupreskic. The indictment against Kupreskic was that he had been involved with others in an attack on Muslims in the village of Ahmici on 16 April 1993. During the alleged incident over 100 Muslims were killed and all of the Muslim houses and mosques burnt and razed

to the ground. The alleged attack was carried out by forces of the Croatian Defence Council (HVO) and began with shelling at 05:30 in the morning. Men, women and children of all ages were said to have been killed in the attack. The attacks were coordinated with wider attacks on the town of Vitez and villages of Donja Vecenska, Sivrino Selo, Santici, Nadioci, Stava Bila, Gacic, Pirici and Preocica, all within 10km (6 miles) of Ahmici.

In view of the resistance offered by Simo Drljaca, SFOR forces certainly knew what to expect. He had not offered himself voluntarily for arrest, unlike some of his cousins who had also been indicted, and it was therefore possible that he would continue to resist arrest.

DUTCH 108TH KORPS *COMMANDOTROEPEN*

Following the invasion of Holland by German forces in World War II, a Dutch commando group was set up in Achnacarry, Scotland, as part of No. 10 Inter-Allied Commando. The Dutch Commando participated in major engagements, including the D-Day landings. The Commando was split initially into six groups, namely the 1st, 2nd, 3rd, 4th, 102nd and 103rd. In 1953 these groups were disbanded and the 104th, 105th and 108th Commando Companies were raised to replace them. In 1965 the 104th was designated the Long Range Reconnaissance Patrol while the other two companies became reserves. Another reorganization in 1993 made the 108th the active company and it was officially designated the 108th Special Operations Company (SOC).

The 108th SOC has essentially the same role as the British SAS and it is also involved in training other Dutch Army units in relevant skills. It has a capability to be active in peace-support operations while carrying out the full spectrum of special operations activities. Counter-terrorism is another important aspect of KCT training. Similarly to other countries, the Dutch special operations force has a close relationship with a particular aerial unit, in this case the 11th Air Mobile Brigade.

Selection and training for the KCT is as rigorous as one would expect for an elite special operations

unit. The introductory period comprises a 12-month commando training course for soldiers already on active duty and a 14-month course for civilian recruits. Preparatory training is designed for those unfamiliar with basic military skills and includes weapons training, physical training including forced marches, as well as a range of other courses.

Basic commando training includes a selection course similar to that run by the British Royal Marine Commandos, at the end of which a green beret is earned. Training includes escape and evasion (E and E) and reconnaissance.

Advanced commando training is designed to equip each recruit with a range of skills in addition to the particular specialization he may have chosen. Each recruit is therefore trained in free-fall parachuting, fighting in built-up areas, communications, field medicine and demolitions.

The training is rigorous and few recruits make it to the final stages.

Specialized training also includes arctic warfare, mountain, jungle and desert training to complete the full sphere of global operations in which the KCT may be required to operate. The counter-terrorism team is trained specifically for missions in urban terrain that may include hostage rescue or capture of suspects.

As with all such operations, the indictee was the object of a careful surveillance operation to track his movements down to the last detail. As an HVO soldier, he was assumed to be armed and potentially dangerous and it was also known that he had at least one bodyguard who kept watch outside his house at night. The observations appear to have been carried out by members of the Dutch 108th Special Forces Company who had been parachuted into a location near Vitez.

The 108th Special Forces Company linked up with a British team who were already in the country for the final phase of the operation.

On Thursday 18 December, after midnight, the team moved in on Kupreskic's house. Some accounts indicate that there was a guard at the door of the house who was overcome and gagged by the soldiers. No doubt Kupreskic would have chosen his bodyguard with care, but he was unlikely to have been a match for members of the world's elite special operations group. The next task was to capture Kupreskic himself alive.

There were many good reasons for the time and care taken to carry out this and other similar operations. The obvious one was to minimize the risk of injury to the soldiers and to reduce the risk of collateral effects. No matter how appalling the alleged actions of some individuals, certain communities had a talent for turning a blind eye to them. The abduction of these men was therefore seen as wrenching away one of their own. The major reason, however, was to bring out the suspect alive so that he could stand trial. Each indictee that appeared before the tribunal added to the body of evidence and this had important implications for the process as a whole. Much of the evidence that enabled cases to be brought against perpetrators of genocide and other crimes came from the testimonies of previous indictees. For the jigsaw of evidence to be built up, it was important for each indictee to be brought to trial.

Placing a guard on the exits, the soldiers entered the building and quickly isolated Kupreskic's wife and children. It is said that Kupreskic tried to resist and fired at the soldiers with a sub-machine gun. The soldiers were unhurt but managed to shoot Kupreskic in the arm and in the leg. It was

enough to immobilize him and he was quickly overwhelmed.

There is little doubt that Kupreskic owed his life to the high level of training of the Dutch commandos as they could have easily killed him to preserve their own safety. Shots to the torso and head would most likely have been fatal but their carefully aimed shots to the limbs were instead designed to be temporarily disabling.

On 14 January 2000 Vlatko Kupreskic was sentenced to six years' imprisonment. On 23 October 2001 he was acquitted on appeal and immediately released.

ARREST OF GENERAL STANISLAV GALIC

On 21 December 1999 the British forces, acting on behalf of SFOR and the ICTY, arrested General Stanislav Galic. Galic was one of the officers who commanded the Bosnian Serb Romanija Korps (SRK) from September 1992 to August 1994. During this period, the city of Sarajevo was besieged and was subjected to shelling, constant sniping, mortar attacks and other incursions, all committed against the civilian population of the city, although there were Bosnia-Herzegovina (BiH) forces also present.

The citizens of Sarajevo were effectively subjected to a deliberate terror campaign. Schools, homes and hospitals were subjected to attack and there were numerous no-go areas and death traps in the city. Civilians were shot on trams in order to stop the services running and they were also shot at whenever and wherever they queued at water stands or for food. There were no-go areas, such as 'sniper alley', where every time civilians attempted to cross the road they would be fired at, either with sniper rifles or with automatic weapons. High-rise blocks in the Grbavica district, which was controlled by the SRK, provided excellent vantage points for the snipers. The snipers were armed with state-of-the-art rifles with telescopic and infrared sights. On one occasion a little boy of four was hit by a bullet while on a tram; on another a woman was killed crossing

Facing page: Armed with an M4 carbine, a member of the US special forces working in Bosnia-Herzegovina communicates with fellow soldiers.

the street with her son-in-law; and on another a woman was killed in her apartment at night in front of her husband due to the fact that they had lit a candle which the sniper, probably using an infrared sight, had used as an aiming point.

In July 1993, a crowd of people waiting to fill canisters from an emergency water supply received a direct hit from a mortar shell. About 11 people were killed instantly and 13 others were wounded. One witness saw his wife and two daughters die.

On 22 January 1994, three mortar shells were fired into a residential area, Alipasino Polje, which killed six children and injured several others.

In all these cases, the court found that there was clear evidence that civilians had been deliberately targeted by SRK forces. General Van Baal, UNPROFOR chief of staff in Bosnia-Herzegovina in 1994, testified that women and children were the predominant targets for snipers. It was also

Swedish and Danish soldiers in a UN armoured personnel carrier on their way to take control of Tuzla airport from government troops.

said by other UNPROFOR officers and others that sometimes the snipers would deliberately aim to wound a victim so that rescuers would be drawn to the scene. The rescuers would then be attacked.

Between 1992 and 1994, minimum estimates for the number of civilians killed by sniping, shelling and other attacks were 1399, with 5093 wounded. At least 670 women, 295 children and 85 elderly people were killed. At least 2477 women, 1251 children and 179 elderly people were wounded.

During this period, General Galic was in direct control of the soldiers who perpetrated the sniping and shelling campaign against civilians as part of a deliberate campaign to terrorize the local population and to influence the BiH forces. Due to the rigid chain of command in the SRK, General Galic's influence was all the more direct. The sniping would stop if a particular representation had been accepted by the SRK command, which indicated the sniping was under direct and immediate control of the SRK chain of command and not some form of freelance activity.

A French special forces soldier (right) introduces a US special tactics airman to the mysteries of the FAMAS assault rifle in preparation for combined operations in Bosnia in 1995.

General Galic was a man of considerable influence who resided in the Banja Luka area of Bosnia-Herzegovina, about 65km (40 miles) south-east of Prijedor. Having retired from the army, Galic became military adviser to Nikola Poplasen, who was elected President of Republika Srpska. There is evidence to suggest, however, that, aware of being on the ICTY wanted list, Galic was making inquiries about moving to the Federal Republic of Yugoslavia so that he could have a better chance of evading capture. Such a man had a strong influence in the area and could call on powerful support. His arrest was therefore potentially fraught with danger.

Once again, the indictee was the object of a careful surveillance operation, during which his movements would have been carefully recorded. As he was aware that he was on a wanted list and had not voluntarily given himself up, the soldiers responsible for his capture could expect evasive tactics and active resistance. If the arrest were to become protracted, they could also expect aggressive reactions from local supporters and bodyguards. As in all these cases, a careful assessment would have been made by intelligence operatives and the special operations commandos as to the point of least resistance, which varied from case to case.

The plan to arrest Galic was perhaps one of the most daring of all as it was to take place in broad daylight in one of the busiest streets in Banja Luka. As Galic left his home and drove to work that morning, he was unaware that he was being tailed by an unmarked car and a van. Divided between the two vehicles were British security forces. The van moved into position behind Galic's car and, at a given signal, the car swept round in front of Galic's car and forced him to stop. The soldiers in the vehicles gave Galic little time to react. Although he is said to have reached for his gun, a British soldier smashed the driver's door window with the butt of his rifle and Galic was unceremoniously bundled out of his seat and onto the road. A sack was placed over his head and handcuffs put on. He would have been body-searched and taken to British military headquarters. Soon Galic was on a flight to The Hague where he would stand trial. On 5 December 2003 he was found guilty of one count of violations of the laws or customs of war and on four counts of crimes against humanity.

ARREST OF A DOCTOR

Not all of the arrests of ICTY indictees were carried out by British forces. On 17 June 1997 Slavko Dokmanovic was arrested by members of the United Nations Transitional Administration for Eastern Slavonia (UNTAES).

Slavko Dokmanovic had been President of the Vukovar municipality between 1990 and 1991 and he resumed this position after the fall of Vukovar. Dokmanovic's indictment was based on his alleged involvement in events said to have taken place after the capture of Vukovar on 18 November 1991. During the siege, several hundred people took refuge in Vukovar hospital. But when JNA and Serb paramilitaries arrived they took at least 400 non-Serbs from the hospital, and about 300 of these were said to have been transported to a farm at Ovcara where they were subjected to beatings.

Slobodan Milosevic, former President of the Republic of Yugoslavia, adopts a confident stance during his trial at the ICTY in the Hague.

After this, the prisoners were taken in groups of between 10 and 20 to another site where they were executed and buried in a mass grave. The known murders amounted to 198 men and two women.

In the period prior to his arrest, Dokmanovic was living in the Federal Republic of Yugoslavia and therefore outside the jurisdiction of UNTAES. He did, however, have a lure to get him to cross the border. ICTY officials had already interviewed him at his residence in FRY about other suspects on their list without, however, making him suspect that he was also wanted for questioning.

Eventually Dokmanovic came across the border in a UN vehicle, ostensibly to meet with UNTAES officials to discuss issues regarding his property. Once across the border, the car drove off the road and he was quickly overwhelmed before he could reach for a weapon he was carrying concealed in his briefcase.

Dokmanovic was taken to The Hague for trial, but on 29 June 1998 he was found hanging in his cell. Arrests continued and were carried out by either British, French or US troops. On 22 January 1998, a US-led force arrested Goran

THE SAS IN KOSOVO

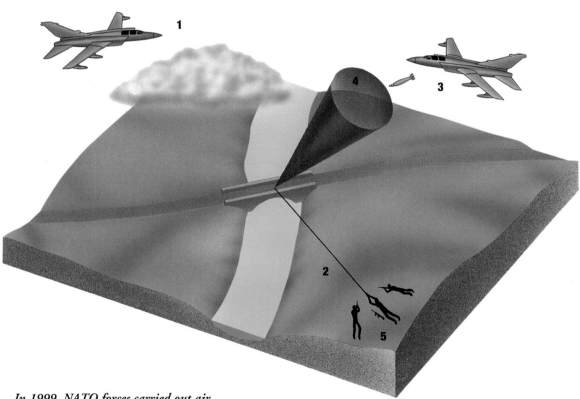

In 1999, NATO forces carried out air strikes against Serb targets in Kosovo, following Serb aggression in the province. SAS teams were deployed to identify targets. They used laser designators to pinpoint their targets. The laser light was reflected off the target, forming a 'cone' or 'basket', into which the bomb was dropped. The bomb's seeker head followed the reflected laser to the target.

Key
1 RAF Tornados arrive overhead.
2 SAS troopers designate the target.
3 The laser-guided bomb is released.
4 It follows the 'cone' to the target.
5 The SAS troopers withdraw.

A Bosnian refugee grieves outside the Omarska detention camp, 1995.

Jelisic. He had been indicted for his alleged activities surrounding the capture of Brcko in Bosnia-Herzegovina by Serb forces. Between 7 May and July 1992, the Serbs kept hundreds of Muslim and Croat men and women in inhuman conditions at Luka camp. Jelisic is said to have come in each day to select detainees for interrogation, during which they were almost invariably beaten up and often killed.

The operation mounted to capture Jelisic would have taken into account the possibility that he was armed and prepared to use a weapon to defend himself. Careful attention would have been paid to his movements and he was apprehended in the early morning after he was seen in Bijeljina.

British forces were active again in the Prijedor region when they arrested Dragoljub Prcac. Prcac had been deputy commander of the Omarska detention camp near Prijedor between 1992 and 1995. Between April and August 1992 at least 6000 Muslims, Croats and other non-Serbs were rounded up and distributed between the concentration camps of Omarska, Trnopolje and Keraterm, where there were regular beatings, interrogations and murders.

The arrest of Prcac, which is assumed to have been carried out by members of the British SAS, was similar to that of Galic, When Prcac was driving his car with his wife and neighbour, he was tailed by three unmarked vehicles. At a given signal, Prcac's car was boxed in by the vehicles;

soldiers smashed the car windows with their rifle butts and Prcac was dragged out. He would then have had a bag placed over his head and been handcuffed before being taken to a holding point prior to transport to The Hague.

On 3 April 2000, French SFOR soldiers were involved in the arrest of Momalo Krajisnik, ex-speaker of the Bosnian Serb Parliament and close associate of Radovan Karadzic. He was indicted for participation with others, including Slobodan Milosevic, in the planning and execution of a wide-ranging programme of persecution against the Bosnian Muslims and other non-Serbs of a wide range of municipalities in Bosnia-Herzegovina. These persecutions included detentions, beatings, killings and other inhumane acts.

In this case the arrest took place at 03:30, when Krajisnik and his family would have been asleep. The soldiers blew open the door, tied up members of Krajisnik's family then swiftly arrested Krajisnik before transporting him to The Hague.

KARADZIC AND MLADIC

Two of the most wanted men on the list of indictees were Radovan Karadzic and Ratko Mladic. Karadzic was a founder member and president of the Serbian Democratic Party (SDS) and was a member of the Supreme Command of the armed forces of the Serbian Republic. He was president of Republika Srpska from December 1992. He was indicted for genocide, complicity in genocide, extermination, murder, wilful killing, persecutions, deportation, unlawfully inflicting terror upon civilians and the taking of hostages. He was indicted twice for complicity in the genocide at Srebrenica in which 7000 Bosnians were killed. Several attempts were made to arrest Karadzic but he remained at large, often assuming a disguise and protected by friends, until 21 July 2008.

According to SFOR, two attempts were made to arrest Karadzic near Celebici in 2002. This operation involved special forces and regular troops as well as aerial assets. The raid was carried out at dawn on 28 February with a substantial force arriving in helicopters. The whole village of Celebici was thoroughly searched and explosives were used to blow down doors. Karadzic could not be found. The next day, troops returned, again by helicopter, and combed the hills round Celebici but without success.

In January 2004, NATO troops attempted another arrest in Pale, raiding Karadzic's house, a Serb Orthodox Church and other buildings. The area was searched by British, American and Italian troops. Once again, there was no sign of Karadzic. On 1 April 2004, British troops raided the house of a Serb Orthodox priest, using explosives to break in. The priest and his son were seriously injured in the operation. Weapons were discovered but Karadzic himself was nowhere to be seen. The operation continued the following day and once again drew a blank.

It was thought that Karadzic was based near the border with Montenegro in mountainous country. If any unusual activity by the security forces was seen, he escaped across the frontier into a safe house. The eventual arrest of Radovan Karadzic was probably due to the considerable reward money on offer for a tip-off as to his whereabouts.

Ratko Mladic was commander of the main staff of the Bosnian Serb Army (VRS) between 1992 and 1996. He was indicted for genocide committed in several municipalities of Bosnia–Herzegovina, including Prijedor and Srebrenica. He was also held responsible, along with others, for the continued attacks on Sarajevo, including the shelling and sniping of civilians.

Mladic was said to have been popular with the soldiers who served under him and there is little doubt that he had a wide network of safe houses to which he could escape. Ratko Mladic was eventually arrested on 26 May 2011 in an operation involving Serbian police officers. Mladic was armed with two pistols but was brought under control before he had a chance to use them.

The US invested a great deal of time and money in the search for Karadzic and Mladic. The National Security Agency carried out a sophisticated programme of electronic eavesdropping, while FBI agents and US marshals also visited Bosnia in efforts to identify possible hideouts and to follow likely trails.

DRUG HUNTING IN SOUTH AMERICA

About five per cent of the world's population use drugs at least once a year and about half of those use drugs regularly. There are about 25 million drug addicts in the world. The most widely used drug is cannabis, taken by about 162 million people, and this is followed by amphetamines, ecstasy and opiates. The most widely used drug in South America, based on treatment statistics, is cocaine.

The coca plant is most prevalent in Colombia, Peru and Bolivia. In 2009, the area of coca cultivation in Colombia was thought to be 116,000 hectares (940,427 acres), while in Bolivia it was 35,000 hectares (283,747 acres). This is a significant increase on production from the 1990s. Cocaine production remained relatively stable up until 2005, but had increased by 70 per cent by 2010. The UN believes that in 2011 Colombia produced about 42 per cent of the world's coca, only slightly more than Peru. In recent years reports have suggested that Columbia's cocaine production had fallen behind both Peru and Bolivia, partly as a result of improved law enforcement.

Mexico remains the world's largest opium poppy cultivator. Marijuana cultivation there increased

Facing page: A Colombian rapid reaction force carries out a riverine patrol designed to interdict drug runners.

by 45 per cent to 17,500 hectares (141,873 acres) in 2009. Mexico is a major supplier of heroin and home to some very powerful drug syndicates. By 2013, the official death toll of the Mexican Drug War was at least 60,000.

COLOMBIA

The trafficking routes for cocaine from South America are mainly from Colombia and other parts of the Andes to either the United States, usually via Mexico, or to Europe, usually via the Caribbean or Africa. Seizures of cocaine have shown a steady increase, with the largest number of seizures taking place in Colombia. Colombia remains a major exporter of cannabis and Brazil has been the largest producer of herbal cannabis in the world.

The drugs trade in Colombia and other South American countries has been largely conducted by highly organized criminal cartels, some of the most notorious of which were based in Colombia. These included the Medellin Cartel, the Cali Cartel and the Norte del Valle Cartel. As the world drugs trade was worth at least $400 billion, these cartels were often ruthless in their quest to get a bigger slice of the profits.

The Medellin Cartel, operating from the town of Medellin in Colombia, was set up and run by Pablo Escobar and was said to be earning in the region of $60 million per month at the height of

Pablo Escobar, leader of the Medellin Cartel, attempts to escape with his henchmen shortly before being shot and killed by Colombian police.

its operations in the 1980s. When Colombia and the United States arranged a mutual extradition treaty over drug trafficking, some of the Colombian justice officials involved were gunned down. The Colombian justice minister, Rodrigo Lara Bonilla, was shot by motorcyclists while his car was stuck in traffic. Later a guerrilla group raided the Palace of Justice and took hostages, many of whom died in gunfire exchanges with the police.

The US Drug Enforcement Agency was heavily involved in the fight against the Cartel and managed to turn one of its runners, Barry Seal. His information led to many successful interceptions of drug pipelines and, as a result, the Cartel tracked down Seal and murdered him. With the capture of Pablo Escobar, however, the Medellin Cartel declined, though some of its former members are thought to be associated with other cartels.

The Cali Cartel was founded by Gilberto Rodriguez Orejuela in the 1970s and was thought at its height to control 80 per cent of cocaine exports from Colombia. The Cali Cartel were fierce rivals of the Medellin Cartel, each fighting for greater control of the drugs market.

Like most of the cartels, the Cali Cartel ran a sophisticated network of distributors through which cocaine powder was taken from Colombia, often via Mexico, to the United States. Due to the huge sums of money involved, the Cartel was able to buy aircraft and ships, build remote airfields, hire guerrilla forces and bribe corrupt officials.

Constant campaigns against the Cartel by Colombian and US drug enforcement agencies resulted in many of its major operators being brought to justice but it is still thought to function through other associates.

The Norte del Valle Cartel benefited from the decline of both the Medellin and Cali cartels and became one of the most powerful cartels in the 1990s. Led by Diego Leon Montoya and Hernando Gomez Bustamente, the Norte del Valle Cartel made substantial use of guerrilla organizations to enlarge and protect its distribution networks. This included terrorizing anyone who should get in its way and dealing ruthlessly with rival cartels.

The Norte del Valle Cartel began to self-destruct when some of its members proposed to enter into negotiations with the authorities by way of reducing their chances of being extradited. Gang warfare ensued in which about a thousand people were killed. The authorities took advantage of the disarray to arrest some of the most ruthless members of the cartel and to seize its assets, which included a fibreglass submarine some 8m (26ft) long, designed to smuggle drugs into the United States.

Fuerzas Armadas Revolucionarias de Colombia (FARC)

The largest armed rebel group in Colombia, the FARC is a Marxist organization purportedly dedicated to the support of the poor against the wealthy. A large proportion of its funds come through the drugs trade. It is thought to have between 10,000 and 15,000 armed personnel at its disposal, about 20–30 per cent of whom are children. Those children who refuse to join or who try to escape are tortured and killed. The FARC carries out a programme of assassinations, hijackings and bombings and has also kidnapped

many foreigners for ransom, many of whom are then executed. The FARC also organizes protection rackets and mounts roadblocks to steal money and valuables.

Efforts by the Colombian Government to assuage the FARC have included the demilitarization of 42,000 square km (16,000 square miles) of Southern Colombia. This olive

Security police gather round as the head of the Cali Cartel is arrested in Bogota in June 1995.

Members of the Colombian paramilitary group
Auto-Defensa Campesina (AUC) prepare for a
patrol near La Hormiga, Colombia.

branch failed to achieve any results and, as the
kidnappings and other atrocities continued, the area
was remilitarized.

Outrages continued, including the massacre of
34 rural farmers on the grounds that they were said
to have right-wing sympathies.

Autodefensa Unidas de Colombia (AUC)

This paramilitary group was formed in April 1997
for the purpose of protecting its adherents from
other insurgent organizations, thus filling a vacuum
left by the state. Like many organizations of its kind
in South America, the AUC relies heavily on drug-
related earnings to support itself.

Far from 'protecting' people, as it claims, the
AUC has assassinated 804 people, killed over 500
in several massacres and kidnapped over 200. The
organization is a law unto itself and on the whole
avoids direct confrontation with government forces,
preferring to carry out campaigns against anyone it
considers to be an enemy, mostly among the civilian

and indigenous population. The leader of AUC,
Carlos Castano, treads a fine line between supposed
cooperation with Government security forces and the
rules of war and a fiercely guarded independence.
The vicious reality that underlies this is that ordinary
people have their lives ruined by such organizations.

Ejercito de Liberacion Nacional (ELN)

Widely regarded as a terrorist organization in
both the United States and Europe, the ELN is a
Marxist insurgent group similar to FARC in many
ways but on a smaller scale. It is known to carry
out kidnappings for ransom as well as massacres
and other atrocities. They are also known to have
extorted money from multinational companies.
The ELN has had some leaders with a muddled
relationship between Christianity and Marxism,
including Father Camillo Torres.

Ejercito Popular de Liberacion (EPL)

Formed in 1967, this is another Marxist-Leninist
group whose agenda is ostensibly to promote the
Socialist revolution but whose major preoccupation,
as with other groups of this type, is the ongoing
round of extortion, kidnappings and drug-related

Colombian Army special forces soldiers line up at Factativa, west of Bogota. A Black Hawk helicopter lifts off behind.

activities. The group experienced a deadly rivalry with FARC and several EPL members have been murdered by FARC over the years.

COLOMBIAN SPECIAL FORCES
Agrupacion de Fuerzas Especiales Urbanas (AFEAU)

Colombia has continued to be bedevilled by numerous terrorist groups, many of whom have links to the drugs trade. In the 1970s the M-19 terrorist group carried out several high profile assaults against banks and other economic targets and also pulled off high profile publicity stunts designed to cause shock, such as the theft of Simon Bolivar's sword and armour from a national museum.

In 1980 the M-19 group pulled off its biggest coup when it took over the Dominican Embassy in the midst of a cocktail party, taking 14 ambassadors and many other high-ranking officials hostage. The siege ended eventually with a negotiated settlement whereby the terrorists were allowed safe passage to Cuba. There were rumours that the rebels were demanding between $1–2 billion from the Colombian government.

The M-19 terrorist assault did not end there. In November 1985 they took some 300 judges, magistrates and lawyers hostage in the Palace of Justice. Although there were some attempts by the Government to negotiate with the terrorists, in the heat of the moment the military quickly took over command of the operation and attempted to storm the Palace of Justice. In the ensuing battle, over 100 people were killed and the building caught fire. It was apparent that Colombia urgently needed to create a specialist anti-terrorist group that could handle such crises in a more incisive way and with less risk to the hostages.

Like many special operations units of its kind, the AFEAU is relatively small, with about 100 members drawn from the armed forces and police. There are six squads consisting of 15 soldiers each. Entry to the unit involves a tough seven-day pre-selection course followed by further training at Factativa near Bogota where they undergo specialist training in various aspects of anti-terrorist work, including rescues from ship, aircraft or buildings, fast roping, parachuting and other disciplines.

PLAN COLOMBIA

In an attempt to defeat the widespread cultivation of drugs in Colombia, the US Government carried out a number of initiatives between 1998 and 1999 under Plan Colombia. This included both military and development aid, along with plans for the eradication of drug crops through fumigation from the air and by manual uprooting.

In 2000 the United States offered to put on the ground up to 500 military personnel to train local forces to fight the insurgents and to counter drug-related activities. In 2004, the United States expanded the programme to the Andean Counter-drug Initiative and increased the number of military personnel to 800.

Not surprisingly, organizations such as FARC reacted with violence. When peasants trooped out accompanied by police to uproot coca plants, the FARC would plant mines in their path or kill them in other ways. Although in 2005 over 30,000 hectares (74,130 acres) of coca plants were said to have been uprooted, much like pulling up weeds, it was likely that they would grow again. Also, while some areas were cleared, the growers would move to other areas in the Andean region and start again.

Fuerzas Especiales de Infanteria de Marina

The concept of a Colombian naval unit capable of carrying out a range of anti-terrorist operations was first aired in 1966. Since then a Marine Infantry brigade has been established at Sincelejo on the Atlantic Coast and the second Marine Infantry Brigade at Buenaventura on the Pacific Coast.

Cartagena naval base is the base for the *Grupo de Comandos Anfibios* (GCA). This unit is said to have received training from elements of the US Navy SEALs and it has a similar mission profile to the US Navy SEALs or British SBS, namely insertion from the sea to neutralize enemy assets, combat diving and hostage rescue. The Colombian force has a special focus on counter-drug operations.

In 2003 Naval special forces carried out a successful combined operation against drug runners in the Canal del Dique in the Atlantico department of Colombia.

In order to trap drug runners using the canal for transport, naval units from Yati Combate Fluvial 30–30 sealed off the Calamar and Estanislao areas of the canal. The GCA moved in and detected three fast-boat launches that were ready to put to sea. Further inland they located two four-wheel drive vehicles hidden in the undergrowth.

Continuing their searches, the special forces unit found caches of cocaine amounting to 3.5 tonnes (3.44 tons). Large amounts of weaponry and ammunition were also found and at least four arrests were made.

In a similar operation on 19 October 2006, 8500kg (17,600lb) of cocaine were found by units from the navy, police, and other anti-drug squads. The cargo of cocaine, worth at least $170 million, was found on board three high speed 'Go Fast' launches not far from the mouth of the River San Juan on the Pacific Coast of Colombia.

Lanceros

In order to create an effective counter-insurgency force, the *Escuela de Lanceros* was set up in December 1955. Named after a famous unit

Facing page: A Colombian commando undergoes riverine training, 2003.

that fought in the 1819 campaign, the *Lanceros* grew from studies in irregular warfare that were in part carried out at Fort Benning USA. Having undergone training with the US Rangers, officers returned to Colombia to train men of various ranks for counter-terrorist challenges. In 1966, elite counter-insurgency groups were created which, though consisting of smaller teams, were even more highly trained in specialist skills than previously.

Colombian Army Commando Battalion (BACOA)

Created in 2003, the new commando battalion was trained by US Green Berets in techniques such as surveillance, operations involving night-vision devices and laser target designation. As the US special forces personnel are not allowed themselves to participate in combat missions, personnel from units such as the 600-strong commando battalion are used to accompany conventional forces in raids against the FARC and other insurgency groups.

Operation Liberty-1 based in the Cudinamarea region of Colombia involved members of the Commando Battalion and the army 5th Division. In five months, the military operation resulted in the deaths of 165 FARC paramilitaries, the capture

Bolivian paratroops wait to board a C-130 Hercules transport during **Fuerzas Unidas Bolivia, a joint exercise with the United States.**

of a further 155 and the seizure of at least eight tons of explosives. Four senior FARC field commanders were also killed in the fighting.

Training
In Arauca region the elite 18th Brigade also receive training from US Special Forces. Americans are not allowed to accompany them on combat missions, but the Colombian soldiers benefit from the extra hours of training on new weapons and in honing their rapid reaction skills. Training may also involve reorganization of the existing forces in order to make them more effective, for example creating a reconnaissance section in addition to the assault sections so that they have more effective 'eyes and ears' in the dense jungle.

The special forces training unit also includes a PSYOPS detachment, bearing in mind that the 'hearts and minds' aspects of special operations can be 80 per cent of the battle. Some of the work involves trying to re-educate youngsters who have been indoctrinated by the rebels to regard the Colombian Security Forces and their allies as sworn enemies.

Another aspect of training imported by the US Special Forces is in lowering the command threshold in the Colombian forces. With a different social structure in Colombia, the lower ranks are not used to taking the initiative and tend to wait for orders from the 'officer class'. This does not work in special operations where each man has to think for himself and where NCOs have to be able to give orders with or without officers present.

BOLIVIA
Despite ongoing attempts to reduce the amount of coca plants grown in South America, there is strong resistance from traditional coca farmers who sell the crop for legitimate purposes.

The election of President Evo Morales, a former coca farmer, in Bolivia was a signal that the tide of coca crop destruction might soon cease. While ordinary farmers might welcome this, the drug cartels would also be jostling for position in order to benefit. Having had their activities frustrated in countries such as Colombia, the drug cartels sought alternative sources of income. An ominous

---

US ARMY CIVIL AFFAIRS AND PSYCHOLOGICAL COMMAND (AIRBORNE) (USACAPOC)

Based at Fort Bragg, North Carolina, USACAPOC consists of about 10,000 personnel, many of whom are reservists with professional civilian careers.

The purpose of psychological operations is to provide an interface between the military presence and the official civil structures and civilian population of a particular nation. The reservists' professional skills can be especially useful here as it allows them to engage with the relevant civil organizations, whether it be law, medicine, public affairs or engineering.

By creating a dialogue as well as providing practical assistance, the PSYOPS teams can create an environment of cooperation and collaboration with the local population. This can extend from small-scale medical assistance, dealing with wounds or illnesses, to large-scale engineering projects such as building or repairing roads.

PSYOPS soldiers are heavily engaged in media and all forms of publications, disseminating counter-propaganda information and keeping the local population informed of political and civil developments.

Language skills are one of the priority requirements for successful PSYOPS soldiers.

---

development was that Mexican cartels began to establish a presence in Bolivia, bringing with them a high level of organization as well as ruthless methods.

The Bolivian anti-drug agency, FELCN, working closely with the US DEA, continues to mount a strong and effective campaign against drugs proliferation. Unlike the large Colombian cartels, the Bolivian drugs traffickers tend to be organized in small groups that are easier to intercept and neutralize.

Bolivia is the third largest producer of coca leaf in the world and the security forces are presented with a huge challenge in attempting to stem the tide of cocaine production. Apart from the infiltration of Mexican drug dealers, there are also thought to be strong links between Bolivian drug dealers and FARC guerrillas in Colombia. Due to the

GRUPO DE FUZILEIROS NAVAIS

Within the main corps of the *Grupamento de Fuzileiros Navais* there is a special operations battalion, *Batalhão de Operacoes Especiais de Fuzileiros Navais* (Tonelero). The battalion is also known as the *Comandos Anfibios* (amphibious commandos) or COMANF.

The battalion's duties include both reconnaissance and assault and the unit is split up into separate companies. There are two amphibious reconnaissance companies (ReconAnf), a command and services company, a land reconnaissance company (ReconTer) and two companies of amphibious commandos. There is also a company designated for hostage rescue and similar duties, known as the *Grupo Especial de Retomada e Resgate* (GERR).

Once selection has been passed for the Toneleros battalion, the fusilier goes through a two-year period of training, taking the *Cursos Especiais de Comandos Anfibios* (CESCOMANF), a special course for amphibious commandos, the special operations course (CESOPESP) and the free-fall course, *Curso Expedito de Salto Livre* (CEXSAL). The budding commandos also learn submarine infiltration and underwater demolitions. They also do mountaineering and jungle-training courses. Some Toneleros are then designated to participate in specific courses abroad, such as the Royal Marines All Arms Commando Course, the Spanish Navy *Comando de Operaciones Especiales* course, the US Ranger course or the US Marine Corps Amphibious Reconnaissance Course.

On home territory the Comanfs carry out exercises in various climatic and geographical regions, including cold climate, mountainous, swamp and river.

'squeezed balloon' effect, the drug problem in Bolivia may be increasing as the anti-drug and anti-insurgency campaign in Colombia becomes more effective.

Bolivian Special Forces

There are strong training links with the United States for military, naval and air force officers and other ranks. Company grade officers receive specialist training at the Escuela de Especializacion de Armas and field grade or staff appointments are made via the Escuela de Comando y Estado Mayor Mariscal Andres Santa Cruz at Cochabamba. This is also the location of the Centro de Instruccion de Tropas Especiales, which is the home of a paratroop battalion.

Other special operations schools include the Centro de Instruccion de Operaciones en la Selva, which is a jungle training school at Riberalta, and the Special Forces school at Santa Cruz, which includes staff from the United States.

The Bolivian Air Force has bases at La Paz, Cochabamba, Santa Cruz, Robore, Tarija and Trinidad.

The Bolivian Navy is, understandably for a landlocked country, modest in size. The major emphasis is on patrolling the river system which, as elsewhere in Latin America, provides a fast highway for drugs movement. There are patrol craft based at Riberalta, Trinidad, Puerto Guayaramerin, Tiquina, Puerto Suarez and Cobija. There is also a Marine Infantry battalion based at Tiquina on the western border of Bolivia.

Military anti-narcotics forces include the army Green Devils Task Force (GDTF), the air force Red Devils Task Force (RDTF) and the navy Blue Devils Task Force (BDTF).

The Green Devils Task Force collaborates with the police, providing transportation and protection for units involved in the eradication of coca plantations. The Red Devils similarly provide air transport for counter-narcotics operations and fly aircraft provided by the United States. These include helicopters and fixed wing transport aircraft, such as the C-130. The Blue Devils are located at the naval bases of Trinidad, Puerto Villaroel, Riberalta and Guayaramerin.

The success of the interdiction operations by special forces and other counter-drug units is such that the potential production of pure cocaine has been reduced between the mid 1990s and 2006 from 255 to 70 tonnes (251–69 tons).

The eradication programme was not, however, successful in reaching all regions, particularly the Yungas region, and between 2005 and 2006 coca production actually increased. The Yungas region is characterized by steep and difficult terrain which makes access difficult. In 2005 the FELCN seized 11.5 tonnes (11.4 tons) of cocaine/base, 31.4 tonnes (30.9 tons) of cannabis, 540,774 litres (118,970 Imp gal) of liquid precursors and 298,815 tonnes (294,034 tons) of solid precursor chemicals (sulphuric acid, bicarbonate of soda). It destroyed 2619 base labs and made 4376 arrests in over 6294 operations. The fact that, despite all this, the drug trafficking industry continues to thrive is a measure

Brazilian Jungle Brigade soldiers disembark a military transport aircraft during Operation Timbo, an exercise centred on the defence of the Amazon region.

of the scale of the problem, and consumption rates for cocaine in the urban population of Bolivia more than doubled between 2000 and 2005.

BRAZIL

The extensive borders of Brazil, its huge jungle areas and vast waterways, particularly in the Amazonas region, make it liable to be used as a hideout and routeing area for drug traffickers. Also, in order to escape government forces, rebels in countries such as Colombia would occasionally slip across the border

Elite Brazilian soldiers prepare to round up clandestine gold miners in the Pic de Neblina area of Brazil.

into Brazil to seek refuge. A major priority for Brazil is therefore to establish a presence in its border areas that will deter illegal entry. The Brazilian National Public Safety Secretariat is designed to combine a range of military, police and civil organizations to further this goal. The Brazilian Air Force operates a zero tolerance shoot-down policy against any aircraft suspected of carrying drugs over its territory.

The Brazilian Navy has bases at Belem, at the mouth of the River Amazon, and also at Manaus, about halfway up the Amazon. The Navy elite forces include the *Grupamento de Fuzileiros Navais*.

The Brazilian regional naval command in the Amazonas region, *Comando Naval da Amazonia Ocidental* (CNAO) has continued to establish an

1ST BATALHÃO DE FORCES ESPECIAIS

Part of the Army Parachute Infantry Brigade, the 1st Special Forces Battalion originated in 1957 as a paratroop rescue unit, with a specialism in jungle rescue. The unit worked closely with a US Army Special Forces Mobile Training Team (MTT) to carry out its training programmes. By 1968 the unit had evolved into a recognizably modern special forces detachment with a broader range of specialist skills, including those needed for anti-terrorism operations.

The initial selection course lasts 14 days and has a very high attrition rate, with only about 10 per cent passing through to the next stage. This is followed by a 13-week counter-terrorist training course which also includes parachuting, helicopter insertions, fast-rope skills, shooting and close-quarter combat (CQB). The Brazilian Army CIGS jungle school also provides training in amphibious operations, mountain warfare, HAHO/HALO operations and long range reconnaissance.

Long-range reconnaissance is a particularly important skill for this unit, which often operates in the vast Amazon jungle. Typical unit strength for these operations is normally larger than usual for special operations units due to the need to provide effective back-up and communications in such remote areas.

ever more substantial presence over recent years. It includes an aerial arm (DAEFLotAM) to provide helicopter support for the ships.

The *Grupo de Fuzileiros Navais* based at Manaus is being transformed into a 900-strong river operations battalion (*Batalhão de Operacoes Ribeirinhas* – BtlOpRib) under a river command headquarters (*Centro de Adestramento de Operacoes Ribeirinhas* – CADOR).

From 1985 a programme was carried out to develop the northern border regions of the Amazon, the frontier with Colombia, Venezuela, Guyana, Suriname and French Guiana. Up to 1999 at least 36 aerodromes were either constructed or overhauled so that they could take C-130 aircraft and therefore host rapid troop deployments. The programme also included the construction of barracks, while 19 frontier posts were constructed under five Special Frontier Battalions.

Jungle Brigades

There are four Jungle Brigades in the Amazon, namely the 1st, 16th, 17th and 23rd Jungle Brigades, comprised of 14 battalions and supported by the 4th Air Squadron. They also work in conjunction with paratroop brigades or such special operations units as the Naval Fusiliers.

A full-scale exercise was carried out in the Amazon border region in 1999, designed to deter FARC guerrillas and narco terrorists. The main force for the operation came from the Jungle Brigades already on the ground. The operation involved 5000 personnel and covered the entire 1644km (1023 miles) of the frontier with Colombia. The operation was not entirely an exercise as there had been reports of Colombian special forces using Brazilian aerodromes in their operations to counter FARC guerrilla activity in adjacent parts of Colombia.

In the Brazilian operation, two Hercules C-130 aircraft inserted at least 240 special forces soldiers into the region. At least 120 commandos were landed to protect an airstrip at Querari, close to the Colombian border. They were quickly supported by the 5th Battalion, from one of the Jungle Brigades.

This show of force may have been temporary but was not far from reality. In 1991 FARC guerrillas attacked a Brazilian outpost in the River Traira region, killing three men and wounding others. The Brazilians reacted swiftly. Only 48 hours later, Brazilian special forces entered Colombian territory, killed seven FARC guerrillas and recovered armaments and ammunition that had been stolen in the FARC raid.

Grupo de Mergulhadores de Combate (GRUMEC)

First formed in 1970, these special operations divers undergo the Brazilian Combat Diver Course

Chilean army special forces prepare to board a plane heading for Haiti in March 2004 to form part of an international peacekeeping force.

and also learn a variety of other specialist skills, including HALO/HAHO parachute jumps and explosives work. Part of their training includes operations in river and jungle environments where, like the US Navy SEALs or British SBS, they carry out raids from water to land. Recruits are also given courses in mountain climbing and other specialist skills to enable them to be fully adaptable across a spectrum of operational environments.

GRUMEC's specializations makes them a useful tool in the war against drugs, particularly in view of the fact that the rivers and coastal areas are an important transport route for the narco traffickers. The unit can quickly deploy on fast boats such as the Zodiac CRRC.

Centro de Instrucao de Guerra na Selva (CIGS)

The Brazilian jungle training school, based in Manaus, has courses divided by ranks, namely COS Cat A for senior officers, COS Cat B and COS Cat B1 for middle-ranking officers of different services and COS Cat C and COS Cat C1 for NCOs. The courses are attended by members of various services, including the navy and police. A range of jungle-related issues are covered, including clothing, equipment, communications, rations, operations and logistics.

CHILE

Although drugs are not grown or produced in significant quantities on Chilean territory, because of its extremely long coastline, excellent road system and the fact that it has an inland border that is difficult to patrol, it is an important transhipment point for heroin and cocaine. Large amounts of drugs are carried over the border from Peru and Bolivia and a certain amount comes from Argentina.

The carabineros, investigative police (PICH) and the coast guard (DIRECTEMAR) play key roles in drugs interdiction, and operations are often carried out in collaboration with the United States Drug Enforcement Authority (DEA).

In 2005, the authorities seized 2777kg (6123lb) of cocaine hydrochloride, 2173kg (4791lb) of cocaine, 5.4kg (12lb) of heroin, 5846kg (12,980lb) of marijuana and 122,740 marijuana plants.

Buzos Tacticos

This unit comes under the *Comando de Fuerzas Especiales* of the *Armada de Chile* (Chilean Navy). The *Buzos Tacticos* unit is about 200-strong and is based at Vina del Mar and Valparaiso. Members of the unit are trained in reconnaissance, underwater demolition and shore raids.

The attrition rate for early recruits is extremely high, with only 10 per cent passing initial selection.

During training, a system of equality is imposed and the students only know each other by number. A large part of the course is carried out in a marine context and endurance exercises are carried out both in and under water. This may include swimming 50m (164ft) without coming up for air.

Another exercise involves underwater swimming between oxygen bottles on the bottom of the pool. The recruits have to swim between the bottles,

Commandos from Ecuador cross a river using a rope during Exercise Blue Horizon with the United States.

taking a gulp of air from each one and then rise to the surface in a controlled manner. Some exercises are also carried out in water with the recruits' hands and feet tied.

Grupo de Operaciones Policiales Especiales (GOPE)

This is an elite section of the Chilean Carabineros (*Carabineros de Chile*). The unit is trained in much the same way as a military special operations unit to carry out counter-terrorism operations and hostage rescue as well as intervening in narco-trafficking and similar crimes. The unit works in coordination with the *Patrullas de Acciones Especiales* (PAES) on special operations patrols. Training involves a wide range of disciplines, including mountain rescue, maritime operations and urban operations.

The drug control aspects of GOPE operations come under the broad heading of counter-terrorism. In this respect the GOPE have trained with C Company of the US 7th Special Forces Group. Joint training has included sniper training, tactical parachuting and assault and rescue, including rescue of hostages from aircraft, ships and buildings.

ECUADOR

Located on the Pacific coast of South America, sharing borders with the major drug-producing countries Colombia and Peru, Ecuador is a major

Facing page: Peruvian police special forces guard the presidential palace in Lima in October 2000, after rebel soldiers took the mining town of Toquepala.

transit point for drugs. And interceptions of vessels leaving Colombia with drug shipments has led to increasing use of vessels with an Ecuadorian flag. Another problem is that the northern border with Colombia is closest to the area in which FARC has its greatest influence.

The US Government has cooperated with the Government of Ecuador in various counter-drug initiatives and 2438 Ecuadorians and 314 foreigners were arrested for drug trafficking in 2005.

US Naval Special Warfare Unit 4 has worked with the Ecuadorian Cuerpo Infanteria de Marina (Ecuadorian Marine Corps) at bases at Guayaquil and Quito to maximize their riverine interdiction skills. The US Marine Corps have also worked with Ecuadorian Special Operations Forces and national police while the 16th Special Operations Wing and 720th Special Tactics Group have helped to train the Ecuadorian Ala de Combate (combat wing).

PERU
Sendero Luminoso – Shining Path

This is a Peruvian revolutionary organization which sought to indoctrinate people with purified Maoist teaching and which exercised a reign of

7TH SPECIAL FORCES GROUP (AIRBORNE)

This specialist unit was first formed on 9 July 1942 as a joint United States/Canadian commando. It was intended to deploy the group against Nazi missile and nuclear weapons facilities in Scandinavia but the group was diverted to a campaign in the Aleutian Islands. From there it went to southern France and Italy. At this time the nickname 'Devil's Brigade' was coined.

Having been stood down in 1945, the group was reactivated in September 1953 at Fort Bragg. In 1960 it was officially named the 7th Special Forces Group (Airborne), 1st Special Forces. In 2005 the 7th Special Forces was moved to Florida.

From the 1960s, the 7th were given responsibility for training and advising foreign military forces and they were deployed to South Vietnam for this purpose in 1961 and also to Laos and Thailand. The Group also moved into Latin America during the same period as 3rd Battalion, 7th Special Forces Group. Here they were active in countering the spread of communism in countries such as El Salvador and Honduras. From the end of the 1980s onwards, the main focus of activities for 7th Special Forces Group became counter-drug operations in the Andes region and this also included direct action in Panama during Operation Just Cause in January 1990.

US Marines assigned to Special Purpose Marine Air-Ground Task Force conduct a live-fire exercise in Matuntugo, Colombia, 2011.

terror over the local peasantry. Like many such organizations, it funded itself on the drug trade, especially cocaine. Its leader, Abimael Guzman Reynoso, was captured by the authorities in 1992 and sentenced to life imprisonment, but nevertheless the group continues to exist, though on a smaller scale.

After a lull in activity, however, the *Sendero Luminoso* has shown a resurgence, with at least 291 incidents caused by the group in 2004. By 2005 this had jumped to 426 incidents, an increase of 46

per cent over the previous year. At least 13 police officers were killed over a period of only two weeks. The *Sendero Luminoso* is organized on a 'voluntary' basis whereby its members go about their ordinary legal business until called up. They then assemble at prearranged remote locations in order to carry out operations, where they have access to stores of weapons, ammunition and other supplies.

Sendero Luminoso operations are largely funded by drugs traffickers, and their murders of police and their other atrocities are closely linked to the objectives of the drug gangs.

The US-backed destruction of coca plantations has not only damaged the drug traffickers but also harmed the local peasantry who grow coca for its other traditional legitimate uses and who have lost a valuable source of subsistence. Having terrorized the local population in the past, *Sendero Luminoso* is now clever enough to ally itself with this latent disaffection. Since one of the first rules of counter-insurgency is to win the 'hearts and minds' of the local population, the Government forces are now at a disadvantage.

Members of 16th Special Operations Wing (SOW) offload special forces and their equipment during an operational mission at night.

US SPECIAL FORCES DEPLOY

A large component of the military personnel that went into the Andean region were special forces. Special forces personnel were ideal for this kind of environment. They had the training that would enable them to not only survive a jungle and high altitude environment but also to maintain the initiative. They were trained in specific linguistic skills and in 'hearts and minds' techniques to win over the local population and deter them from the siren songs of the insurgents. They were able to train local military personnel in advanced counter-

insurgency techniques, intelligence gathering and tactical manoeuvres and would also be a conduit for state-of-the-art weaponry and other equipment that would enable Government forces to maintain the advantage. Such equipment included helicopters and fast patrol boats.

In 1984 alone, 2700 special operations soldiers were deployed in South America from United States Southern Command (SOUTHCOM). The units involved included army Green Berets, US Rangers, Special Operations Aviation Units, Psychological and Civil Affairs Units, US Navy SEALs, Special Boat units and US Air Force special operations squadrons.

Joint Combined Exchange Training (JCET)

The JCET programme was primarily designed to enable US special forces and other military personnel to become acquainted with the topography and geography of the countries to which they were deployed as well as familiarizing

themselves with the political, military, social and humanitarian issues on the ground and to form relationships with the appropriate military, political and other useful contacts.

United States Southern Command and Special Operations Command, South (SOCSOUTH)

Based at Naval Station Roosevelt Roads, Puerto Rico, SOCSOUTH has three subordinate operational units in forward base areas. These are C Company, 3rd Battalion, 7th Special Forces Group (Airborne); Naval Special Warfare Unit 4; and D Company, 160th Special Operations Aviation Regiment (Airborne).

There are about 200 SOF deployments per year, covering at least 16 countries. The activities of the special forces commands and units are coordinated with the major concerns of the regional nations, which mostly involve counter-insurgency, drug trafficking and natural disasters or other

US SEABORNE SPECIAL FORCES – CENTRAL AND SOUTH AMERICA

Cyclone Class Patrol Coastal Ships

These ships are designed for coastal patrol duties and interceptions and for transporting SEAL or coast guard teams. They are capable of transporting the Combat Rubber Raiding Craft as well as a rigid inflatable swimmer delivery craft. They are armed with a Mk96 mounting with a 25mm (0.98in) gun and 40mm (1.57in) grenade launcher, and two 12.7mm (.50 cal) gun mounts.

Patrol Boat Light

This boat is based on the Boston Whaler and is manufactured from fibreglass with a reinforced transom and gun mounts. It is 7.62m (25ft) long and has a shallow draft, making it ideal for river operations. It can carry either 12.7mm (.50 cal) or 7.62mm (0.3in) machine guns. It is not armoured.

Naval Special Warfare Group 2

Based at Little Creek, Norfolk, Virginia, NSWG 2 operates across Europe, the Atlantic and in South

America. Under its control are SEAL Team 2, SEAL Team 4, SEAL Team 8, SEAL Delivery Vehicle Team 2 and Naval Special Warfare Unit (NSWU) 8. NSWU 8 is based in Rodman, Panama.

It comprises two SEAL platoons and Special Boat Unit 26. Apart from its training duties, NSWU 8 can provide the basis of a Naval Special Warfare Task Unit.

Special Boat Squadron 2

Based in Little Creek, Virginia, SBS Two comprises Special Boat Unit 20, Special Boat Unit 22 as well as nine Patrol Coastal Class Ships, namely the USS *Cyclone* (recently retired), USS *Tempest*, USS *Typhoon*, USS *Scirocco*, USS *Chinook*, USS Firebolt, USS *Whirlwind*, USS *Thunderbolt* and USS *Shamal*.

Special Boat Unit 22 is equipped with two Patrol Boat Riverine detachments, two mini armoured troop carrier detachments and two patrol boat light detachments, each consisting of two patrol boats and crews.

humanitarian issues. Where there is rivalry between the different nations, US military elements have to take care to remain detached so as not to be seen to be supporting a particular nation in their regional ambitions.

Special operations commands are keen to play up the humanitarian aspects of their missions, such as post-hurricane flood rescues as opposed to the more delicate matters of military training and counter-insurgency intelligence.

Since much of the movement of drugs is by boat, and this is especially the case in a jungle

US Special Forces Special Boat Unit 26 (SBU-26) use the Patrol Boat Light (PBL) on Operation Unitas 37-96, in combined operations with Panamanian forces.

environment where waterways provide a swift means of transport, units such as the US Navy SEALs and Special Boat units have a particularly important role to play. There is also close coordination with offshore coastal patrol vessels, either operated by special forces commands, the US Coast Guard or local national navies.

SPECIAL FORCES UNITS IN SOUTH AMERICA

2004 data

Country	Title of Training	No. of Trainees	Location	Students' Units	US Units
Colombia	Advanced CSAR Doctrine	100	Tolemaida, Apiay, Melgar, Bogota, Rio Negro	COLAF CATAM, COLAR Helicopter Bn, COLAF CACAM 2/4/5	16th SOW
Colombia	Advanced Light Infantry	510	El Espinal, Larandia, Tolemaida	CNP, DIRAN	7th SFG
Colombia	Advanced Light Infantry	557	Tolemaida, Apiay, San Jose de Guiviare	COESE, SF Commando	7th SFG
Colombia	Advanced Light Infantry	560	Larandia, Bogota, Tolemaida, Sibate, Tress Esquinas, Melgar, Apiay, Espinal, Cartagena, Cali, Tumaco	CD Bde, Cadre, BACNA Bn	7th SFG
Colombia	Advanced Light Infantry	510	Espinal, Larandia, Tolemaida, Bogota, Melgar, Sibate, Santa Maria, Tulua, Arauca, Barrancon	CNP Carabineros	7th SFG
Colombia	Advanced Light Infantry	797	Espinal, Larandia, Tolemaida, Bogota	COESE HQ, Cdo Bn, Lancero Bn, SF Bde, FUDRA, Mobile Bdes	7th SFG
Colombia	CNT	25	Tumaco, Bahia Malaga, Buenaventura, Cali, Covenas,	Naval Special Dive Unit, Submarine Cdos, Army SF Comd, Marine SF Cartagena, Barrancon, Tolemaida Army SF Bde, Army Aviation Bde, Lancero Bn, Marine Riverine Bn 50	Special Boat Team, NSWG 2, Combat Bn 1, Army SF School, Service Support Team
Colombia	CNT	300	Tolemaida, Larandia	Colombian Mobile Bdes	7th SFG
Colombia	CNT Battle Staff	857	Tres Esquinas, Tumaco, Tulua	COESE, Commando Bn, Lancero Bn and SF Bde, FUDRA or Mobile Bdes	7th SFG
Colombia	CNT Riverine Interdiction	60	Barrancon, Tolemaida, Cali, Marine Medellin, Cartagena, Covenas, Santa Marta, Corozal, La Pita	SF Bn 1, Army SF Bde, Army Aviation Bde, Army SF Command, Navy Urban Anti-Terrorist SF Unit, Marine Riverine Bn 50N	SWD South, Special Boat Team, ST NSWG 2
Colombia	CNT Riverine Training	60	Barrancon, Tolemaida, Cali, Medellin, Cartagena, Covenas, Santa Marta, Corozal, La Pita	Marine SF Bn 1, Army SF Bde, Army Aviation Bde, Army SF Command, Navy Urban Anti-Terrorist SF Unit, Marine Riverine Bn 50	NDW Detachment South, Special Boat Team, NSWG 2
Colombia	JPAT	0	Bogota, Arauca, Barrancon, Cano-Limon, Espinal, Facativa, Fortul, La Esmeraldas, Larandia, Saravena, Tame, Tolemaida, Yati, Cartagena, Cali, Tres Esquinas	1st Cdo Bde, 12th Bde, SF Bde, 18th Bde, Colombian National Police (Carabineros) and (Diran) or other CO vetted units	Naval Special Warfare
Colombia	JPAT	NA	Arauca, Barrancon, Cano-Limon, La Esmeralda, El Espinal, Facativa, Fortul	1st Cdo Bde, 12th Bde, SF Bde, 18th Bde, Colombian National Police (Carabineros) and (Diran)	7th SFG, USACAPOC Tactical CA Component NTE USASCO
Colombia	Light Infantry	500	Bogota, Arauca, Apiay, Saravena, Fortul, Tame, Las Esmeralda	Colombian Army Personnel	7th SFG, 96th CA BN, 12th AF, 4th PSYOPBN, 112th Signal Bn, 16th SOW, USAOC
Colombia	Light Infantry	615	Bogota, Espinal	CNP, Diran	7th SFG
Ecuador	JPAT	0	Quito, Coca, Machachi, Lago Agrio, Latacunga, Santa Cecilia, Puyo, Tulcan, Puerto El Carmen, Esmeraldas	N/A	US Army SOC, 7th SFG
Panama	Light Infantry	80	Panama City, Cerro Tigre, Colon City	Darien-Kuna Yala Border Security Police (DARKUN)	7th SFG, USACAPOC, US Army SOC
Paraguay	Riverine/ Urban	40	Asuncion, Ciudad Del Ester, Puerto	SENAD, Marine Cdos	NSWD South Rosario
Peru	Advanced Light Infantry	35	Lima, Satipo, Huanuco, Tacna	First SF Bde	7th SFG
Peru	Riverine	6	Lima, Ica, Tacna, Loreto	Fuerzaz de Operaciones Especiales	NSWD South NSWD Central
Peru	Riverine Waterborne Tactic	30	Loreto, Ucayali, Madre De Dios	Escuela de Operaciones Riverenas (EOR)	NSWD South, NAVSCIATTS

2003 data

Country	Title of Training	No. of Trainees	Location	Students' Units	US Units
Bolivia	Riverine	20	Chimore	Blue Devils Task Force	USMC
Bolivia	Riverine	30	La Paz	Fuerza Contra Terrorista Conjunctas (FCTC)	NSWU 4, NSWG 2
Bolivia	Riverine	100	La Paz	Bolivian Navy and Special Operation Police	NSWU 4
Bolivia	Staff Training	40	Chimore	Ninth Division - Chipiriri	Bn 7th SFG
Chile	JCET	50	Santiago	Grupo Operaciones De Policia Especial 7 SFG (GOPE) of the Carabineros De Chile	7th SFG
Colombia	Huey II Training	30	Melgar	COLAR	Contractor (Lockheed Martin) and Aviation Training Technical Assistance Field Team

Country	Title of Training	No. of Trainees	Location	Students' Units	US Units
Colombia	Light Infantry	80	Espinal	CNP Counter Narotics Division (DIRAN)	7th SFG
Colombia	Light Infantry	80	Facatativa and Sibate	CNP Counter Narotics Division (DIRAN)	7th SFG
Colombia	Light Infantry	195	Espinal	Colombian National Police	7th SFG
Colombia	Light Infantry	450	Arauca	18th SF Bde	7th SFG
Colombia	Light Infantry	450	Saravena and Arauca	18th SF Bde	1st Op Det, 7th SFG, 96th Civil Affairs Bn, 16th SOW, 4th PSYOPS Gp
Colombia	Light Infantry	450	Tolemaida	1st SF Bde	7th SFG
Colombia	Light Infantry	450	Tolemaida	1st SF Bde	7th SFG
Colombia	Light Infantry	550	Larandia	1st Cdo Bde	7th SFG
Colombia	Light Infantry	550	Larandia	1st Cdo Bde	7th SFG
Colombia	Light Infantry	1500	Espinal - Larandia - Tolemaida and Sibate	CNP Carabineros-Gp 1 and Diran	7th SFG
Colombia	Panning and Assistance	200	Bogota - Barancon	BAFLIM 60 - 70 - 80 - 90	NSWU 4
Colombia	Planning Assistance	50	Bogota	COLMIL	7th SFG
Colombia	Riverine	200	Arauca - Yati	COLMAT Riverine Combat Elements	U.S. Marines
Colombia	Riverine	30	Cartagena	Colombian Marine SF Bn 1NSWU 4	
Colombia	Riverine	31	Puerto Carreno	Marine Riverine Bn 40	NSWU 4, NSWG 2, Special Boat Team
Colombia	Riverine	40	Yati	Colombian Marine Riverine Bn	NSWU 4
Colombia	Riverine	40	Puerto Inidria	Marine Bn 50	NSWU 4 NSWG 2
Colombia	Riverine	45	Bogota and Yati	Colombian Marine Riverine BN	NSWU 4
Colombia	Riverine	50	Cartagena - Covenas	Colombian AFEAU, Marine SF Bn and Barrancon	NSWTT (NSWU 4, Combat Service Support Team, TCS Element)
Colombia	Riverine	50	Cartagena	Colombian Navy Special Dive Unit - Submarine Cdo	NSWU 4
Colombia	Riverine	60	Cartagena	Colombian Navy, Marines SF Bn 1	NSWU 4
Colombia	Riverine	60	Cali	Selected members of Colombian Cdos	NSWU 4
Colombia	Riverine	100	Cartagena	Colombian Atlantic Coast Guard	NSWU 4, Special Boat Team Detachment CARIB
Colombia	Riverine	200	Cartagena - Covenas - Barrancon	Colombian Cdos Especiales del Ejercito (CEE)	Naval NSWU 4, NSWG 2
Colombia	Search and Rescue	126	Tolemaida - Apiay - Melgar	COLAR Heli Bn/COLAF CACOM 2 & 4 Tactics Gp	16th SOW & 720th Special Tactics Gp
Colombia	Staff Training	80	Larandia - Tres Esquinas - Cali	Colombian 12 Bde Tactics Gp, 96th Civil Affairs Bn	7th SFG, U.S. Army SOC, 116th SOW, 720th Special
Colombia	Staff Training	550	Larandia - Tres Esquinas	1st CN Bde, BACNA Staff, Support Bn,	7th SFG 2nd Cdo Bn
Costa Rica	Maritime Interdiction	35	Murcielago	Costa Rican National Coast Guard	NSWU 4
Dominican	Republic Maritime Interdiction	50	Salinas	Cdos Navales	NSWU 4
Ecuador	Riverine	40	Guayaquil	Ecuadorian Marine - Cuerpo Infanteria De Marina	NSWU 4
Ecuador	Riverine	50	Guayquil	Ecuadorian SOF and national police	USMC Riverine Operations Seminar Team
Ecuador	Search and Rescue	100	Quito	Ecuadorian ALA DE	720th Special Tactics Gp
Honduras	JCET	50		Honduran Navy, Puerto Castilla, Honduras, 15th Bde, (50)	SEAL Team 4, NSWU 4, NSWG 2
Nicaragua	JCET	47		Brigada De Fuerzas Especiales	SEAL Team 4, NSWU 4
Panama	JCET	36	Panama	Panamanian National Police (PNP) (13) Panamanian National Maritime Service (SMN) (13) Institutional Protective Service (SPI) (13) / 36	NSWU 4, 160th SOAR, NSWG 2
Panama	JCET	40	FT Sherman	Panamanian Grupo De Operaciones Especiales (GOE)SEAL Team 8,	NSWU 4
Panama	Light Infantry	60	Panama City Colon	Panamanian National Police	7th SFG
Panama	Riverine	60	Panama City Colon	SPI Special Reaction Gp	NSWU 4, NSWG 2
Panama	Staff Training	100	Former Howard AFB - and Fort Sherman	Panama National Police	7th SFG
Paraguay	JCET	100	Asuncion	CIMOE, SENAD, Marine Cdos	7th SFG
Paraguay	Riverine	30	Asuncion - Ciudad Del Este	SENAD and Cdos	NSWU 4
Peru	JCET	32		Fuerzas De Operaciones Especiales (FOES) Peruvian Naval Special Forces	7th SFG
Peru	Light Infantry	40	Santa Lucia	Directiva Nacional Antidrogas	7th SFG
Peru	Riverine	30	Loreto	Instructors from the Riverine Operations School	NSWU 4
Peru	Riverine	100	Lima - Pucallpa - Contamana	Peruvian National Police - Peruvian Coast Guard	NSWU 4, Special Boat Unit

SIERRA LEONE

Sierra Leone faces the Atlantic Ocean and has one of the largest natural harbours in the world next to the capital, Freetown. The mountains that surround Freetown were named by the Portuguese navigators of the sixteenth century the Serra Leoa, or Lion Mountains. Most of the coast consists of swamps and lagoons, the Peninsula mountains around Freetown being an exception.

Inland, the northern part of the country is largely savanna, while the south consists of rolling woodland interspersed with hills that rise abruptly from the forest. There is a mixture of savanna and hill country with some substantial mountains in the northeast.

There are nine major rivers running through the country, which are not navigable in their inland sections. The rivers contain crocodiles, alligators, manatees and hippopotamuses.

The rainy season runs from May to October and the dry season from November to April. In general, the climate is warm and humid.

The various villages now tend to be arranged along a road and less frequently in the traditional circular manner. Freetown itself contains two cathedrals, Roman Catholic and Anglican, as well as mosques. Otherwise, Freetown has all the other administrative buildings typical of a capital city, including government offices, law courts, a university and various embassies.

Facing page: A soldier of the 1st Battalion The Parachute Regiment on patrol near Yeliwor Island, Sierra Leone in May 2000.

There are various indigenous tribal groups as well as the creoles, who were free blacks that populated the coastal area in the nineteenth century.

Sierra Leone gained its independence from Great Britain in April 1961. The country remained divided into four administrative units, namely the northern, southern, western and eastern provinces. The provinces were in turn subdivided into districts and the districts into chiefdoms. Although effective power lay with officials in the city, the chiefs continued to exert an important cultural and to some extent administrative influence based on tradition.

In 1971 the country was declared a republic within the Commonwealth. Although Siaka Stevens' All People's Party (APC) had won the 1967 election, the army took over and set up a military government under Lieutenant Colonel Andrew Juxon-Smith. Stevens came back to power after the army officers had been overthrown.

Government under Stevens became more and more corrupt until in 1978 he introduced one party rule. Joseph Saidu Momoh took over in 1985, but the corruption continued. In 1992 there was coup after which the National Provisional Ruling Council (NPRC) took over, with Captain Valentine E.M. Strasser as head of state.

The Revolutionary United Front (RUF) was set up in Liberia in the 1980s and it began a campaign against Momoh's corrupt government in Liberia. The RUF found many recruits among the disenchanted unemployed local population in Sierra Leone. Young children, among others, were either enticed or forced to take up arms. Due to the proliferation of small arms in Africa, firearms were one of the few commodities that were not lacking.

Strasser was in turn overthrown in January 1996 by Brigadier Julius Maada Bio. Then the Sierra Leone People's Party under Ahmad Tejan Kabbah managed to negotiate a return to civilian rule, after which the Government attempted to negotiate a ceasefire with the RUF, but to no real avail.

In May 1997, Lieutenant Colonel Johnny Paul Koroma and the Armed Forces Revolutionary Council (AFRC) overthrew Kabbah's administration and the RUF were invited to participate in the new government. At this point the international community took action. The United Nations imposed sanctions by Security Council Resolution 1132, the Commonwealth suspended Sierra Leone's membership and Kabbah was able to return to power in March.

On 13 July 1998, the United Nations Observer Mission in Sierra Leone (UNOMSIL) was established. Its mission was, in collaboration with the Economic Community of West African States Monitoring Group (ECOMOG), to disarm the combatants and restore the nation's security forces. Fighting and atrocities, however, continued. RUF gang leaders would lead raids into Freetown and elsewhere, amputating limbs and raping and killing those who were thought to oppose them. The build-up of RUF forces was such that they soon controlled half of the country and by December 1998 were ready to make a full-scale attack to take Freetown itself.

In January 1999 the RUF overran Freetown, forcing many of the UNOMSIL representatives to withdraw. ECOMOG forces counter-attacked later the same month and managed to gain control of Freetown but the RUF remained at large. After negotiations with the rebels, an agreement was signed in Lome on 7 July, calling for a government of national unity.

On 23 September 1999, UNOMSIL was replaced by a more powerful peacekeeping mission, the United Nations Mission in Sierra Leone (UNAMSIL), which was to consist of 6000 military personnel. In February 2000, the military component of the mission was expanded to 11,100 military personnel.

In May 2000 the RUF broke the ceasefire and captured hundreds of peacekeepers in a move that threatened to undermine the whole mission. It was at this point that Great Britain intervened with its own forces to both deter the rebels and to retrain the local security forces.

OPERATION PALLISER

On 8 May 2000, Great Britain despatched the spearhead battalion of the Joint Rapid Reaction Force (JRRF) to Sierra Leone. Four RAF Chinook helicopters were deployed and an Amphibious Ready Group, led by the support carrier HMS *Ocean*, departed Marseilles for Sierra Leone via Gibraltar. Apart from HMS *Ocean*, the Amphibious Ready Group comprised the frigate HMS *Chatham*, the assault ship HMS *Fearless*, and the logistic support ships RFA *Sir Bedivere*, RFA *Sir Tristam*, RFA *Fort Austin* and RFA *Fort George*.

The British spearhead battalion consisted of 1st Battalion, The Parachute Regiment. Landing in Senegal, the battalion then moved in to secure Lungi airport in Sierra Leone and to enable the evacuation of British, Commonwealth and EU nationals. Once this was completed, they continued to hold the airport so that humanitarian supplies could be flown in.

Embarked on HMS *Ocean* was a 600-strong Royal Marine Commando Group, which included 42 Commando Royal Marines, 20 Commando Battery Royal Artillery, Special Boat Service detachments and 539 Assault Squadron.

As close air support would be required, the aircraft carrier HMS *Illustrious* was also re-routed from Lisbon to Sierra Leone, carrying six Harrier FA2s of 801 Naval Air Squadron, Sea King ASW and AEW helicopters, two Lynx ASW helicopters of 847 Naval Air Squadron and two Royal Marine AH Mk 1 Westland Gazelle helicopters.

The deployment of the JRRF Spearhead Battalion was carried out via Lockheed Tristar and Hercules C-130 aircraft. Eight C-130 aircraft remained on station and there were four Joint Helicopter Command Chinook helicopters in theatre. The initial movement was by Tristar from RAF Brize Norton in Oxfordshire to Dakar in Senegal. Onward movement to Sierra Leone was by C-130 Hercules.

Although there was no official confirmation in the battle order, following British practice, SAS units may have been deployed at this advanced stage. The airport and its environs had been secured from 8 May and the Royal Marines Commando Group, which had heavier weaponry and supporting equipment, were due to take over from 26 May.

Prior to the arrival of the Parachute Regiment, 16 Air Assault Brigade Pathfinder Platoon had already been deployed to carry out reconnaissance. They'd also engaged in combat with RUF rebels.

Lieutenant Colonel Johnny Paul Koroma, leader of the Armed Forces Revolutionary Council (AFRC), at a press conference in 1997.

The Pathfinder Platoon's mission is to conduct covert reconnaissance and to mark suitable drop zones and landing sites, including helicopter landing areas.

Members of the Pathfinder Platoon are effectively an elite within the elite Parachute Regiment. Its members are almost entirely drawn from 2nd and 3rd Battalions of The Parachute Regiment.

Working in four-man teams and with specialist training in both High Altitude Low Opening and High Altitude High Opening parachuting techniques, Pathfinders are not a million miles away from the SAS, and transfer from Pathfinders to the SAS is not infrequent.

On the night of 17 May, RUF guerrillas made a move against the village of Lungi

Royal Navy Sea Kings land at Aberdeen Beach, Sierra Leone, north-west of Freetown to disembark members of 42 Commando Royal Marines.

Loi, which was about 60km (37 miles) from Lungi airport. Their intention was to surprise and wipe out the British contingent in the village. Unfortunately for the rebels, they did not realize that members of the Pathfinder Platoon had taken up defensive positions around the village or that the British soldiers were equipped with night-vision goggles (NVG), which gave them a clear view of the approaching enemy. The RUF guerrillas suddenly found themselves under a storm of fire from British small arms and general purpose machine guns. Up to 30 rebels are thought to have been killed and there were no British casualties. It might have been even worse for the rebels if some of the British soldiers had not had problems with their SA80 automatic rifles. It is said that in some cases the safety catch jammed and the weapons could not be fired.

SPECIAL FORCES DEPLOY

While the deployment of the Pathfinder Platoon was openly acknowledged by the British Ministry of Defence, there was a black curtain hanging over another substantial deployment that took place at about the same time. This was a small unit of SAS, a troop of SBS and the Joint Special Forces Aviation Wing, flying Chinook helicopters and C-130 Hercules transports.

Deployment from the temperate environment of England to sub-equatorial jungle, especially when large amounts of equipment need to be carried, can in most cases require acclimatization. For rapid response units, this acclimatization period has to be minimized so that they can effectively hit the ground running. This is the purpose of constant training in different climate zones, including preparation for jungle deployments at the British Army Jungle Warfare Wing in Brunei, on the island of Borneo.

four Kenyan soldiers were killed. On 3 May the RUF captured 49 peacekeepers. At one point, a Zambian column of soldiers, including no less than 13 armoured personnel carriers, fell into rebel hands.

On 11 May the Quick Reaction Company (QRC) of the Indian Armed Forces came to the aid of Kenyan troops held hostage by the RUF and a breakout was staged. The Indian QRC had travelled 290km (180 miles) in BMP armoured personnel carriers through the jungle to conduct the rescue, and four British military observers, including an officer from the Parachute Regiment, also made their escape.

On 7 May, Indian Air Force helicopters deployed to evacuate three Kenyan casualties from Makeni and UNAMSIL and ECOWAS forces remained hard pressed around the Makeni area. On 11 May UNAMSIL forces were heavily engaged again, this time involving Guinean troops.

In order to warm things up and to make it clear that the rebels would meet determined force, the Royal Marines staged a landing exercise on 19 May, preceded by a fly-over of a Harrier aircraft and several helicopters. The RUF leader, Faraday Sankoh, was captured by a British unit and taken

ROYAL MARINES TAKE OVER

The Royal Marines Amphibious Ready Group landed on 25 May in a state of maximum readiness. The firefight between the Pathfinders and the RUF at Lungi Loi left little doubt that there was ever-present danger in and around Freetown itself, not to mention the large concentrations of rebels further inland which were being engaged at the time by forces from UNAMSIL and the Economic Community of West African States (ECOWAS).

On 19 May, in Resolution 1299, the UN Security Council had authorized the increase of the UNAMSIL contingent to 13,000. On 1 May, Nigerian soldiers from ECOWAS had been ambushed by guerrillas near Porto Loko. A Nigerian sergeant was shot in the leg and the patrol were fortunate to survive the encounter. On 2 May RUF fighters surrounded an ECOWAS base at Makeni and demanded that 10 of their soldiers be released. When the demand was refused, the RUF attacked the camp as well as another nearby and

WESTLAND LYNX HELICOPTER

The Lynx was first designed and built by Westland in 1971 and has been adapted to become an advanced military and naval operational asset. It is currently supplied to the Royal Navy Fleet Air Arm (FAA) in the Mark 8 version as an anti-surface and anti-submarine helicopter. It is fitted with a Central Tactical System, radar and a Passive Identification Device. The British Army Air Corps (AAC) operate the aircraft as an attack helicopter. The Fleet Air Arm deploy the Lynx AH Mk 7 as an attack helicopter in support of the Royal Marines. Naval versions can carry four Sea Skua missiles. Attack versions can be armed with eight TOW anti-tank missiles. Other armament may include a general purpose machine gun (GPMG). The version of the Lynx deployed on Operation Palliser and Operation Barras was the Lynx HAS Mk 3.

to a secure location. There is little doubt that the capture was carried out by British special forces.

When 42 Commando, 20 Commando Battery Royal Artillery, 539 Assault Squadron and Special Boat Squadron deployed, part of their reconnaissance included the island of Pepel. Here a firefight took place, mainly involving members of 20 Commando Battery RA, after which 15 'West Side Boys' were captured.

OPERATION KHUKRI
Despite the success of the raid conducted by the Indian Army QRC to rescue Kenyan troops, two companies of the Indian Army's 5/8 Gurkha Rifles (GR) Infantry Battalion Group remained surrounded at Kailahun. The aim of Operation Khukri was to enable the 5/8 GR to stage a breakout and to link up with the main battalion at Daru.

A 5/8 Gurkha Rifle patrol, which was commanded by the Battalion Second in Command, had been detained at Kuiva by about 200 rebels. Eventually, after a certain amount of diplomatic pressure, the patrols were released and the main focus of attention was switched to the battalion at Kailahun.

The Indian Army reinforced its in-country contingent with INDBATT-2, an artillery battery, a special forces company and attack helicopters. The rescue operation would involve a variety of Indian Army and Aviation units, two companies of the Ghanain Army, two companies of the Nigerian Army, two Chinook helicopters and one C-130 Hercules of No. 7 Squadron Royal Air Force and elements of D Squadron SAS. Between 13 and 14 July 2000, the combat elements moved out from the Freetown and Hastings area by road and air.

Contact had been maintained with the embattled Gurkha companies so that the breakout could be coordinated with the arrival of the relief force. On 15 July ground troops cleared the area of guerrillas and the two RAF Chinooks landed exactly on time

Facing page: A soldier of the Parachute Regiment watches an RAF Chinook fly in over the village of Lungi Loi.

HMS OCEAN

This amphibious helicopter carrier was launched on 11 October 1995 and commissioned on 30 September 1998. The primary role of HMS Ocean is to carry an Embarked Military Force (EMF) along with amphibious and aerial assets. These typically comprise 12 medium support (EH101 Merlin or Sea King) helicopters, six attack (Lynx) helicopters and four Mark 5 Landing Vehicle Personnel (LCVP). The ship can also be used as a base for anti-terrorist operations; in other words, she can be used as a platform for special forces operations. Otherwise, her usual complement is 480 Royal Marines and 206 aircrew in addition to her own crew of 255. HMS Ocean can potentially take Harriers, though her systems are not designed to provide support for such aircraft.

HMS Ocean has a range of 12,900km (8000 miles) with a maximum speed of 18 knots.

at 06:20 and embarked 44 military personnel plus their stores.

The rest of the operation was successfully carried out, largely under the auspices of the Indian Army. The operation involved an advance on the village of Pendembu, where RUF weapons caches were found and, after frequent engagements with the enemy, the rescue force linked up with 5/8 GR and moved back to Daru.

As the columns moved back to Daru, the RUF attempted to ambush them at Kuiva, Bewabu and Mobai. These attacks were also defeated. The operation as a whole was hailed as a significant collaboration success for the forces involved, including the Indian Army, Indian Air Force, UNAMSIL, British Army and Royal Air Force.

OPERATION BASILICA
The presence of the Parachute Regiment and the Royal Marines along with crucial support from the Royal Navy and Royal Air Force contingents resulted in a rapid military stabilization in Freetown and the surrounding area. British military forces were not under UN Command and the RUF discovered early on that any attempts to bully the

DISARMAMENT, DEMOBILIZATION AND REINTEGRATION (DDR)

An important part of the UNAMSIL project was the DDR programme. The aim of the programme was to persuade guerrillas, including members of the RUF, to lay down their weapons and former way of life in return for a range of benefits, including cash, education, skills training, tool kits for a variety of crafts and support for entrepreneurial endeavours.

By the end of 2005, some 75,490 combatants had been disarmed and demobilized through the DDR programme, including 6845 child soldiers and 4651 women. More than 12,000 of these chose to go through an educational process, though due to the poor state of the Sierra Leone economy, there was no guarantee of a job at the end of it.

The key to the DDR programme was that the incentives provided by the peacekeeping forces proved stronger than the lure of drugs and drink that characterized life as a rebel.

The DDR programme together with the presence of a determined military force to a large extent broke the spell that the rebel leaders had over their men. As their members began to melt away, the rebel leaders became increasingly restive.

British, as they had done with some success to other UN contingents, would result in a swift and decisive response.

British officers coordinated their operations with the local UNAMSIL command and there is little doubt that the UN operation as a whole benefited from their expertise.

Operation Palliser, designed to intervene in the immediate crisis in Sierra Leone, provide safe passage for British and other nationals and protect the civilian population and government in Sierra Leone, had achieved its aims and by 30 May the Amphibious Ready Group was preparing to depart.

The departure of the ARG was as significant as its arrival. They left behind them a Military Advisory and Training Team (MATT) which signified that the British had no intention of protecting the Sierra Leone population on an

open-ended basis but, once the immediate crisis had been dealt with, the aim was to enable the people of Sierra Leone to manage on their own.

The plan was to man, train and equip the Sierra Leone Army, Air Force and Navy. This would include the supply of such basics as shoes, boots and uniforms, not to mention the powerful L1A1 7.62mm (0.3in) Self Loading Rifle that had been standard issue to the British Army up to the mid-1980s. The MATT would also be involved in creating sustainable organizational structures, covering command, administration, supply, maintenance and personnel management. Much of this, of course, depended on finding able and incorruptible people of the required level of education if the structure that was put in place was not to collapse like a pack of cards. A training programme was therefore also put in place in coordination with institutions in Britain, including, for example, the training of civil servants. Processes such as these, however, take time.

The British contingent would continue to maintain its offensive and defensive capability, either on its own or through the use of local forces that it had trained. The RUF rebels would find themselves confronted, therefore, with motivated, determined forces.

The initial training was carried out by 2nd Battalion, The Royal Anglian Regiment. On 22 July 2000 they were relieved by 1st Battalion, The Royal Irish Regiment (RIR).

THE WEST SIDE BOYS

The West Side Boys or West Side Soldiers were a renegade rebel group associated with the Armed Forces Revolutionary Council. The group had been involved in earlier incidents in 2000, including the capture and hostage taking of UN peacekeepers.

Recruitment into the West Side Boys included the abduction and dehumanization of children, some of whom were even forced to participate in the torture and murder of their parents. Any traces of conscience were erased by palm wine, marijuana and heroin. The group was able to sustain itself financially largely through the sale of illegal conflict diamonds. Though almost constantly either drunk or high or both, the West Side Boys were regarded as effective jungle fighters and in all circumstances highly volatile and dangerous.

CAPTURE

On 25 August 2000 a patrol of three Land Rovers from the 1st Battalion, The Royal Irish Regiment, including one Land Rover WMIK (Weapons Mount Installation Kit), carrying a hefty 12.7mm (.50 cal) machine gun, headed for the village of Magbeni. The RIR patrol was under the command of Major Alan Marshall. Although the village was not on the patrol itinerary and known to be in an area under the control of the West Side Boys, accounts suggest that Marshall may have decided to pay it a visit following a conversation with his opposite number in the Jordanian UNAMSIL contingent nearby.

Things seemed to be progressing well with the DDR programme and the British commander may have felt confident enough to check out what sort of progress was being made in Magbeni.

In normal circumstances the 11 British soldiers,

armed with automatic SA80 rifles, would have been more than a match for enemy guerrillas more than twice their number. This was not, however, in military parlance a 'contact' with the enemy but a close-up fact-finding mission that was to develop into something else.

About 25 members of the West Side Boys were in the village and came out to meet the patrol. According to accounts, the initial exchanges were fairly good humoured. Everything changed, however, when the West Side Boys' commander arrived. This was Brigadier Foday Kallay, a 24-year-old commander with a reputation for ruthlessness. A Bedford truck mounting a heavy machine gun emerged to block the route south and the mood of the crowd suddenly changed.

Although heavily armed, the British soldiers now had little control. They were in the midst of the now hostile crowd and at too close range to allow their weapons to be effective. There was no room for tactical manoeuvre and to open fire would have resulted in a bloodbath. Major Marshall was

The West Side Boys display an array of weaponry at Masiaka, including a rocket-propelled grenade launcher and a 12.7mm (.50 calibre) machine gun. They proved to be highly volatile and dangerous opponents.

assaulted and the rest of the soldiers had little choice other than to hand over their weapons and endure the humiliation.

Once the rebels had taken control, the British soldiers were put on canoes and taken upriver to the West Side Boys' base at Gberi Bana.

The West Side Boys, otherwise known as members of the AFRC/ex-SLA, were largely based around the Occra Hills and imposed a reign of terror on the villages within their range, broadly the Port Loko and Masiaka districts. According to Human Rights Watch, their daily routine consisted of 'rape, murder, torture, abduction, massive looting, forced labour, and indiscriminate ambushes along a major highway. The AFRC/ex-SLA murdered numerous civilians for not having enough money, for being unable to carry looted items or for refusing to have sexual relations with a combatant.'

The rebels appeared to have a particular taste for Christian missionaries as hostages. Though several

were released for ransom, a group of nuns was murdered by one gang leader.

The West Side Boys were no less ruthless with their own members. The climate of reconciliation created by UNAMSIL and the increasing numbers of people choosing to make a go of a normal civilized life created an atmosphere of increasing suspicion and retribution within the rebel cadres. A mass execution of men he considered to be waverers was carried out by the same rebel leader who had captured the British soldiers.

As the UN contingents were deployed under more complex rules of engagement than would be expected of conventional forces, and as some of the contingents were not as highly trained as others, the ability to hit back at the perpetrators of these atrocities had been somewhat limited. The Indian Army had shown what could be achieved through determined action and professionalism. The British Army had the added advantage of being outside the UN chain of command.

Now, however, the tables had apparently turned. The British were suffering the same humiliation that had been meted out to UN contingents in the

Soldiers of 1st Battalion Royal Irish Regiment in a Land Rover WMIK who later lost their tactical advantage when surrounded by West Side Boys.

Soldiers from the Economic Community of West African States Monitoring Group (ECOMOG) on patrol in Freetown, Sierra Leone.

past. Their weapons and vehicles had been taken away and even prized personal possessions such as wedding rings removed and flaunted in front of their faces. They could do little more than bite their lips.

The humiliation and capture of serving members of the British Army threw down a gauntlet which had a resonance perhaps even greater than the occupation of an embassy in London. The West Side Boys and others had spent years torturing and humiliating innocent civilians as well as the members of peacekeeping forces who were often constrained by their rules of engagement. The British Army had lost face. The lives of its soldiers were in danger. How would the British respond?

PRELUDE

The immediate reaction of the British was to open negotiations with the rebels. These were conducted through the commanding officer of 1st Battalion, The Royal Irish Regiment, Colonel Simon Fordham. Soon he had negotiated the release of five of the captive soldiers in exchange for supplies

and technological equipment. That left six soldiers at the mercy of the West Side Boys, who used the opportunity to posture in the limelight of world media attention. It turned out that the men dressed in shower caps and psychedelic clothing had been involved in some of the previous coup attempts in Sierra Leone but it remained unclear how exactly they would benefit from this latest hostage taking.

While the clock ticked away and the talking continued, A Company of 1st Battalion, The Parachute Regiment was put on standby to move, along with attachments for signals, snipers and mortars. Many of the men were familiar with Sierra Leone from their stint in Operation Palliser. Meanwhile, in Sierra Leone, the West Side Boys were already being observed. Information was being fed back to headquarters about their movements, equipment and possible lines of attack. The SAS and SBS were taking control.

Soldiers from 1st Battalion the Parachute Regiment patrol the United Nations compound in Freetown, May 2000.

A SPECIAL FORCES OPERATION

Just as 1st Battalion, The Parachute Regiment were returning to familiar territory so were members of 22 SAS who had reputedly formed a significant contingent of Operation Palliser.

A rescue operation was being planned, to be known as Operation Barras. Owing to the specialist nature of such an operation and its very high risk value, there is also little doubt that the lead command for Operation Barras was Director Special Forces. A Company, 1st Battalion, The Parachute Regiment would have taken the lead from the special forces command, first in England and then in Sierra Leone, in an arrangement that would later become formalized with the creation of the Special

Forces Support Group (3 April 2006). This would include members of the Parachute Regiment as well as Royal Marines and the RAF Regiment.

The special forces elements included members of 'D' Squadron SAS along with the men from the SBS. There was an amphibious element in the operation as the two rebel camps were separated by a river while much of the rest of the physical environment consisted of mangrove swamps.

That operation had allowed them to ascertain that an amphibious approach for the main operation was not an option as the river was full of sandbanks and the observation teams themselves were able to confirm that a land attack was also not possible due to the dense undergrowth. A Company, 1st Battalion, The Parachute Regiment would discover to their discomfort what the terrain round the village and camp was really like. The SAS and SBS would work with the observation units on the ground, reinforced by special forces elements carried in a CH-47 Chinook helicopter. The main force for Operation Barras arrived on Thursday 7 September 2000. The die was cast.

THE PLAN

There would be two elements to the attack. One target was the village of Magbeni, where the RIR soldiers had been captured in the first place, and the other was the rebel camp itself at Gberi Bana, where the British hostages and others were now held.

The village of Magbeni was an important target as, having been mostly cleared of civilians by the West Side Boys, it was mainly occupied by the WSB along with heavy weaponry and ammunition stores. If the village were not neutralized, the contingent there would be able to provide heavy fire support to the Gberi Bana contingent.

The attack on the village of Magbeni would be akin to a conventional assault on a built-up area at which the Parachute Regiment were well practised. The attack on Gberi Bana would require the pinpoint location and extraction of hostages which was what the special forces were trained for. In both attacks, transport would be provided by CH-47 Chinooks of No. 7 Squadron RAF and aerial fire support by two British Army Air Corps Lynx helicopters.

The question remained how to move the rescue force into position faster than a drugged West Side Boy could pull a trigger and kill all six hostages. This is precisely what the rebel leader had said he would do the moment he heard the sound of

British Royal Marine Commandos test their weapons on board the helicopter carrier HMS Ocean, off the coast of Sierra Leone, May 2000.

While the SAS successfully rescued the British hostages held in a camp at Gberi Bana, 1 Para attacked the main force of the West Side Boys at Magbeni.

approaching helicopters. Identification of the precise location of the hostages was crucial. The SAS and SBS teams on the ground would provide covering fire at the critical point.

GO-AHEAD

Negotiations with the West Side Boys continued but it was becoming clear to the British that, however, much they gave or promised to the West Side Boys, including food and equipment, there was no sign of the hostages being released. Discussions had even extended to vocational training for the West Side Boys.

As with Operation Nimrod and the attack on the Iranian Embassy in Princess Gate, authority for the rescue operation to go ahead would be sanctioned by the Cabinet Office Briefing Room (COBR), known as 'Cobra', along with permission from the Prime Minister. Military advisers received the required permission. The operation would go ahead on Sunday 10 September.

ACTION

Having been brought in by RAF C-130 Hercules and assembled at Lungi Airport, the two Mk 7 Lynx helicopters had been initially moved to HMS *Argyll*, where one of them had a new engine fitted, and then on to a landing strip at nearby Hastings, on the Freetown Peninsula, which was controlled by the Indian Army. They were joined by three CH-47 Chinook helicopters of No. 7 Squadron RAF. At 06:16 on Sunday 10 September 2000 the helicopters, having embarked SAS troopers and Paratroopers, lifted off.

Two CH-47 Chinooks headed for a point south of the village of Magbeni. These helicopters carried A Company, 1st Battalion, The Parachute Regiment and their support units. The other helicopter headed north of the village to a drop zone near the Gberi Bana camp. This helicopter contained elements of D Squadron SAS as well as some paratroopers.

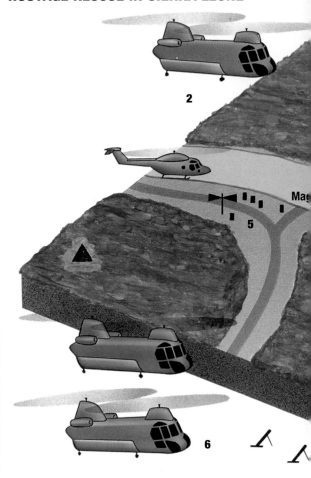

HOSTAGE RESCUE IN SIERRA LEONE

Key
1 SAS and SBS units secure the river.
2 The SAS Hostage Rescue Team flies into Gberi Bana by Chinook.
3 The hostages are rescued and evacuated.
4 SAS Land Rovers provide fire support for the rescue.

The two Lynx helicopters were available for command and control duties as well as aerial fire support.

GBERI BANA

If the West Side Boys heard the helicopters coming in, they did not have much time to take action, for

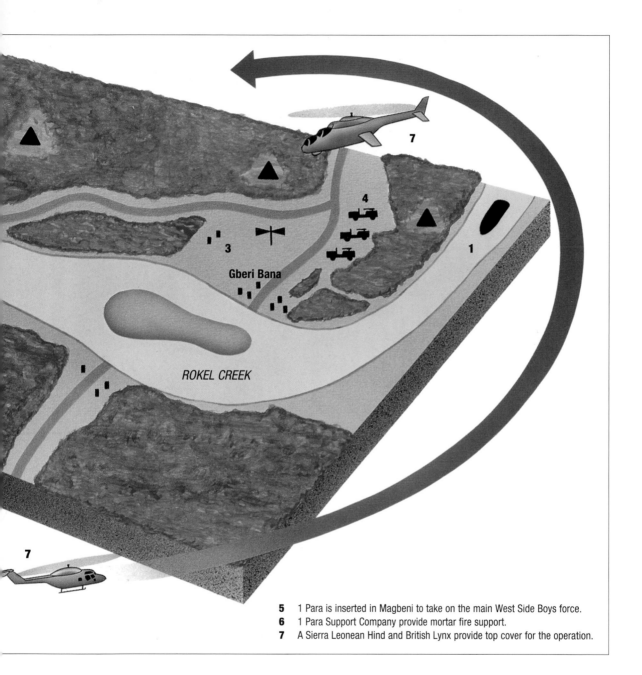

ROKEL CREEK

Gberi Bana

5   1 Para is inserted in Magbeni to take on the main West Side Boys force.
6   1 Para Support Company provide mortar fire support.
7   A Sierra Leonean Hind and British Lynx provide top cover for the operation.

something else was incoming, namely rounds put down by the SAS and SBS observation patrols who had kept them silent company incognito over the last few days.

In the whirl of sound and bullets, quick thinking was certainly necessary but barely possible. In such circumstances experienced soldiers act on automatic pilot, or, to use the oft repeated phrase, 'the training takes over'. But it was early morning and, with drugs and alcohol hanging like a wet blanket on the mind, the likely outcome was confusion.

Once they had grabbed their weapons and got outside, the West Side Boys began to fire back. The Chinook helicopter offered an enormous target but

131

A soldier from the British Pathfinder Platoon in training. The Pathfinder Platoon are an elite force providing advance reconnaissance.

in the panic, and due to the dodging antics of the pilot, no serious damage was done.

The SAS were fast-roping down and one of the West Side Boys managed to get off an accurate shot at one of the men, who was unfortunately fatally wounded. Once they hit the ground, the joint teams of SAS either killed or captured those members of the WSB who had not managed to hide or run away. Kallay himself was found alive under a pile of dead bodies. The hut housing the hostages had been located by the SAS ground teams who neutralized the opposition and protected the hostages until the moment came to load them on to the helicopter, along with the Sierra Leone hostages and several WSB captives.

MAGBENI

As the main complement of A Company exited the ramps of two CH-47 Chinooks, they found themselves up to their armpits in a swamp. This was not an ideal position to be in for a fast tactical manoeuvre, especially when under fire. Being under fire no doubt helped to concentrate the mind. Being drenched in water and covered in sticky mud was an inconvenience but the main concern was the potential jamming of weapons, particularly the belt-fed GPMGs.

As the paratroopers reached dry ground and took stock, the Lynx helicopters came overhead and started to strafe the heavy machine gun position in the village until it was put out of action. Then the platoons began to move through the village towards their objectives, many of them coming under heavy fire. At one point the HQ team were hit by a mortar, with Major Lowe, Officer

Commanding going down with severe leg injuries. Six other soldiers were also injured. While the Paras quickly reorganized their command structure, the CH47 Chinook that had picked up the SAS and hostages did a rapid detour to pick up the wounded at Magbeni, landing on the main track before roaring off again.

The remaining Paras continued to clear the village, gradually pushing the remaining West Side Boys out of the east side of the village. The Paras then dug in to await a possible counter-attack.

The counter-attack, however, was not forthcoming. The West Side Boys had encountered the SAS, the SBS, the Parachute Regiment, the RAF

A Royal Marine door gunner keeps watch on board a Royal Navy Westland Sea King helicopter flying over the bay of Freetown.

and Army Air Corps. Those that survived certainly did not want to come back for more.

AFTERMATH

The use of initiative is encouraged in the British Army. It is this kind of initiative that enabled the Paras to carry on with the operation in Magbeni despite losing their Officer Commanding. Major Marshall had used his initiative in attempting to gather information while on patrol. It proved to be a mistake. Like many errors of judgment, however, a certain amount of good came out of it. Apart from the British hostages, there were several Sierra Leone captives who would probably have been brutalized or murdered if the British had not come to the rescue. And many people in the surrounding area would go about their business with greater security now that the West Side Boys had gone.

Operation Enduring Freedom (Invasion of Afghanistan)
Operation Anaconda (Assault on Taliban and al-Qaeda)
Operation Red Wings (US Navy SEAL reconnaissance mission)
Operation Commando Wrath (Battle of Shok Valley)
Operation Neptune Spear (Assassination of Osama bin Laden)

AFGHANISTAN

The US-led operations in Afghanistan that continue at the time of writing were instigated by the most devastating terrorist assault in history. On 11 September 2001 Islamic terrorists hijacked four US commercial airliners. Two of the airliners (United Airlines Flight 175, a Boeing 767-222, and American Airlines Flight 11, a Boeing 767-223) were flown into the two towers of the World Trade Center in New York, and a third (American Airlines Flight 77, Boeing 757-223) was crashed on the Pentagon in Washington. The fourth airliner (United Airlines Flight 93, a Boeing 757-222), which may have been intended for the Capitol in Washington, crashed in open country as the passengers heroically attempted to take control of the plane.

The fatalities in the attacks included every single person on all four airliners, including children as young as three, amounting to 246 lives. The death toll in the World Trade Center was 2602, including 343 firefighters and 23 policemen who had entered the building after the initial impacts. They put themselves in the way of danger in an attempt to rescue the people in the towers. There were 125 killed in the Pentagon.

The US Government identified al-Qaeda and Osama bin Laden as responsible for the attacks

Facing page: An Afghan National Army commando with the 3rd Commando Battalion scans the surrounding mountains while providing security during a clearing operation in the Maiwand district of Kandahar Province, 2011.

and in a number of video recordings Osama bin Laden himself claimed responsibility as part of a jihad, or holy war, against the United States. The sheer horror of the attacks was such that the entire civilized international community stood by the Americans at this terrible hour, the mood summarized by a headline in the French newspaper *Le Monde*: 'We are all Americans now.'

The UN Security Council passed Resolution 1368 in which it reiterated the right of individual or collective self-defence.

TALIBAN AND AL-QAEDA

The Taliban, otherwise known as Students of Knowledge Movement, took over in Afghanistan from the Mujahideen. By February 1996 they had captured Kabul and taken control of the country. The Taliban had an extremely purist view of Islamic law and, although there was a measure of stability in the country under Taliban rule, its relations with the outside world were cold and limited. Human rights violations were rife. Some resistance to the Taliban regime remained in the country, mainly centred around the Northern Alliance.

Despite having received some aid from Pakistan and the West, it soon became clear that the Taliban regime was a pariah, underlined by the fact that the country became a haven for Islamic militants, including Osama bin Laden and al-Qaeda.

When the Taliban regime refused to agree to the extradition of Osama bin Laden and thus effectively associated themselves with al-Qaeda, they made themselves into a target for American retribution.

OPERATION ENDURING FREEDOM

After the 11 September 2001 attacks, the United States launched a global war on terror. The phrase underlined the difficulties with which the United States and its allies were faced, for terrorists by nature did not stand up and fight, and it would be a challenge for conventional forces to take them on.

The alliance between al-Qaeda and the Taliban, however, at least provided a concrete objective and a definable enemy, albeit in one of the most rugged and difficult environments.

The British and Russian Empires had clashed in the rugged Afghan mountains in the nineteenth century, one empire probing downwards from the vast expanses of the Russian steppes and the other pushing upwards from the Jewel in the British Imperial Crown: India. What came to be known as the Great Game ended in stalemate but the activities of British and Russian officers, often bearded and disguised as local tribesmen, prefaced the kind of covert operations that would take place in the same mountains a century and a half later.

5TH SPECIAL FORCES GROUP (AIRBORNE)

Originating as the First Special Service Forces founded in the Second World War on 5 July 1942, the unit saw action in Italy and was disbanded at the end of the war in France in 1945.

On 21 September 1961 the 5th Special Forces Group (Airborne) was activated and by the following year it was seeing action in Vietnam. The specialized and high-risk nature of their work in Vietnam resulted in a clutch of medals.

In 1988 the unit base was moved from Fort Bragg to Fort Campbell.

In 1990 5th Special Forces Group (Airborne) provided a significant contribution to Operation Desert Shield and Desert Storm, where they carried out both reconnaissance and direct action missions. In 1992 they were deployed to Somalia.

The deployment of the unit to Afghanistan in 2001 was to prove one of their most challenging and far-reaching missions.

In 1979 the Soviet Union made one of the biggest mistakes in its history. Provoked by the constant attempts of the Afghanistan Mujahideen to push out the Soviet-supported Marxist People's Democratic Party of Afghanistan, it moved major forces into the country, including the Fortieth Army with three motorized rifle divisions, an airborne division, an assault brigade, two independent motorized rifle brigades and five separate motorized rifle regiments. Not only did the Mujahideen command the mountains and mount constant pinprick attacks against the Soviets, but they also had a steady supply of weapons supplied by the CIA, including the easy-to-use hand-held Stinger anti-aircraft missile.

If the United States learned anything from watching their rival superpower kicking and writhing under the Mujahideen assault it was that large conventional forces were not the way to deal with fast-moving small groups that know the ground well. Even large weaponry such as cruise missiles would simply bounce off the mountainsides.

SPECIAL FORCES DEPLOY

It is significant and a key to the success of Operation Enduring Freedom in Afghanistan that the initial deployment of US forces consisted of a large special forces contingent. One of the first of these was the 5th Special Forces Group (Airborne), based at Fort Campbell, Kentucky.

Ironically, the US deployment was greatly aided by an agreement to use bases in Uzbekistan, which had formerly been part of the Soviet Union. The 5th Special Forces Group were part of Joint Special Operations Task Force North, otherwise known as Task Force Dagger. They were accompanied by 160th Special Operations Aviation Regiment.

Although large numbers of conventional forces were deployed to Afghanistan, the configuration of the operation was such that its success or failure

Facing page: Soldiers of 1st Battalion, 187th Infantry Regiment, 101st Airborne Division (Air Assault) on patrol during Operation Anaconda.

JOINT TASK FORCE TWO (JTF 2)

This unit has its roots in the US/Canadian 1st Special Service Force of Second World War fame, otherwise known as the 'Devil's Brigade'.

JTF 2 was activated on 1 April 1993 when the force took over counter-terrorist responsibilities from the Royal Canadian Mounted Police (RCMP).

JTF 2 takes recruits from across the spectrum of the Canadian armed forces, the only stipulation being a minimum of two years' service. At the Dwyer Hill Training Center, recruits are assessed for physical stamina as well as for mental aptitude and overall psychological profile. Only about two out of 10 candidates pass the selection process.

Like many special operations teams, the JTF 2 are trained in a range of specialisms, including scuba, fast-roping, HALO/HAHO parachuting, amphibious assault and mountain, arctic, jungle and desert environments.

JTF 2 was deployed to Afghanistan in December 2001 and completed its mission in November 2002.

Soldiers of 20th Special Forces Group (SFG) Operational Detachment Alpha (ODA) 342 patrol with members of the Afghanistan Military Forces.

depended almost entirely on the performance of the special forces in theatre.

Apart from US special forces, a detachment of British SAS was also thought to have been deployed in theatre from the outset, and over the course of Operation Enduring Freedom a number of other countries would also deploy special forces assets. These included contributions from Canada (Joint Task Force Two [JTF 2], in addition to its large conventional forces contribution); from Australia (the Australian SAS were deployed under US command); from New Zealand (the New Zealand SAS worked in conjunction with the Australian SAS); from France (1er Régiment de Parachutistes d'Infanterie de Marine and Detachement Alat des Opérations Spéciales); from Germany (the German Kommando Spezialkräfte [KSK] is said to have been deployed in theatre, though, like the British SAS, there is no official confirmation of this); from Denmark; from Norway; from the Czech Republic; from Lithuania; from Poland (*Grupa Reagowania Operacyjno-Manewrowego* [GROM]); and from Portugal (commandos).

Their task was to liaise with the members of the Northern Alliance and to successfully coordinate those forces with US and Allied ground forces. This would involve a high level of task coordination with the US Air Force as well as considerable leadership skills, as the use of air power and ground forces needed to be coordinated to achieve the maximum effect. Special forces would be required to identify al-Qaeda camps and hideouts, destroy them and choose the most favourable approaches for any attack.

The commanders of the Northern Alliance were General Abdur Rashid Dostum, General Mullah Daoud and General Fahim Khan, and to add to the challenge for the special forces, although these leaders were in a temporary alliance, they had also in the past been rivals.

INSERTION

The 12-man special forces units were inserted by 160th SOAR flying CH-47 Chinook helicopters at night in the Afghan winter. The terrain was extremely hazardous and the insertions were at high altitude. The severe Afghan winter was setting in, with unpredictable wind gusts through the high mountain passes. The enemy was ever present and impossible to spot. The whole operation would be carried out in extreme darkness, aided only by the use of night-vision goggles (NVGs).

After the insertion, each team faced a daunting march with heavy equipment loads. This would have included not only their personal kit such as cold weather gear and other essentials but also the communications equipment and target illuminators that would magnify their potential power a thousandfold.

Soldiers of B Company, 2nd Battalion 504th Parachute Infantry Regiment (PIR) are inserted by CH-47 Chinook into the Baghran valley.

The first SF team was dropped within a few miles of the city of Mazar-e Sharif. It split into two teams, Alpha and Bravo, and liaised with the local General Dostum in order to attack the Taliban in both the city and the Darya Suf Valley.

Mazar-e Sharif had been General Dostum's stronghold until he was pushed out by the Taliban and he had a strong incentive to get it back. The two-pronged approach by the special forces team was designed to pin down the garrison at Mazar-e Sharif and to prevent reinforcement from reaching them from the south. Team Alpha began calling down aerial support to interdict Taliban

forces at Mazar-e Sharif and this was provided by B-1 and B-52 bombers as well as F-14 , F-15, F-16 and F-18 fighters. Large numbers of enemy vehicles and other assets were destroyed.

Team Bravo had a similar effect further south, bringing in aerial support to destroy up to 65 vehicles, 12 command bunkers and an ammunition storage bunker. The special forces teams enhanced their popularity by joining the Northern Alliance

US Army Special Forces ride with the Northern Alliance. They achieved considerable success in the opening stages of Operation Enduring Freedom.

forces on horseback, which, in the absence of other forms of transport, added significantly to their mobility.

Moving to a forward observation post (OP) in a pass south of Mazar-e Sharif, the special forces called in aerial support against a large concentration of Taliban forces, including vehicles as well as troops. B-52s took part in a massive air strike that devastated the Taliban forces in the region.

The combined forces of General Dostum and General Atta, along with their special forces companions, were then able to move in and take over the city of Mazar-e Sharif, receiving a rapturous welcome. Many of the surviving Taliban forces fled in panic eastwards towards Kunduz.

The capture of Mazar-e Sharif, along with its two airfields and other military assets, signalled the effective destruction of Taliban power in the north.

FIRST RAID ON KANDAHAR

Kandahar, founded by Alexander the Great, is one of the oldest cities in the world and it is situated to the southwest of Kabul, near to the Pakistan border. It has had great strategic importance over the centuries, partly due to its location on the trade routes.

In modern history, Kandahar has been occupied by various powers with an interest in Afghanistan, including the British during the First Afghan War (1839–42) and the Soviets from 1979–89, when it was the Soviet command centre. The Taliban also used the city as a power base from which to spread out and dominate the country.

On 19 and 20 October the US Rangers, along with special forces elements, carried out a series of raids against this Taliban stronghold. The 3rd Battalion, 75th Ranger Regiment was dropped into a zone south-west of the city. Special operations forces also landed and a number of incursions and engagements were conducted, though at this stage they were more by way of probing attacks to test the enemy's strength and not powerful enough to take the city itself.

Special forces were landed in northeast Afghanistan to make contact with Northern

SPECIAL FORCES WEAPONS AND ANCILLARY EQUIPMENT

Aiming devices
Aimpoint Comp M Close-quarter battle sight
M68 Aimpoint
AN/PEQ2 Infrared Target Pointer/Illuminator/Aiming
Laser (IPITAL) dual beam aiming device

Personal weapons
Colt M4 assault rifle
SOPMOD (Special Operations Peculiar Modification)
M4A1 Assault Rifle
CAR 15 assault rifle
Stoner SR-25 self-loading rifle
Colt Model 733 assault rifle
Walther MPK sub-machine gun
HK MP5 SO sub-machine gun
Uzi sub-machine gun
M249 SAW light machine gun
HK13E light machine gun

M60 medium machine gun
Browning M2 heavy machine gun
Remington 870 combat shotgun
Mossberg Cruiser 500 shotgun
HK PSG sniper rifle
M40A1 sniper rifle
M24 sniper rifle
Barret M82A1 12.7mm (.50 cal) heavy sniper rifle
Beretta 92F handgun
SIG SAUER P-228 handgun

Support weapons
M203 40mm (1.57in) grenade launcher
M79 'Blooper' 40mm (1.57in) grenade launcher
81mm (3.17in) mortar
Carl Gustav 84mm (3.28in) recoilless rifle
66mm (2.6in) LAW
MK-19 40mm (1.57in) automatic grenade launcher
Stinger MANPAD
M136 AT-4 anti-tank rocket

Alliance forces. The Panjshir valley was about 80km (50 miles) north of Kabul and the Northern Alliance had the advantage of controlling the old Soviet air base at Bagram. This was where the special forces team decided to set up an OP. From here for some weeks they called in almost continual aerial missions against the Taliban forces further down the valley.

By 13 November, the Taliban forces had been weakened enough for the Northern Alliance to carry out an assault on the Taliban forces in the Kabul area. Following a B-52 strike, the Northern Alliance swept forward, creating panic and confusion among the Taliban forces, many of whom decided to change sides.

The Northern Alliance and their US allies entered the capital city in triumph. Only two months after the destruction of the twin towers in New York, the capital city of the host nation of the perpetrators of that atrocity had fallen.

A US special forces soldier confers with members of the Afghan Northern Alliance during Operation Enduring Freedom.

TALOQAN

Special forces teams were inserted into the central and northern area, following Taliban resistance

A US Navy SEAL from SEAL Team 8 armed with an M60 medium machine gun trains in the Kuwaiti desert prior to operations in Afghanistan.

around the town of Taloqan. In this case their mere presence seemed to give the Northern Alliance forces the confidence they needed to launch an all-out assault and take the town.

KUNDOZ

Special operations forces provided leapfrog cover for Northern Alliance forces advancing towards the city of Kundoz. On each day of the advance, a special forces team would position itself in front of the front line, in the best possible position to observe the developing battle.

The Taliban forces in the area proved to be a hard nut to crack and it was to take 10 days of repeated air strikes, destroying dozens of tanks and dumps, before the Taliban resistance began to crumble. By 23 November, the Taliban force in Kundoz had surrendered, resulting in about 3500 prisoners. The overwhelming success of the operations and the large numbers of prisoners that resulted created a secondary problem. The prisoners become an unpredictable, seething mass and there were not enough trained soldiers on the ground to properly search and control them. In the prison at Mazar-e Sharif, there was a revolt in which a US intelligence officer was murdered.

US Special Forces and British SAS attempted to regain control but in these circumstances what was required was large numbers of trained soldiers. Lacking sheer numbers of troops to support them,

the special forces called in aerial support but the ranges were so close that friendly forces were also wounded.

The 1st Battalion, 87th Infantry, 10th Mountain Division were brought in from Uzbekistan to provide the necessary manpower.

SECOND RAID ON KANDAHAR

Having tied up the north, special forces began to move southwards, as did the Northern Alliance

1ER REGIMENT DE PARACHUTISTES D'INFANTERIE DE MARINE

Despite its name, this French special forces unit is in fact part of the French Army as opposed to the Navy. They are not dissimilar to the British Marines, although Marines in Britain are under naval command.

The unit owes its inception to the Free French Special Air Service Regiment, which played a full and distinguished role in the earliest SAS operations under David Stirling in North Africa and thereafter in Crete, France, Belgium, Holland and Germany. The unit carries the same motto as the SAS 'Qui Ose Gagne'.

After the war, the unit served in Indochina until 1954, following which it became a training unit. In 1974 the unit was given a special forces role and became part of the French Army *Brigade des Forces Speciale Terre* (BFST).

The unit is organized in three airborne research and special action companies (RAPAS), each of which has a particular speciality, such as mountain skills, jungle skills, HAHO/HALO parachuting or counter-terrorism. There is also a training company, a communications company and a command company.

Aerial transport, insertion and extraction is provided by the French Special Forces Aviation Regiment (DAOS).

The *1er Regiment de Parachutistes d'Infanterie* was deployed in Afghanistan for Operation Enduring Freedom and served under US command. Tasks included securing the airfields at Mazar-e Sharif and at Kabul. French Navy Super Étendard attack aircraft flying off the French aircraft carrier *Charles de Gaulle* provided close air support for coalition special forces on the ground.

---

allies. Karzai came down from the north and Gul Agha Sharzai came across the Pakistan border to approach from the south. The US Marine Corps operated south-west of Kandahar.

Special forces A-team 574 and Karzai's forces moved towards Kandahar from Tarin Kowt, which was directly north of the city. Alliance forces under Gul Agha Sharzai moved up to the city from the south. A friendly fire incident occurred at Shawali Kowt when Karzai himself and several of his fighters were wounded. Three US soldiers were also killed.

What was clear was that Karzai and his allies would have been wiped out well before now without SF support, but close air support could, as it had proved, be dangerous to both sides when the adversaries were so close.

The special forces team moving from the south with Gul Agha Sharzai came across the Taliban at Takht-pol. As there appeared to be a possibility of a surrender, Sharzai sent a delegation into the town to investigate. The Taliban took this opportunity to attempt to overcome their enemies. At this point, the special forces observers brought in another air strike, though again there was risk to both sides from the munitions that were dropped. After negotiations between the Northern Alliance

and the Taliban, Kandahar was taken without the need for more fighting, which could have proved extremely costly if the Taliban had chosen to defend the city.

TORA BORA

The ongoing defeat of Taliban forces in major cities in north and central Afghanistan suggested that it would be only a matter of time before the country was completely taken over by Allied forces. Unfortunately, the Taliban and al-Qaeda forces had a fall-back plan. They moved back into some of the most rugged and intractable mountain networks in Afghanistan, known as Tora Bora.

The Tora Bora mountains are located in the east of Afghanistan, south-east of Kabul, near the Pakistan border. The overall difficulty of access to the region by land and, indeed, any other form of transport, has made it an ideal hiding place for guerrillas at odds with the administration in the rest of the country. Over the years a sophisticated network of bunkers and tunnels are said to have been constructed in the hills and there are also a large number of natural caves to provide refuge.

This was the place where, in all probability, Osama bin Laden himself had taken refuge.

A British special forces soldier sets out on patrol wearing a mix of civilian and military high performance clothing and carrying the characteristic large capacity SF Bergen.

Plumes of smoke rise from the mountains of Tora Bora during US aerial bombardment of the area, witnessed by a group of local men.

Despite the prodigious nature of the obstacle, special forces made their approach, set up OPs and, when they located the enemy, called in air strikes. The enemy forces were moved further and further back. The attacks were unrelenting so as to create a descending spiral among Taliban forces. The enemy, however, remained tenacious and there was no sign of a mass surrender that would bring the conflict quickly to a close.

This tenacity, added to the fact that hundreds of Taliban fighters were slipping over the Pakistani border to avoid capture did not bode well for the future.

Reinforcements began to come in, including special forces from Britain, Australia, New Zealand and elsewhere, as the battle continued to locate and root out pockets of resistance.

OPERATION ANACONDA

Another refuge of Taliban and al-Qaeda fighters was the Shahi Kowt region of Afghanistan. This was a remote range of mountains located south of

Kabul. With an overall elevation of around 2450m (8000ft) and with peaks rising to up to 3700m (12,000ft), it was clear that the operation was going to be complex and hazardous.

The difficulty of the terrain made it difficult to estimate the number of enemy concealed within the mountain range but available intelligence suggested that this operation would require both additional special operations assets as well as extra regular forces. The special operations component included three command and control units, six 12-man A teams and three special operations task forces. The 10th Mountain Division and 101st Airborne Division were also deployed, along with substantial US-trained Afghan forces.

The Australian SAS made a significant contribution to advanced reconnaissance and forward observation, including the coordination of air strikes. The Australian SAS played a key role in interdicting Taliban and al-Qaeda forces that were attempting to escape the battle area.

Other special forces and regular army units along with significant air support focused on creating an encirclement of the enemy forces, followed by a series of attacks that would either eliminate the enemy forces or force them to take a particular escape route which would also be intercepted.

The Australian SAS (Task Force 64) was one of the first units into the area, deploying on 27 February. On 2 March the main operation got underway.

Difficult terrain and another friendly fire incident made for a poor early start and it was obvious that the enemy themselves had effective skills in forward observation as they began to shower mortar and artillery fire on the advancing allied troops.

The 1st and 2nd Platoons, 1st Battalion 10th Mountain Division took heavy enemy fire soon after being dropped off and the company as a whole began to take casualties as it fought off enemy attacks during the day.

TAKUR GHAR

The Takur Ghar is a 3191m (10,470ft) peak in the eastern part of the Shahi-kot valley and was the scene of one of the most harrowing incidents of the whole Anaconda operation.

The mountain provided excellent potential for observation posts. A US Navy SEAL team, along with an Air Force combat controller was therefore airlifted onto the mountain in an MH-47E helicopter, flown by 160th SOAR. The special operations Chinook MH-47E had a fully integrated adverse weather cockpit, forward-looking infrared, terrain following radar and the capability for low altitude, high-speed flight for rapid infiltration and extraction. As it reached the drop zone, the helicopter came under fire from Taliban/al-Qaeda who had also chosen the same spot for observation work. The helicopter was hit by a rocket propelled grenade (RPG) and by machine gun bullets that severed hydraulic cables. As the helicopter lurched, one of the Navy SEALs slipped on hydraulic fluid that had leaked on to the deck and fell out of the

helicopter into the snow about 3m (10ft) feet below. As it was badly damaged, the helicopter left the area and the pilot managed to fly it about 7km (4.4 miles) before carrying out a crash landing.

Having survived the fall, the US Navy SEAL was left to defend himself from the enemy forces on the mountain. He turned on his emergency beacon and could only hope that a reaction team reached him before his luck and ammunition ran out. Tragically this was not to be.

Another helicopter was immediately deployed to pick up the team from the damaged helicopter, then head back up the mountain to rescue the downed Navy SEAL and continue with the mission. Once again, the helicopter came under fire as it approached the drop zone but it managed to drop the team.

The SEAL team and Air Force combat controller then engaged in a firefight with the enemy on the hill but the Air Force CC was killed and one of the SEALs was wounded. With an AC-130 gunship providing covering fire, the team had to pull back and await reinforcements.

RANGERS TO THE RESCUE

At this point the rescue mission was switched to a US Army Ranger Quick Reaction Force (QRF) based at Gardez. Having been informed that the SEALs were still embattled on the hill, one Ranger helicopter headed straight for the drop zone. When it arrived at the location, the helicopter was fired upon with RPGs and heavy machine guns. Both pilots were wounded and the door-gunner was killed. The helicopter crashed and two Rangers were killed as they exited the downed helicopter, while another was killed while still inside. The remainder of the Rangers managed to get out and set about defending their position.

The other Ranger Chinook had landed about 610m (2000ft) further down the hill, and the team came up the hill on foot to join the other Rangers at the top of the hill. Having regrouped, the two teams then carried out an assault on the enemy positions and managed to clear the enemy of the hill.

Despite dominating the mountain, the Rangers continued to take fire from enemy positions on

A memorial at the National Memorial Cemetery, Hawaii to nine members of US Navy SEAL Delivery Vehicle Team One (SDVT-1) who died on operations in Afghanistan in 2005.

other peaks and sustained another casualty. Due to the high attrition rate for helicopters coming in to the area, there was to be no extraction attempt during daylight and as the Ranger Quick Reaction Force held out during the day, one of the casualties died. They were lifted out after dark.

The fatalities on Takur Ghar were two Air Force (TSgt John Chapman; Senior Airman Jason Cunningham), one Navy (Petty Officer 1st Class Neil Roberts) and four Army (1st Battalion 75th Rangers Regiment Sergeant Bradley Crose, Specialist Marc A. Anderson and Private First Class Matthew A. Commons; 160th Special Operation Aviation Regiment (Airborne) Sergeant Philip J. Svitak). These men had died attempting to rescue the US Navy SEAL alone on the mountain.

The United States armed forces do not leave their colleagues on the battlefield, whether they are alive or dead. It is a code of honour underwritten in blood. 'Greater love hath no man than this: that he lay down his life for his friends' (John 15: 13).

COMPLETION OF ANACONDA

Despite the trials at Takur Ghar, the overall operation continued to advance, with large numbers of caves being cleared and the enemy gradually squeezed out of the valley. US commanders continued to place as much emphasis as possible on the use of Northern Alliance forces and a 700-strong force under experienced Afghan General Gul Haidar was brought in. Special forces carried out a final clearance of the region to confirm that the enemy had been defeated.

BRITISH SAS IN AFGHANISTAN

The British SAS were heavily involved in Afghanistan from the outset but maintained their independence and were not written into the US chain of command. There have been reports that this resulted in some friction between SAS and US commanders.

The British SAS are trained to have a high level of responsibility and initiative on the ground and it has been suggested that they felt constrained by the American habit of referring upwards to command centres based in the US. Due to the quicksilver movements of Osama bin Laden and his henchmen, any delays could result in missed opportunities.

The maverick activities of the SAS, however, were most disturbing to the enemy. Not only did the Taliban and al-Qaeda have the campaigns led by US Special Forces to contend with, they also had the wraith-like SAS out looking for them as well, away from the main concentrations of US forces and their Afghan allies.

As there are no official accounts of SAS activities, their activities are more shrouded in mystery than those of some other special forces deployed in the region. At Kandahar on 26 November 2001, at

Facing page: Soldiers of the Canadian Army, US Army and Afghan military await extraction from the Tora Bora mountains by a CH-47 Chinook.

least 100 members of the SAS are said to have been involved on a raid on a Taliban/al-Qaeda training camp where it was suspected that Osama bin Laden himself was hiding. During the assault, the SAS are said to have been nearly outflanked by Taliban/al-Qaeda forces and, although they gained control in hand-to-hand fighting, at least four of their members were injured.

AUSTRALIAN SAS

In March 2002, the existing Australian SAS forces in Afghanistan that had been involved with Operation Anaconda were supplemented by another squadron. In view of the fact that many of the Taliban/al-Qaeda fighters had slipped over the border with Pakistan to escape the ongoing US and Northern Alliance advances, it was necessary to mount effective patrols in the border region to locate any remaining enemy hideouts and to deter fighters from coming back over the border.

Operation Mountain Lion involved Australian, British, Canadian and US personnel, and occasional contacts were made with the enemy.

Members of the Australian Special Air Service Regiment (SASR) during Operation Slipper in Afghanistan, July 2002. The vehicles are 4x4 and 6x6 Land Rover Perenties.

On 16 May, in the mountains of the Paktia province in southeast Afghanistan, an Australian SAS patrol had a major contact with the enemy that developed into an extended firefight. The Taliban/al-Qaeda were using RPGs and heavy machine guns and the Australians called for support. This was provided by British forces in theatre, mainly comprising 45 Commando Royal Marines supported by 7 (Sphinx) Commando Battery Royal Artillery. The Marines and the RA unit were lifted in by No. 27 Squadron RAF on 17 and 18 May.

Previous to this incident, 45 Commando had been engaged in Operation Snipe. This involved clearing caves in the south-east of the country in association with friendly Afghan forces. Although once again the al-Qaeda high command proved elusive, the operation resulted in the destruction of over 100 mortars, 100 recoilless anti-tank guns, 200 anti-personnel mines and thousands of rounds of heavy and light ammunition.

Apart from the destruction of Taliban weaponry, the operation also provided an opportunity for ongoing 'hearts and minds' operations among friendly Afghan villagers. This included the provision of medical care by highly trained Royal Marines medics.

Between 29 May and 9 July, 45 Commando carried out a similar operation in the Khowst

NEW ZEALAND SAS

The New Zealand SAS was formed on 7 July 1955, building on the close associations and major contributions New Zealand forces had made in the Second World War to the Long Range Desert Group and the nascent SAS unit formed by David Stirling. New Zealanders seemed to have plenty of the right kind of qualities for these operations.

New Zealand special forces also draw on their unique national history, including units such as the Taranaki Bush Rangers of colonial times.

The New Zealand SAS were deployed to Malaya in 1956 when they made a major contribution to the defeat of the communist insurgency. They were also deployed in Borneo alongside the British and Australian SAS. In Vietnam the New Zealand SAS operated under Australian command and both forces liaised closely with US Special Forces in operations against the Viet Cong.

The New Zealand SAS accepts candidates from all branches of the New Zealand Defence Force, the only stipulation being at least four years prior military service. Most candidates come from the army. The successful recruits are trained in counter-revolutionary warfare (CRW), hostage rescue, Combat Search and Rescue (CSAR), reconnaissance, HALO/HAHO parachuting, indigenous recruitment and operations in the arctic, mountain, jungle and desert environments.

The NZ SAS liaise closely with the British SAS as well as other special forces units. They bring to these exchanges particular skills of their own, including high level combat tracking.

The New Zealand SAS encompasses a boat troop, similar to the British SBS. The boat trip is manned on a rotational basis from the main unit.

The New Zealand SAS is organized in two squadrons, each comprising three troops that focus on different specialities, namely boat, mountain and air.

region of south-east Afghanistan. Again the mission was to find enemy pockets of resistance, destroy any military assets and carry out humanitarian operations on behalf of the local population.

British regular forces operating in these regions could be instantly identified by their mix of desert and temperate camouflage uniforms due to shortages of equipment supply from Britain.

The SAS were not limited to conventional military equipment and wore instead a range of high performance clothing better suited to the climate, the high level of physical activity and extremes of heat and cold. This included high wicking base layers, with sleeveless gilets that were designed to carry a range of equipment. Shemaghs were also carried which were useful for guarding the face in sandy or high heat conditions and for adjusting body temperature. Tough military trousers were the order of the day along with high performance walking boots.

The Taliban/al-Qaeda clearly decided not to take on the Royal Marines, preferring instead to focus their intentions on smaller groupings when they could find them. The importance of special operations was that they were better placed to

interdict the elusive Taliban and al-Qaeda fighters before they had a chance to slip away.

AFTERMATH OF EARLY OPERATIONS

The first phase of Operation Enduring Freedom had achieved its objectives. The Taliban regime had been effectively removed as a political entity and it had no major power bases left in Afghanistan. Having been ousted from the cities, the Taliban and al-Qaeda fighters were also effectively hounded out of their mountain and cave hideouts, an operation that it would have been impossible to perform without the effective use of special forces.

What the Coalition had not managed to achieve, however, was the capture of the man who was more than anyone responsible for the 11 September attacks in the United States, namely Osama bin Laden. He had always contrived to remain one step ahead of the advancing coalition forces and it may be the case that the closest the Coalition came to capturing him was at Tora Bora. Seeing the writing on the wall, the Taliban had asked for a truce during the Tora Bora operation and it is thought this may have been a ruse to allow Osama bin Laden to slip across the Pakistani border.

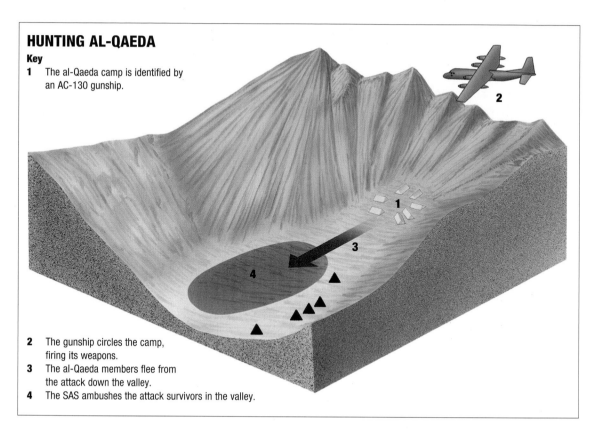

HUNTING AL-QAEDA

Key

1 The al-Qaeda camp is identified by an AC-130 gunship.

2

3

4

2 The gunship circles the camp, firing its weapons.
3 The al-Qaeda members flee from the attack down the valley.
4 The SAS ambushes the attack survivors in the valley.

American AC-130 gunships were used to 'flush out' al-Qaeda members from their base camps. As they retreated, they were ambushed by the SAS. Any survivors were taken to Camp X-Ray in Guantanamo Bay, Cuba.

What the Coalition had also not achieved was the total breakdown of all Taliban and al-Qaeda resistance throughout the country. In 2006 operations against the Taliban were still ongoing and Coalition service personnel were still in combat and getting killed.

While the country as a whole cried out for reconstruction and development, the Taliban continued to cynically infiltrate villages to carry out their attacks, often using villagers as human shields. They would then disappear again into the great expanses of the Afghan plains and mountains or across the border into Pakistan.

In some cases the Taliban fighters did change sides and joined their fellow countrymen of the Northern Alliance. Others chose to die in their hundreds or to continue fighting in pockets of resistance and from safe havens in Pakistan.

The Taliban leader Mullah Omar used again the familiar word 'jihad' to rouse his forces to renewed attacks and insurgency. The religious schools or madrassas would produce new recruits and the Taliban would come over the border in groups of 50 to carry out attacks and then split up into fragments of about five men to disappear once again into the landscape.

They would never fight powerful US, British or other coalition patrols but wait their chance to carry out carefully planned ambushes before disappearing again. Between 1 May and 12 August, according to the British Royal Statistical Society, an average of five members of the Coalition forces were killed per week by the Taliban.

Meanwhile, Afghanistan remained one of the poorest countries in the world with over six million Afghans not receiving minimum nutritional requirements. The country is regularly affected by a range of natural disasters such as floods, droughts, earthquakes and other extreme weather conditions, including the Afghan winter.

These appalling weather conditions are exacerbated by war, the presence of mines and by insurgency. Operations at the time of writing were ongoing but, as in Iraq, the real challenge was not so much to defeat an army of insurgents as to defeat an ideology.

A rare appearance by the British SAS. They were called in to help suppress a revolt at the Qala-e-Jhangi fortress near Mazar-i-Sharif.

A photograph taken prior to the operation showing the Navy SEALs who died during Operation Red Wings. From left to right: Matthew Axelson, Daniel R. Healy, James Suh, Marcus Luttrell, Eric S. Patton and Michael P. Murphy.

OPERATION RED WINGS, 2005

On 28 June 2005, a four-man US Navy SEAL team embarked on a reconnaissance mission to track a Taliban insurgent leader named Ahmad Shah who commanded a group known as the Mountain Tigers. The team was inserted by an MH-47 Chinook helicopter and then moved to an observation position under cover of darkness. The ground was not ideal for the purposes of the mission and it was very difficult for the team to both observe and remain concealed.

Their predicament was similar to that of the British SAS team Bravo Two Zero, where again there was little cover and enemy forces were too close for comfort. The SEAL team were also spotted by some goatherds. There was some debate among the team about whether to kill the goatherds as they had no equipment with which to tie them up. The

other problem was that the goats stayed close to the goatherds and threatened to signal their position.

In the event, the SEALs let the herders go and, as they feared, about an hour later a Taliban force appeared and began to engage them. Attempts to arrange extraction by helicopter failed due to faulty communications. The four SEALs now had to defend themselves against the Taliban as best they could in the exposed environment while taking fire from three sides.

Inevitably, due to the weight of fire and although they were hitting the enemy hard, the SEALs began to take casualties. Despite sustaining wounds, however, they fought on, while still trying to signal for assistance. After a two-hour firefight, three of the SEALs were dead and only Marcus Luttrell remained alive.

Eventually, six helicopters did arrive to provide assistance, but tragically an MH-47 was hit by a rocket-propelled grenade (RPG) and lost control, crashing to the bottom of a ravine. All 16 crew and US Special Forces on board were killed.

Luttrell managed to hide and was eventually found by local villagers who took him into their care. Their Pashtun rules of hospitality were proof against attempts by the Taliban to capture him. Weeks later, a US rescue team found him and took him back to base.

The operation had revealed the extreme fighting qualities and courage of the US Navy SEALs but it also revealed how even the best-trained soldiers could be caught out by bad ground, accidental discovery, sheer weight of numbers and the vulnerability of sophisticated military helicopters to the simple but devastating RPG.

HOSTAGE RESCUE IN WESTERN AFGHANISTAN, 2007

In September 2007, two Italian intelligence operators who had been working undercover in western Afghanistan in Herat Province were captured by the Taliban. The prospects for the Italian soldiers looked very grim as it became apparent that the Taliban planned to interrogate them to death before ransoming their bodies to the Italian Government. The whereabouts of the hostages was known to ISAF forces through the use of Predators drone and other surveillance assets.

The rescue operation was assigned to the British Special Boat Service (SBS) and Italian commandos.

The SBS had been deployed in Afghanistan from the beginning of Operation Enduring Freedom in 2001. They had first worked with Northern Alliance fighters against the Taliban and were involved in search and destroy missions before joining the operation against Osama bin Laden's base in the Tora Bora mountain complex. The SBS had the main special forces responsibility in Afghanistan during this period while the Special Air Service (SAS) focused on operations in Iraq.

On 24 September, the SBS commandos embarked on four Army Air Corps Lynx Mk 7 helicopters and headed towards the target area, accompanied by a team of Italian commandos. Reconnaissance had shown that the Taliban were in the process of transferring the two hostages to a new location and had set off from their base near Farah in two vehicles.

As the helicopters approached the convoy, SBS snipers took aim from their aerial positions and fired into the vehicle engine blocks with 8.59mm (.338) calibre rounds from their L115 sniper rifles, fitted with Schmidt and Bender 3-12x50

British Special Boat Service (SBS) soldiers practice a beach landing somewhere in the UK.

SPECIAL FORCES WEAPONS: USSOCOM WEAPONS INVENTORY

SCAR

Introduced in 2009, the Special Operations Combat Assault Rifle (SCAR) is a modular system that includes a sniper rifle, close-quarters-battle rifle and grenade launcher. It was developed due to reports of failures in the M4A1 design, which made it unreliable in the intense combat experienced by special forces. The SCAR comes in a 5.56mm (0.219in) Mk 16 'light' version and a 7.62mm (0.3in) 'heavy' variant. Both versions are available in three barrel lengths – short, standard and long. The SCAR has a rate of fire of 625rpm.

Mk 13 Grenade Launcher

The Mk 13 grenade launcher has a telescopic buttstock that allows the weapon to be used independently. Alternatively it can be clamped to one of the SCAR rifles. The Mk 13 is designed to fire 40mm (1.57in) grenades to an effective range of 100m (109yd) for single targets and 300m (328yd) for area targets. The MAAWS (Multi-role Anti-armor Anti-tank Weapon System) capability provides an 84mm (3.3in) recoilless, shoulder-fired, man-portable, line-of-sight, anti-armour and anti-personnel weapon system.

M14 Enhanced Battle Rifle (EBR)

Developed directly from the M14 sniper rifle at the request of the Navy SEALs for a more compact squad marksman rifle, the M14 EBR is used by Delta Force, the Navy SEALs, and ODA units.

FN 17 SCAR-H specifications:
Calibre: 5.56mm (0.219in)
Operation: Gas operated, rotating bolt
Weight: 3.49kg (7.7lb)
Barrel length: 400mm (16in)
Magazine: 20 round or STANAG box magazine
Range: 500–600 metres (1640–1970ft)

Mk 13 Grenade Launcher specifications:
Calibre: 40mm (1.56in)
Range: 100 metres (109yds) single target

M14 Enhanced Battle Rifle (EBR) specifications:
Calibre: 7.62mm (0.3in) NATO
Operation: Gas operated, rotating bolt
Weight: 5.1kg (11.24lb)
Barrel length: 457mm (18in)
Magazine: 10 or 20 round detachable box magazine
Range: 800 metres (2624ft)

PM II telescopic sights. This brought the convoy to a halt. While Italian commandos of the *Folgore* Parachute Brigade stormed the building used by the Taliban insurgents, two Lynx helicopters landed the SBS commandos, who attacked the Taliban with their C8 SFW carbines and other weapons. The special forces killed all the insurgents and rescued the two hostages, both of whom were wounded, one seriously.

BATTLE OF SHOK VALLEY: OPERATION COMMANDO WRATH, 2008

The omens were not good. During the nineteenth century, when India was part of the British Empire, British and Russian agents had conducted dangerous espionage operations in the mountains of the Hindu Kush. The British invaded Afghanistan in 1838–42, and again from 1878–80, both with limited success, and leading to eventual withdrawals. After the Soviet invasion of Afghanistan in December 1979, the Russians also treated the region with wariness. The average altitude of the Hindu Kush is 4500 metres (14,800 feet). Its sheer cliffs and ravines are the almost impregnable home of the local tribesmen and a death trap for invaders.

Despite the dangers, Operational Detachment Alpha (ODA) 3336, 3rd Special Forces Group (Green Berets) had a mission. In a village nestled in a fastness of the Shok Valley in Nuristan Province, the Hezb-e-Gulbuddin (HIG) insurgents were stockpiling weapons and posed a severe threat to the stability of the region. Their weaponry was thought to include Russian PKM machine guns, rocket-propelled grenades (RPG), DShK heavy machine guns, ZPU anti-aircraft guns and even surface-to-air missiles. Moreover, one of their senior commanders, Haji Ghafour, was a Tier Level O target for Allied forces. That put him on the same level as Osama bin Laden.

On 6 April 2008, Special Forces ODA soldiers set out with a unit of the Afghan National Army 201st Commando *Kandak*. The combined assault force numbered more than 100 men. Transported by MH-47 Chinook helicopters, they reached the objective, where the soldiers jumped to the ground as the helicopters could not land.

Special Forces from Operation Detachment Alpha (ODA) 3336 patrol in the Shok Valley, following a seven-hour firefight with insurgents.

*An Afghan National Army commando from the 2nd Company, 205th **Kandak**, coordinates forces via radio during a four-day security operation in the Tagab Valley.*

The minute the attack force had assembled and the helicopters had pulled away, they came under withering fire from insurgents hidden among the rocks all around them. In the initial confusion they had to take rapid cover, before they could set about laying down suppressive fire.

The nine members of the ODA had with them on attachment a Joint Tactical Air Controller (JTAC), Sergeant Zachary Rhyner, who would co-ordinate aerial fire support from F-15E Strike Eagle aircraft of the 335th Tactical Fighter Squadron (TFS), a flight of AH-64 Apache attack helicopters and close air support A-10 Thunderbolt ground-attack aircraft. In the initial confusion Rhyner lost radio contact, but once he had found it again he began calling in air strikes.

However, at this point the ODA started taking casualties. Sergeant Morales was hit twice, first in the thigh and then through his boot, shattering his ankle. Sergeant John Walding was then shot through the leg, almost severing it. Having given himself first aid with a tourniquet and morphine and secured his injured leg with his bootlaces, Sergeant Walden continued firing at the enemy. One of the Afghan commandos was also hit, and combat cameraman specialist Michael Carter went out in the open to rescue the Afghan soldier.

Such was the intensity of enemy fire that the team decided to call in the F-15E strike aircraft for 'danger close' fire missions. This meant that there was the great likelihood of friendly fire casualties due to the proximity of the exploding munitions. As the fight continued to escalate, about seventy 'danger close' fire-support missions were called in by the JTAC. Taking their turn with the F-15Es, AH-64 Apache helicopters used their chain guns to sweep insurgents off the roofs of nearby buildings. Following the helicopters the A-10 close air support aircraft also attacked, firing 30mm (1.18in) GAU-8/A Avenger Gatling-type cannon at a rate of 3,900 rounds per minute.

Although things were getting hot for the insurgents, an F-15E Strike Eagle pilot had spotted insurgent reinforcements running down the hillside. The weather was also beginning to turn and darkness beginning to fall, which would compromise the ability of the air assets to support the ODA and Afghan commandos.

In the circumstances, having lost all forward momentum, the ODA decided to withdraw. As most of them were now wounded, some severely, movement down the sheer hillsides, slippery with melting snow, was in itself a challenge, and even more so while under constant enemy sniper fire. While organizing the medevac, Sergeant Ford took a hit in his body armour and then in his arm, which temporarily knocked him over. He managed to get up again and continue with the medevac while Staff Sergeant Seth Howard provided covering fire with his M24 sniper rifle to keep the insurgents' heads down.

The ODA exfiltrated to safety, where the casualties could be treated. At an awards ceremony some months later, ten Silver Stars were awarded to the members of ODA 3336, 3rd Special Forces Group, while the JTAC, Sergeant Zachary Rhyner, received the Air Force Cross.

THE ASSASSINATION OF OSAMA BIN LADEN, 2011

Following the terrorist attack on the twin towers of the World Trade Center on 11 September 2001, Osama bin Laden became the most wanted man for United States intelligence and military forces. They were backed by United Nations Security Council Resolution 1368 (2001), which called on 'all states to work together urgently to bring to justice the perpetrators, organisers and sponsors of these terrorist attacks' and also said 'that those responsible for aiding, supporting or harbouring the perpetrators, organisers and sponsors of these acts will be held accountable'.

The initial operations in Afghanistan included Operation Jawbreaker, which was the insertion of a CIA Special Activities Division team, the deployment of 5th Special Forces Group (Airborne) into northern Afghanistan and the insertion of British SAS special forces. By 7 October 2001, Operation Enduring Freedom was under way, beginning with aerial and cruise missile attacks on selected targets. So far as Osama bin Laden was concerned, the key battle was the attack on the network of caves occupied by the Taliban at Tora Bora, near the Khyber Pass, between 12 and 17 December 2001. US and British special forces were present along with conventional troops and Afghan militia. A temporary ceasefire negotiated by al-Qaeda fighters with the Afghan militia may have allowed Osama bin Laden time to make his escape from the area.

The search for Osama bin Laden would now involve a painstaking sifting of intelligence, including fragments of information gathered from interrogation, intercepts of phone calls and sheer intuition. Two of the key al-Qaeda leaders captured by Pakistani and US forces were Khalid Sheikh Mohammed and Hassan Ghul. They provided a clue to the existence of an al-Qaeda member known as al-Kuwaiti who was associated with the director of al-Qaeda operations, Abu Farah al-Libi. When al-Libi was captured by Pakistani and US forces, he revealed that he had received a message from a courier that he was to be promoted in order to take the place of the captured Khalid Sheikh Mohammed.

Intelligence operators considered that if a very senior member of al-Qaeda had been promoted then it could only have been by order of the most senior member of al-Qaeda, Osama bin Laden. If the courier had been sent with the message, the courier could only have come from bin Laden.

Osama bin Laden's compound in Abbottabad, after the successful Navy SEAL operation.

Therefore to find bin Laden they had only to follow the courier. This was one of the most important discoveries in the search for bin Laden and now maximum time was devoted to discovering the identity of the courier.

CLOSING IN

It took about two years of careful cross-referencing of intelligence information to narrow down the possibilities of who the courier might be. Eventually the focus fell on Sheikh Abu Ahmed al-Kuwaiti, who had been close to Khalid Sheikh Mohammed and was one of Osama bin Laden's most trusted lieutenants.

A phone tap identified where Abu Ahmed was and then high-technology assets including drones and satellites were deployed to track him. A sophisticated ground surveillance operation was set

A US Special Operations Forces (SOF) soldier watches for enemy movement through the scope of his M4 Carbine somewhere in Afghanistan.

up to follow him to his master's lair. One wrong move could lead to years of painstaking research being lost. It was even more difficult in view of the fact that al-Qaeda operators are trained to be aware of potential surveillance and would be on the lookout for signs that they were being followed.

The surveillance operation was successful and the courier was traced to affluent suburb of Abbottabad in northern Pakistan, which was based upon an original British military settlement from the days of the Raj and was now the site of a Pakistani military academy. Soon the CIA Special Activities Division had taken over a house in Abbottabad in order to provide round-the-clock surveillance of the comings and goings to and from the house. Satellite assets in space were re-directed to provide extra scrutiny of the area and detailed plans were made of the building.

The decision to deploy special forces for the attack was taken at the highest level. Although a bombing mission was likely to be successful, it would be difficult to positively identify Osama bin

Laden among the wreckage and this might become a propaganda tool for al-Qaeda.

SEALS DEPLOY

SEAL Team 6, also called DEVGRU, of United States Naval Special Warfare Development Group was selected for the mission and immediately started rehearsals on a mock-up of the compound set up in the United States. Preparations for the mission left no room for error. Two modified MH-60 Black Hawk 'stealth' helicopters would be the primary mission vehicles but they were backed up by Chinook helicopters carrying additional DEVGRU special forces as well as elite Ranger teams. Fixed-wing jets were on standby to interdict any attempt by the Pakistani authorities to interfere with the

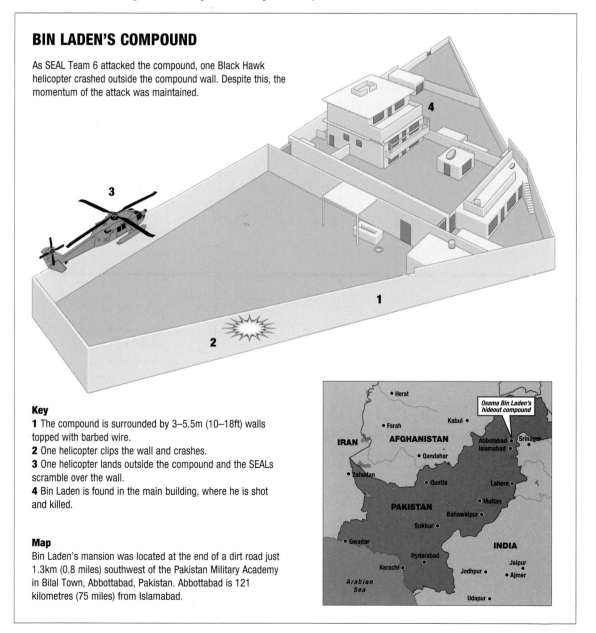

BIN LADEN'S COMPOUND

As SEAL Team 6 attacked the compound, one Black Hawk helicopter crashed outside the compound wall. Despite this, the momentum of the attack was maintained.

Key
1 The compound is surrounded by 3–5.5m (10–18ft) walls topped with barbed wire.
2 One helicopter clips the wall and crashes.
3 One helicopter lands outside the compound and the SEALs scramble over the wall.
4 Bin Laden is found in the main building, where he is shot and killed.

Map
Bin Laden's mansion was located at the end of a dirt road just 1.3km (0.8 miles) southwest of the Pakistan Military Academy in Bilal Town, Abbottabad, Pakistan. Abbottabad is 121 kilometres (75 miles) from Islamabad.

SEAL TEAM 6

SEAL Team 6, officially designated DEVGRU, was founded in 1980, initially under the command of Richard Marcinko. It was created in the wake of the intense questioning that followed the failure of the attempted rescue of hostages from Iran in 1980.

DEVGRU members are selected from operational SEAL units and undergo training in close-quarters battle (CQB) and a range of other skills such as advanced and offensive driving and survival, evasion, resistance and escape (SERE). The attrition rate is high during selection and many applicants are returned to their previous units. DEVGRU operations often include highly sensitive pre-emptive counter-terrorist operations and they sometimes operate together with the army's Delta Force under the umbrella of Joint Special Operations Task Force (JSOTF).

DEVGRU operations have included Grenada in 1983, Somalia in 1992 and Afghanistan from 2001. In 2009, DEVGRU operators rescued Captain Richard Phillips, who was being held hostage by Somali pirates. DEVGRU snipers killed all three pirates and freed Phillips, despite the fact that one of the pirates was holding a gun to Phillips' head and the SEALs were firing from a boat rolling in the swell at 100m (109yd) distance.

mission and combat search and rescue helicopters were also on standby.

Operation Neptune Spear began at 01:15 on 2 May 2011, when two Black Hawk helicopters took off from Bagram air base in Afghanistan. The two helicopters crossed into Pakistani air space undetected and headed towards the compound. On arrival, one of the helicopters suffered an engine failure and crash-landed inside the compound. Although the spectre of Desert One in Iran loomed out of the darkness, the Navy SEALs maintained the momentum.

The second helicopter landed outside the compound and the team on board disembarked and scaled the walls. Both teams stormed the building, placing explosives against doors to break in. The courier who had provided the vital lead tried to defend himself with an AK-47 but was shot down. The SEALs then moved to the third floor of the building where they found bin Laden, who was shot and killed.

Bin Laden's body was positively identified and the house was searched for valuable intelligence information contained in laptops and other electronic equipment. The body and the intelligence stash were then put on the only serviceable helicopter and the teams destroyed the other helicopter before returning to Bagram air base. The body of Osama bin Laden was then flown out to the aircraft carrier USS *Carl Vinson* where a Muslim ceremonial burial at sea was carried out.

HOSTAGE RESCUE IN BADAKHSHAN

In May 2012, four members of the Swiss NGO Medair, including British aid worker Helen Johnston, were captured by rebels while travelling on horseback in Badakhshan, northeast Afghanistan, on a mission to relieve the plight of flood victims.

The hostages were held in a cave in the Shahr-e-Bozorg district near the Tajikistan border. The rebels demanded £7 million for their release. While negotiations continued, British and American special forces established a forward operating base on 28 May near the town of Faizabad, about 30 minutes' flying time from the hostage location. The special forces included 28 members of the British SAS and 28 men from US Navy SEAL Team 6.

When an MQ-1 Predator drone intercepted a mobile phone conversation between the rebels and the Taliban that indicated there might be an imminent threat to the hostages, the special forces were put on stand-by to move. The force would be split to attack two caves, where the hostages were believed to be held.

On 31 May at 17:30 hours, the special forces boarded MH-60L Black Hawk helicopters fitted with M230 chain guns and piloted by 160th Special Operations Aviation Regiment (Airborne). Two USAF Apache helicopters flew in support.

The SAS troopers were dressed in black and carried light assault weapons, such as the C8 SFW carbines fitted with sound suppressors, AN/-PEQ-2

A US Navy SEAL aims an FN SCAR-H battle rifle during a deployment in Afghanistan, 2010.

laser pointer/illuminators and ACOG scopes with mini red dot reflex sights. They also carried handguns, such as the Sig Sauer P226, assault knives and both stun and hand grenades. They were equipped with night-vision devices. They knew that their opponents were armed with heavy machine guns, AK-47 assault rifles and rocket-propelled grenades, and that therefore surprise was essential.

In order not to alert the terrorists, the helicopters landed about five miles away from the target and the special forces completed the rest of the journey on foot through thickly wooded forest. Once both teams were in place, the assault took place simultaneously against both caves. As the rebels rushed out to meet the attack, the special forces troopers rapidly selected their targets and picked off the rebels with pin-point accuracy before they had time to use their weapons. Although well armed, the rebels were up against two of the top special forces units in the world. The result was a foregone conclusion and soon all the rebels were dead.

The hostages were freed unharmed and taken to the helicopters before being extracted.

AUSTRALIAN SASR IN AFGHANISTAN

The Australian Special Air Service Regiment (SASR) was involved in a number of operations in Afghanistan. They set up covert teams in the operation to track down Osama bin Laden and other senior members of al-Qaeda. Whereas other units in similar operations had been compromised by unforeseen circumstances, the Australian SASR managed to maintain a covert presence that enabled them on one occasion to track the attempted escape of a senior al-Qaeda commander. The SASR unit then called in air strikes. Australian special forces support elements, including 2nd Commando Regiment, also made a significant contribution to operations in Afghanistan. Between 10–14 June 2010, Alpha Company of 2nd Commando Regiment was deployed against Taliban positions in the Shah Wali Kot District in northern Kandahar Province. The Australian forces were supported by Afghan national army units and US Army helicopters from 1st Battalion, 101st Aviation Regiment. As the fighting continued and the insurgents prepared to attack, 2nd Squadron Special Air Service Regiment (SASR) was deployed into the region, which had the effect of ultimately turning the tide against the insurgent forces.

IRAQ

The US invasion of Iraq, which began on 20 March 2003, was known as Operation Iraqi Freedom. The British part of the operation was known as Operation Telic and the Australian contribution was Operation Falconer.

Whereas the operations to defend Saudi Arabia and to oust Iraqi forces from Kuwait in 1991 had the full approval of the UN Security Council, and whereas the invasion of Afghanistan was also approved by the UN Security Council, the invasion of Iraq in 2003 had no such authorization and had been deemed by many, including high-ranking members of the United Nations, to be illegal.

In Article 39 of Chapter VII of the UN Charter (Action with Respect to Threats to the Peace, Breaches of the Peace, and Acts of Aggression) it is stipulated that:

'The Security Council shall determine the existence of any threat to the peace, breach of the peace, or act of aggression and shall make recommendations, or decide what measures shall be taken in accordance with Article 41 and 42, to maintain or restore international peace and security.'

Article 41 provides the UN Security Council with a range of options outside the use of force in order to persuade a nation to comply with its requirements. Such measures would include

Facing page: US Army Special Forces, their heads covered with kafiras, sit out a sandstorm on board a Humvee south of Najaf, March 2003.

sanctions and measures such as those already deployed against Iraq.

Article 42 allows the UN Security Council to 'take such action by air, sea, or land forces as may be necessary to maintain or restore international peace and security.' This was the measure that the United States and Britain wanted to use against Iraq but other members of the Security Council were not satisfied that there was sufficient evidence of a 'threat to the peace, breach of peace, or act of aggression' and would veto any attempt to pass a resolution condoning the use of force.

From the US and British point of view, the 'threat to the peace' came from Iraq's supposed Weapons of Mass Destruction (WMD) programme. UN inspectors in Iraq, however, could find no evidence of such a programme.

The United States and Britain invaded Iraq without that nation having performed any act of aggression and without any evidence of the WMD programme. In the early hours of the invasion Coalition forces sent a cruise missile strike into the Iraqi capital Baghdad in order to assassinate the Iraqi head of state, Saddam Hussein.

Although Saddam Hussein was clearly an international pariah who had massacred the Kurds and who ran a regime based on terror, this was not sufficient reason under the norms of international law to carry out a pre-emptive strike against Iraq. Apart from any other reason, there were plenty of other unpleasant leaders around the world.

The problem for the United States and Britain was that, while wishing to be seen as morally and legally responsible nations, they had in fact themselves carried out an armed attack against another member of the United Nations without sufficient reason and without the legal backing of a UN Security Council resolution.

To justify their action, it would have been convenient for the US and Britain to have discovered evidence of a WMD programme once their forces were in Iraq. No such evidence, however, was found.

The armed forces of both countries had acted with their customary professionalism and had carried out their duty as dictated by the governments of the countries involved. The problem was not with the armed forces but with the reasoning and motives of the politicians.

THE INVASION BEGINS
Whatever the justification, the invasion of Iraq went ahead and special forces once again played an important role. From the US point of view, it was

Soldiers of the 10th Special Forces Group (Airborne) on board a US Air Force MH-53M Pave Low IV helicopter during Operation Iraqi Freedom.

the largest deployment of special forces in theatre since the Vietnam War.

Initial reconnaissance was carried out by 2nd Battalion, 5th Special Forces Group in Basra, Karbala and elsewhere, while the 10th Special Forces Group were assigned the vital task of coordinating the advance of Kurdish forces in the north of the country. These included the Patriotic Union of Kurdistan and the Kurdistan Democratic Group.

SPECIAL OPERATIONS IN NORTHERN IRAQ
The original intention for the invasion of northern Iraq had been to deploy heavy forces in the form of the 4th Infantry Division via Turkey. Due to the lack of international consensus about the legality of the invasion and Turkey's sensitivities as a regional power, permission was not granted for the United States to launch this overland operation.

The US was therefore limited to air-transportable forces, which meant special forces and paratroopers. In view of their experience in Afghanistan, this was not such a disadvantage as it might at first

10TH SPECIAL FORCES GROUP

The 10th Special Forces Group was established on 19 June 1952. It was influenced by the Office of Strategic Services (OSS) founded by General William O. 'Wild Bill' Donovan. Colonel Aaron Bank served in one of the 'Jedburgh' teams in France and was later to become the commander of 10th Special Forces Group. The 10th SFG is also influenced by the 1st Special Service Force (FSSF) which was a joint US/Canadian unit.

In the 1950s the Group was stationed at Bad Toelz in West Germany and its mission in the event of an attempted Soviet invasion would have been to get behind enemy lines, as 'stay behind forces'. The Group adopted the unconventional identity typical of many special forces groups, wearing characteristic mountain boots and carrying mountain rucksacks.

The 'hearts and minds' element of special forces operations was a vital element of their training, and was later clearly demonstrated in their operations with the Kurds in northern Iraq. Enthusiastic participation of local forces could mean the difference between success or failure of a mission, and could alter the course of a war.

A detachment of 10th Special Forces Group took part in Operation Desert Shield and Desert Storm in 1991. The team from 1st Battalion took part in a behind-the-lines rescue operation.

In April 1991 the 1st Battalion 10th SFG took part in Operation Provide Comfort to bring humanitarian relief to the Kurds who were being attacked by the Saddam Hussein regime. The major contribution of the Group to the Kurds' survival during this major humanitarian emergency created a seal of friendship with the Kurdish people.

In 1992 the 10th SFG was deployed to Somalia where it acted in support of the 1st Belgian Para-Commando Battalion.

The Group was later deployed to Bosnia and to other parts of Eastern Europe and also operated in Kosovo.

---

seem. During Operation Enduring Freedom in Afghanistan, special forces had successfully collaborated with local forces on the ground to push back the enemy with the use of air power and occasional direct action. By working in collaboration with Kurd forces in the north of Iraq, the expectation was that a similar effect could be produced.

Although the invasion of the north assumed less of a priority once it could no longer provide an avenue for major ground forces, it was still a vital part of US strategy. Two-fifths of the Iraqi conventional strength was dedicated to defending the north and if any of these units were redeployed southwards it would have had a significant impact on the campaign as a whole.

Iraqi forces in the north included Republican Guard divisions, Saddam Fedayeen and Ba'ath Party militia and would be a hard nut to crack. The 10th SFG began by conducting a series of probing attacks against Iraqi outposts in the region. On 26 March they received conventional reinforcements in the form of the 173rd Airborne Brigade. The 173rd Airborne was placed under command of Combined Forces Special Operations Component Command (CFSOCC), which was effectively in control of the whole of northern Iraq.

The operation marked another step upwards in the importance of special forces and in their integration into the overall strategic plan. Whereas in the past special forces had often been seen as a useful adjunct to the main conventional strategy, here to some extent the tables had been turned.

What special forces cannot provide, however, is sheer numbers. Although their attacks on Iraqi positions might be successful, they could all too easily lose the advantage if the ground were not secured by conventional forces. The 173rd would provide that vital backup.

Apart from the ongoing attacks against Iraqi positions across a broad front in the north, Joint Special Operations Task Force–North (JSOTF–North) was also given the objective of securing the important oil-producing city of Kirkuk.

The operations in the north, therefore, were a testament to the success of special forces and to their graduation to leading major operations as opposed to being an adjunct to conventional

US Army special forces in the foreground as a UH-60 Black Hawk helicopter prepares to land near Kirkuk, Iraq, during Operation Iraqi Freedom.

forces. The British had also demonstrated this transformation in the Gulf War in 1991 with the appointment of the Director of Special Forces, General Sir Peter de la Billière, as commander of their land forces. The tables had effectively been turned, and in northern Iraq the conventional forces were under special forces command.

The problem with this arrangement is that special forces by their nature do things differently. They think outside the box and approach problems and objectives in an unconventional way. Combined operations would therefore require a high level of coordination if objectives were to be met. Unfortunately, the organizational systems were to some extent having to be created on the hoof.

The 173rd Airborne Division would be supported in its deployment by the United States Army Europe (USAREUR) Immediate Ready Force (IRF), which included five Abrams tanks

and four Bradley Infantry Fighting Vehicles (BIFVs).

In preparation for the arrival of the Division, special forces cleared the zone near Bashur. An advance reconnaissance team flew into the area in a special operations C-130 Combat Talon. They were then taken by special forces Operational Detachment Alpha on the ground to a safe area inhabited by Kurd fighters. They next day they came back to the area to prepare for the drop.

The 173rd Airborne came in with its associated heavy equipment in C-17 transport planes. Flying at 9150m (30,000ft) as they came over the Iraqi border, the aircraft went into a sharp dive over the drop zone, releasing equipment and men at 300m

(1000ft). At least 963 paratroopers were dropped in the first wave to secure the airfield.

The 173rd had the immediate advantage in its deployment of being able to draw on the extensive contacts and high level of collaboration established by the special forces on the ground with the local Kurdish fighters. The special forces, for their part, had the advantage of conventional force backup, including armoured vehicles and artillery, as they continued to put pressure on Iraqi forces in the northern area.

Special forces in northern Iraq, working with Kurdish forces and the newly arrived 173rd Airborne, carried out a number of coordinated attacks against major Iraqi divisions. Between 30 March and 2 April they attacked and defeated the Iraqi 4th, 2nd, 8th and 39th Divisions. Apart

US special forces working alongside allied Kurd Peshmurga forces fight with members of Ansar al-Islam in northern Iraq.

from taking on conventional Iraqi military forces, JSOTF-North also attacked and defeated an Iraqi terrorist group known as Ansar al-Islam.

Ansar al-Islam was based around a number of villages in the northern region of Iraq, close to the Iranian border. Although largely made up of Kurds, the group was in direct conflict with the Patriotic Union of Kurdistan which was supported by the Americans. Ansar al-Islam was alleged to have direct links with al-Qaeda and even to have provided safe harbour for al-Qaeda members escaping from Afghanistan.

In Operation Viking Hammer, JSOTF-North, working with units of the 10th Mountain Division, carried out a series of raids against the group. Using forward observation skills and employing both close air support and ground attack with conventional forces, JSOTF-North succeeded in neutralizing Ansar al-Islam and removed the actual and latent threat to the backs of the Kurd forces as they pushed southwards to secure their objectives.

THE 'ALAMO' OR THE BATTLE OF DEBECKA RIDGE

Having suffered repeated attacks and numerous defeats and with their own men threatening to desert, the Iraqis carried out a counter-attack at an important crossroads near the village of Debecka. Here, a mountainous ridge provided an important observation point with clear views of the surrounding valley. Some 26 members of 10th Special Forces Group were on this ridge, and had to face an attack from an Iraqi motorized rifle company with hundreds of soldiers, four T-55 tanks, armoured personnel carriers and supporting artillery. Although much fewer in number, the special forces could pack a big punch. They were armed with 12.7mm (.50 cal) machine guns, 60mm (2.36in) mortars, MK-19 automatic grenade

Two members of the 2nd Battalion, 6th US Marines fire a Javelin missile in training. The Javelin would prove to be a deadly weapon.

launchers and Javelin anti-tank missiles. In view of the fact that they had no intention of retreating, the special forces called their position the 'Alamo'.

The Iraqis first attacked early in the morning, no doubt looking forward to wiping the exasperating special forces unit off the face of the earth. After initial unsuccessful attacks with armoured personnel carriers and troop carriers, the Iraqis sent in the heavy units. There was a road leading up into the ridge and an Iraqi T-55 tank platoon started heading up it. Tracked armoured personnel carriers with troops on board spread out on to the fields on either side of the road and trundled steadily forward. It must have been an alarming sight. Many units would have backed off to fight another day. Instead of which the special forces soldiers took aim and fired.

They aimed Javelin missiles at the tanks and knocked out two of them. Other SF personnel opened up with heavy machine guns and grenade launchers on the armoured personnel carriers. Having stopped the tanks, the SF missiles began to hit the APCs. Eight were destroyed and four trucks also went up in smoke. The Iraqi infantry, not having even managed to get within firing range, scattered and headed back to their defensive positions.

After the extraordinary victory at Debecka Ridge, US and Kurd forces continued to move south and eastwards and took Kirkuk on 10 April.

Kirkuk in northeast Iraq is the centre of the Iraqi oil industry and it has major infrastructure connections, including pipelines to ports in the Mediterranean. Kirkuk has traditionally been a Kurdish settlement and the Kurdish community see it as a symbol of their presence in Iraq. The city has also been settled by Turks and Arabs. The Iraqi authorities evicted about 120,000 Kurds and other ethnic groups from Kirkuk between 1991 and 2003 and it was no surprise that the Kurds were eager to take the earliest opportunity to get back.

Guided by US special forces, the Kurdish Peshmerga advanced on Kirkuk. Although the town was defended by Iraqi forces, the presence of the Kurds and the US soldiers on a ridge outside the town helped to foster a popular uprising within the town. The US special forces kept a low profile as the town was retaken by the Kurds.

The Kurds with their US allies then moved on Mosul. The city of Mosul is near the ancient city of Nineveh and is located on the Tigris river. Mosul is claimed by the Kurds of northern Iraq to be part of their regional government, and is now an important routeing point for oil from Iran to Turkey and Syria.

On 11 April 2003, Kurdish forces, guarded by US special forces, moved on the city and took it over. The transfer of power was not so smooth as in Kirkuk, however, and there were clashes between the Kurd occupying forces and the local population.

FGM-148 JAVELIN

The Javelin is a fire-and-forget missile which is locked on to its designated target before launch. After firing it has an automatic self-guidance system which not only takes it to the designated target but configures the flight to approach the target from above. The missile gains a height of about 150m (490ft) before descending on the target. Javelin is fitted with a double warhead to defeat both reactive armour and the base armour underneath.

The missile is ejected from the launch pod before its main motor ignites so that the operator is not harmed by the rocket exhaust. This also makes it more difficult for the enemy to identify the source of the missile from its trail. Typically the operator would move his position before firing another missile.

In due course the Kurdish forces agreed to leave and were replaced by the US 101st Airborne Division, who in turn encountered severe crowd control problems in the city.

Special forces also entered Al Qaim, an important town located on the border with Syria about 400km (250 miles) north-west of Baghdad. The special forces cleared key sites, including and air defence headquarters, the train station and various industrial assets.

SPECIAL OPERATIONS IN WESTERN IRAQ

One of the problems facing the invaders was that Saddam Hussein, seeing the writing on the wall, might decide to create as much havoc and damage as possible in the Middle East before he was toppled from power.

One obvious target in this respect was Israel. This country had been in Saddam Hussein's crosshairs in the first Gulf War, when he had succeeded in lobbing several Scud missiles at both Israel and Saudi Arabia. There was concern now that, in view of Saddam Hussein's much vaunted nuclear and chemical warfare programmes, and in view of the fact that he might feel he had nothing to lose, a catastrophic attack might be launched on Israel.

The most likely location for Scud launchers with any such intent was the same place as they had been in the first Gulf War – the deserts of western Iraq. Similarly, the people best equipped to track down and destroy those launchers were the same people who had done so with some success in the earlier war, namely British and American special forces. In the 2003 campaign, moreover, they would have the added benefit of help from the Australian Special Air Service Regiment (SASR).

COMBINED JOINT SPECIAL OPERATIONS TASK FORCE–WEST (CJSOTF–WEST)

The core unit for CJSOTF–West was US 5th Special Forces Group. Additional forces were provided by the British Special Air Service (SAS) and by the Australian Special Air Service Regiment (SASR). The Australians also provided an additional elite component in the form of the 4th Battalion Royal Australian Regiment (Commando), operating as Task Force 64. There was also a deployment of US Air Force Special Operations Command and

Soldiers of the Australian SASR in a Land Rover Perentie Long Range Patrol Vehicle after capturing Al-Asad air base as part of Operation Falconer.

Naval Special Warfare Command Navy SEALs.

The mission was similar to that in the 1991 Gulf War, the major difference being that, unlike the previous deployment, coalition forces would be invading Iraq. The forward reconnaissance provided by some of the US 'A' Teams and their allied counterparts would therefore have a direct impact on the course of the invasion.

Yet another component of special forces in the western sector, known as Task Force 20, worked with intelligence agents to track down Ba'ath Party activists and members of the Fedayeen. They were also tasked with interdicting other Iraqi irregular activity. For example, a bus was intercepted with several Iraqis who were found to be carrying money as rewards for the murder of US soldiers.

The US Rangers operated in the western sector, both to secure and protect vital infrastructure assets such as pipelines and to locate possible sites for weapons of mass destruction (WMD).

AUSTRALIAN SASR IN IRAQ

The 1st Squadron Group Australian SASR deployed to western Iraq along with elements of the British SAS and US Special Forces. The SASR was supported by the 5th Aviation Regiment, operating CH-47 Chinook, S-70A Black Hawk and MRH-90 helicopters.

Their major role in the primary phase of operations was to track down and destroy Iraqi Scud launchers, either by direct action or by calling in Close Air Support (CAS) missions. The unit had been in the region from February 2003 and it is possible that they went over the border before the invasion began. Australian special forces reported through their own command chain but were interoperable with US and British aerial assets.

The SASR soon found itself operating in extreme weather conditions, with temperatures sometimes plummeting to -5 deg C (23 deg F), even without the wind chill factor. Visibility was reduced by high winds throwing up desert dust. In heavy rain, the ground could become extremely boggy and difficult to traverse.

Insertion was carried out by vehicle and by helicopter, with the ground teams negotiating border defences undetected by Iraqi guard posts.

The unit soon ran into an Iraqi force and, after

AUSTRALIAN SPECIAL AIR SERVICE REGIMENT (SASR)

The Australian SASR was first established as the 1st Special Air Service Company, Royal Australian Regiment in 1957. It was later renamed the Australian Special Air Service Regiment in 1964.

The Regiment is closely allied to its British and New Zealand counterparts and they use the same winged dagger badge with the motto 'Who Dares Wins'. The selection processes and roles are also similar.

Apart from the British SAS, the Australian SAS also has roots in the Australian 'Z' special force of World War II fame as well as the Independent Companies that operated in the Pacific.

The Regiment took part, alongside the British and New Zealand SAS, in operations in Borneo in 1965 against Indonesian incursions and insurgency. In 1966 the Regiment deployed, again with the New Zealand SAS, to Vietnam where it carried out a variety of reconnaissance missions. The excellence of the SASR in jungle fieldcraft gave them a marked advantage over the enemy. Some members of the SASR are said to have worked with MACV–SOG.

The Regiment deployed in a peacekeeping role to East Timor in 2000, again acting in a largely reconnaissance role to deal with incursions from Indonesian forces and insurgency.

The Regiment deployed to Afghanistan in October 2001 where it operated under US command, playing a prominent role in Operation Anaconda. It withdrew in November 2002 but was to deploy again to Afghanistan between 2005 and 2006.

In 2003 the Australian SASR deployed to Iraq with 4th Battalion, Royal Australian Regiment (Commando) and the Incident Response Regiment.

The Australian SAS carries out a number of roles, including reconnaissance and forward observation and counter-terrorism. The Regiment is trained to operate across the full spectrum of environments, namely desert, mountain, arctic and jungle and maritime and they are skilled in such disciplines as HAHO/HALO parachuting.

For selection, the candidates for the SASR must be serving members of the Australian Defence Force. After this there is a three-week selection course which assesses the candidate's physical and mental endurance. Although a candidate may be fit and mentally tough enough to endure the course, this does not necessarily mean he has the right personality to be selected. The Australian SASR, like many other special forces regiments, tends to seek candidates who can walk quietly but carry a big stick.

Having passed selection, the candidate will then go through an 18-month training in the various specialisms. It is possible for a candidate to be failed and returned to unit (RTUd) at any point during this period. Training in the Australian SASR is made as realistic as possible and unfortunately this has resulted in fatalities in the past.

an exchange of fire, the Iraqis were captured. Due to the fact that the special forces could not take prisoners with them, they had to release them, having given medical aid to the wounded. The release of the Iraqis was a calculated risk.

The helicopter insertion was also carried out by 160th SOAR, which took the Australian force deep into Iraq.

The Iraqis, however, had learned their lesson from the first Gulf War and had deployed squads to proactively hunt down the special forces that had done them so much damage. This resulted in a various engagements with Australian and other special forces in which the Iraqis almost invariably came off worse.

One of the Australian SASR objectives was an Iraqi radio relay station. This turned out to be well defended by Iraqi forces, which underlined its importance. The SASR approached the station and carried out an attack, where they defeated the

Iraqi forces and cleared the building. Once this was done they called in CAS to destroy the site. This operation significantly degraded the Iraqi ballistic missile communications system.

As the SASR was deeply embedded in Iraq and is said to have been closer to Baghdad than any other special forces unit, and as the coalition forces had not at this stage fully engaged conventional Iraqi forces in the region, the SASR were in extreme danger of a counter-attack. Sure enough, the following day various Iraqi units were sent out to search for them and an extended firefight ensued. The Iraqis attacked with at least six vehicles but, like the 10th SFG at Debecka Ridge, the Australian SASR took them on with Javelin anti-tank missiles and a range of other heavy weaponry, including

US Army Special Forces in HMWWVs patrol south of Najaf after a heavy battle with Iraqi forces the previous night, March 2003.

12.7mm (.50 cal) machine guns and 40mm (1.57in) Mk-19 grenade launchers. The SASR were also able to call in close air support.

This was not the only engagement of the SASR with the enemy. Another SASR mobile unit was also spotted by Iraqi forces who approached in a range of four-wheel drive vehicles armed with machine guns, rocket-propelled grenades (RPGs) and mortars. No doubt this Iraqi unit intended to give the special forces a taste of their own medicine. It was a big mistake. The Australians did not run away but engaged the Iraqis with a range of weapons systems that destroyed the Iraqi vehicles and forced the Iraqi soldiers to take to their feet. They were then engaged with machine guns.

As with the British SAS in Iraq, the Australians had chosen a mix of deployments: some in vehicles and some on foot. Having vehicles, namely the Land Rover Perentie 6x6 Long Range Patrol

A US Air Force Special Forces airman inspects the 7.62mm (.3in) Minigun on an HH-60G Pave Hawk helicopter of 301st Rescue Squadron.

Vehicle, allowed them to carry a wider range of weaponry, including the Javelin missile. The vehicles were, however, more likely to be spotted and the mobile units found themselves in fairly frequent engagements with the enemy. The units who had been brought in by helicopter, on the other hand, while not having the advantage of such a wide armoury, were more able remain undetected and monitor movement of enemy ballistic missile systems, notably on Highway 10.

Another objective for Australian special forces was a highway intersection at Highway 10 and Expressway 1 where a road joined from the south. There were also airfields at Qasir Amij and Qasir Amij South nearby. The Australian SASR engaged the site first of all through stand-off and CAS missions and then by direct attack on the ground. Most of the Iraqis, however, had taken enough punishment in the aerial strikes and had already departed before the ground forces arrived.

Having neutralized the Iraqi attempts at a proactive response, the Australian SASR were able to police the highways between Ramadi and Ar Rutba to prevent resupply to Baghdad or to prevent high value assets from escaping.

British soldiers from 2/1 Battery 16th Air Assault Brigade drive camouflaged Land Rover Defenders at Camp Viper.

The next major objective was the Al-Asad air base. This was located approximately 180kn (112 miles) west of Baghdad and was the second largest airfield in Iraq. It had 33 hardened shelters as well as hangars and a variety of runways. The security perimeter was 21km (14 miles) long. About 8km (5 miles) to the northeast was a weapon storage area. The Al Asad airfield was the base for three Iraqi fighter squadrons.

On 16 April 2003, the Al Asad base was captured by Australian SASR. As the SASR approached, the Iraqis mounted a pre-emptive attack with machine

guns mounted on sports utility vehicles (SUVs). As before, superior tactics, professionalism and weaponry resulted in the smaller Australian force defeating the enemy. They then took control of the airfield, which had about 50 fixed-wing aircraft, including fighters, as well as large ammunition stores. The force subsequently set about clearing all the buildings and then repairing the bombed airfield so that it could receive a Royal Australian Air Force C-130 Hercules.

SECURING THE OIL FIELDS

One of the most destructive fallouts of the first Gulf War was the Iraqi operation against the oil fields in the region, large numbers of which were set ablaze before the coalition forces could reach them.

Particular care was taken in planning for the 2003 invasion of Iraq that this should not be repeated. Up to 1000 oil fields were located in southern Iraq and there were also oil platforms in the Gulf.

The oil facilities in the al-Faw peninsula included two offshore terminals, three transfer and monitoring stations and two additional support terminals at Mina al Bakar and Khawr Al Amaya.

The special forces operations to secure the oil fields both on land and at sea was shared between the US Navy SEALs and the British Special Boat Service (SBS). They were also responsible for searching the beaches in the al-Faw peninsula.

US Navy SEALs along with SBS were inserted by US Air Force MH-53J Pave Low helicopters in the al-Faw peninsula and they approached the oil rigs Kaabot and Marbot at night in Mk V special operations craft and rigid inflatable boats (RIBs) manned by Naval Special Warfare Command personnel. They climbed the oil platform structures and then overwhelmed the Iraqi guards on the platforms. The Iraqi guards were then tied up and held on the platform until reinforcements arrived to take them away. Backup forces were provided by Royal Marine Commandos. Two oil transfer terminals were also attacked and taken by SEALs.

Such was the stealth of these attacks that casualties in all cases were very low.

On 20 March 2003 United States aerial assets carried out attacks on enemy positions in the al-Faw area. US Navy SEALs were flown in USAF SOF MH-53J Pave Lows to provide reconnaissance and clearance for heliborne landings in advance of the

LAND ROVER PERENTIE 6X6 LONG RANGE PATROL VEHICLE (LRVP)

The Land Rover Perentie 6x6 is a long wheelbase version of the Land Rover 110 with a supercharged Isuzu 4-cylinder diesel engine. It has a front live axle with coil springs and the rear suspension is leaf springs. The LRPV version has two spare wheels on either side of the body. The vehicle is fitted with a machine gun mount on the back and also one at the front. It can carry a trail motorcycle as well as anti-tank weaponry such as the Javelin missile system. Typically special forces personnel hang their Bergens and other personal equipment on the outside of the vehicle to maximize space inside.

GRUPA REAGOWANIA OPERACY JNO-MANEWROWEGO (OPERATIONAL MOBILE REACTION GROUP) GROM

Although officially formed on 13 July 1990, the GROM has roots that go back to World War II. After the German invasion of Poland in 1939, many Poles came to England and joined various parts of the British armed forces. A Polish branch of the Special Operations Executive was set up and the Jacobean house Audley End, south of Saffron Walden, Essex was requisitioned by the British Government to house the unit.

The GROM is formed of personnel from different parts of the Polish armed forces, notably the 1st Commando Regiment and navy combat diving units. Like many special operations units, the GROM is organized in four-man teams.

When the group was set up, advice was taken from British, American and German special forces. Like these forces, GROM recruits are trained to a high level in a number of disciplines, including HAHO/HALO parachuting, sniping and scuba diving. They can also operate across a range of environments and terrain from mountain to urban.

The unit was deployed to Haiti in 1994 as part of Operation Restore Democracy and they have been involved in the ongoing search for war criminals in former Yugoslavia. They were deployed in Afghanistan as part of Operation Enduring Freedom in 2001 and took part in Operation Iraqi Freedom in 2003.

---

assault by 3 Commando Brigade. Marines from 40 Commando Royal Marines and US Marines came in by helicopter to take strategic objectives.

An assault was then carried out further inland by 42 Commando, preceded by a naval bombardment by the Royal Navy and Royal Australian Navy. Conditions proved to be extremely difficult and one helicopter carrying the HQ element of the elite Brigade Reconnaissance Force crashed.

Royal Marines assaulted Um Qasr, the attack preceded by special operations carried out by US Navy SEALs and Polish GROM special forces.

US Navy SEALs and British SBS carried out patrols in the waterways and stopped and searched over 100 vessels.

British forces then moved on to Basra, preceded by special forces including the SAS and SBS. The area north of Basra around the airfield at Ramallah was occupied by 16th Air Assault Brigade, which confronted the Iraqi 6th Armoured Division.

As 7th Armoured Brigade advanced on Basra it came under increasingly heavy attack. The British response was precisely targeted by ground observation provided by special forces forward observers and snipers to pick off areas of armed

Facing page: Polish GROM special forces soldiers on board a US Navy SEAL boat with Iraqis captured during the assault on Um Qasr.

resistance and concentrations of support for the Saddam Hussein regime.

The British approached both Az Zubayr and Al Khasib and in both cases came upon Iraqi resistance. These defences were probed and interdicted by special forces backed up by elite forces in the form of 3 Commando Brigade.

In the confusion of the transfer of power and the smoke of battle, British special forces deployed through the towns to track down members of the Saddam Hussein Ba'ath Party leadership.

SAVING THE DAMS

On 19 March permission was granted to launch 40 Tomahawk cruise missiles at designated sites in Iraq. Some of the targets were within Baghdad itself and it was reported that missiles had been aimed at specific locations where Saddam Hussein and his senior leadership were thought to be located.

The intelligence for these strikes was derived from a number of sources, including previous intelligence gathered over the years, satellite imagery recording buildings and movements of officials and from Allied intelligence agents on the ground. At the same time, special forces from the USA, Britain and Australia were on the ground seeking targets of opportunity, both in the Baghdad area and around Basra, which was the British objective. US Navy SEALs, working with the Polish counter-terrorist unit GROM captured the Mukarayin Dam about 92km (57 miles) outside Baghdad. The teams fast-roped from Pave Low helicopters and held the dam for five days in order to prevent any attempts at sabotage which could have resulted in the flooding of Baghdad.

The town of Hadithah is about 225km (140 miles) to the northwest of Baghdad. Near the town, the Haditha Dam was built on the Euphrates River to create a large reservoir, which is one of the key sources of water supply in Iraq.

In view of the potential wrecking operations that might be carried out by a ruthless Iraqi regime with nothing to lose, the Haditha Dam became a key objective for special forces at the outset of the invasion. If the dam had been blown by the Iraqis it would have released a catastrophic surge of water in the short term and created serious water supply problems in the medium to long term. On the night of 1 April 2003, 3rd Battalion 75th Ranger Regiment seized both the dam and the associated hydro-power complex.

As coalition special forces were discovering throughout the war, Iraqi counter-special forces units were taking an aggressive and proactive approach to hunt them down, and they now began to harass the Rangers with artillery and mortars. The Iraqi forces were mainly operating from the town of Hadithah itself and, due to the presence of civilians, the coalition forces were to some extent limited in their response.

The Rangers did, however, call in CAS missions. The Rangers battled with local Iraqi forces for three weeks in order to protect the dam and were finally relieved by 1-502nd Infantry Battalion of 101st Airborne Division on 19 April 2003.

SPECIAL OPERATIONS CRAFT

The Mk V SOC was developed in the mid-1990s and became fully operational in 1999. It provides high-speed insertion of special operations forces into low- and medium-threat environments. It is also designed to carry out coastal interdiction and patrol.

The boat carries five crew members along with up to 16 special operations force personnel and their equipment. It can also carry rigid inflatable boats (RIBs) or a submersible SEAL delivery unit. These can be easily loaded and offloaded using a ramp at the rear of the boat.

The Mk V SOC has an impressive armoury, including five mounts for 7.62mm (0.3in) machine guns or GAU-17 Miniguns. It can also mount 12.7mm (0.50 cal) heavy machine guns and 40mm (1.57in) grenade launchers. It is also adapted to take Mk 48 25mm (.98in) guns and Stinger surface-to-air missiles (SAMs).

Typically the Mk V SOC is operated in detachments of two craft which can be delivered by USAF C-5 transport aircraft. In Operation Iraqi Freedom, the Mk V SOCs were maintained and refuelled from the high-speed Joint Venture X1 which was used during the operation as a Naval Special Warfare Maritime Forward Operating Base (MFOB).

Specifications:

Beam: 5.33m (17.5ft)
Draught: 1.52m (5ft)
Max speed: 83–130km/h (47–50kts)
Range at max speed: 925+ km (500+ nm)

Special Warfare Combatant-craft Crewmen from Special Boat Team 22 undertake training in Kentucky. Their Special Operations Craft – Riverine (SOC–R) were put to good use in Iraq. They were particularly valuable along the country's inland waterways.

US Air Force special operations forces arrive back at a base in southern Iraq after rescuing a downed USAF pilot (left) during Operation Iraqi Freedom.

Throughout the campaign as a whole, special operations forces could always be found where the trouble was. Knowing that they could not defeat US and British forces in conventional battles, the Iraqis had organized many of their forces in smaller groups deployed in depth. These proactive hunters proved to be more of a challenge to special forces than had been the case in the first Gulf War but almost invariably the high level of professionalism demonstrated by the special forces won the day.

Whereas in the first Gulf War the special operations units had operated largely independently, though with full backing from aerial support units and with full interoperability with aerial strike assets, in the second Gulf War their operations were more closely integrated with the activities of conventional forces.

In the north, 10th Special Forces Group worked closely with the 173rd Airborne Division. In the south, special forces groups acted in advance of the columns of conventional force so that when these forces reached a particular objective they would almost invariably make contact with a special forces group that had already reconnoitred the area, identified targets of opportunity or discovered a way of minimising the conflict by creating a dialogue with the relevant local leaders.

At An Nasiriyah, as the 3rd Infantry Division approached a bridge across the Euphrates, the special forces in the area were able to provide key intelligence and target information that enabled the 3rd ID to take their objective with much greater speed and efficiency.

JSOTF–West, as has been seen, deployed in a variety of configurations. They were flown in as highly covert observation units that kept an extremely low profile and whose effectiveness was shown by directing relevant air strikes or ground attacks but not being seen themselves. They operated in more overt vehicle-mounted groups which allowed them to mix stand-off target observation with occasional direct action. Such patrols were mounted by Delta Force A teams and by British and Australian SAS units. They operated in larger formations, such as 3rd Battalion 75th Rangers in order to seize and hold major strategic and infrastructure assets, such as airfields and water, oil or electricity installations. They also worked closely with ground forces that became increasingly available through the course of the campaign. As they were working with an invading ground force, they could make use of such major assets as Abrams tanks in support of their missions. This mix of 'outside the box' special forces ingenuity with heavy conventional fire power was often a devastating combination.

FIGHTING THE INSURGENCY

Once the invasion of Iraq had been completed, the US and British military authorities found themselves up against intense waves of insurgency that threatened to completely destabilize, and even reverse, the conventional military victory.

Special operations task forces had been set up soon after the 11 September 2001 attacks in New York by both the Americans and the British. In order to maintain secrecy and confuse the enemy, designations of the special units changed periodically, including Task Force 145, Task Force 121 and Task Force 626.

The forces elements making up these amalgamated units included 1st Special Forces Operational Detachment – Delta, United States Naval Special Warfare Development Group

Two 19th Group Special Forces soldiers pose for the camera in Babil Province, Iraq, 2007.

BRITISH L115A

The L115A3 is the British Army's standard long-range sniper rifle, capable, in one record-breaking instance in 2009, of making a kill at a distance of 2475 metres (8119ft).

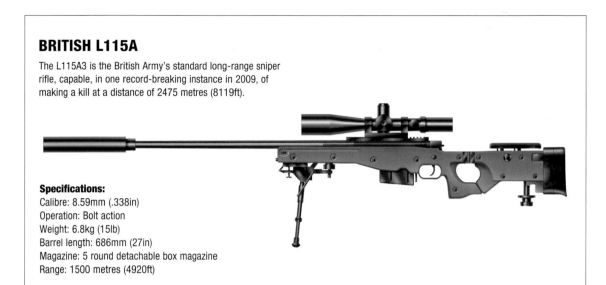

Specifications:
Calibre: 8.59mm (.338in)
Operation: Bolt action
Weight: 6.8kg (15lb)
Barrel length: 686mm (27in)
Magazine: 5 round detachable box magazine
Range: 1500 metres (4920ft)

(DEVGRU), British Special Air Service (SAS), British Special Boat Service (SBS) and CIA Special Activities Division (SAD). The support elements included US 160th Special Operations Aviation Regiment ('Night Stalkers'), USAF 24th Special Tactics Squadron, and British Parachute Regiment soldiers of the Special Forces Support Group.

As al-Qaeda unleashed a campaign of killings, assassinations, kidnappings and suicide-bomb attacks in Iraq, it was decided that the best way to counter the attacks was by getting the retaliation in early and eliminating as many potential insurgents as possible.

The organization of the Task Forces under whichever description was broadly as follows:

- Task Force Black, based largely on British SAS and Special Forces Support Group along with elements of US 1st SFOD–D (Delta Force), was stationed in Baghdad.
- Task Force North, based on the US 75th Ranger Regiment, was located in northern Iraq.
- Task Force West, based on US Naval Special Warfare Development Group, was based in western Iraq.
- Task Force Center, based on 1st Special Forces Operational Detachment – Delta, was based in central Iraq.
- Task Force Orange is believed to have comprised

various assets, notably US Army Intelligence Support Activity (ISA).

The various elements of the Task Forces were to conduct many successful missions against both unknown targets, such as suicide bombers, as well as high-profile targets such as Abu Musab al-Zarqawi. In July 2005, SAS snipers ambushed a group of Iraqi suicide bombers as they were setting out on a mission against cafes and restaurants in the city.

The British Secret Intelligence Service (MI6) had received a tip-off from one of its Iraqi undercover agents and a 16-man British special forces unit staked out a building in Baghdad where the bombers were based. Codenamed Operation Marlborough, the mission involved four teams armed with British L115A sniper rifles, accurate to 1000m (1090yd). The site was monitored by a Predator unmanned aerial vehicle (UAV) controlled by the CIA and the building was wired with listening devices.

It was vital to kill the terrorists before they had a chance to detonate their bombs, causing wounding and death to nearby civilians. As the terrorists emerged, accurate fire by the snipers signalled an operational success and a potential catastrophe was averted.

Abu Musab al-Zarqawi was second only to Osama bin Laden himself in the US most-wanted

list. Task Force 145 was given the job of killing or capturing him and it set about its task with an unblinking eye and pulling together all of its various intelligence and special forces assets.

INTERROGATION TECHNIQUES

A significant contribution to the ultimate success of the operation was made by Matthew Alexander who used a collaborative approach in his interrogation techniques, which was in stark contrast to the rough techniques used in locations such as Guantanamo Bay. Understanding Arab culture and the importance of both the family and respect for authority, Alexander was able to painstakingly steer his detainees to giving away vital information, which brought them ever closer to their main target.

Eventually a Muslim cleric was identified who regularly drove out to visit al-Zarqawi, changing cars on the way. The special forces units staked out the area and al-Zarqawi was killed by bombs dropped from an F-16 fighter-bomber.

US Joint Special Operations Command (JSOC)

A gunsite camera targeting the safe house near Baquba, Iraq, in which Abu Musab al-Zarqawi was reportedly holding a meeting, is seen 8 June 2006. US warplanes dropped 227kg (500-lb) bombs on the house, killing al-Zarqawi and seven others.

was commanded by General Stanley McChrystal. The ex-Ranger and Delta Force soldier soon began to set up a new organization that would maximize the use of available intelligence and break down walls created by different organizational cultures and by rank.

The British Operation Black, relying largely on its own intelligence resources, ran some successful counter-insurgency operations on its own. It was also allocated improved intelligence resources and equipment, including armoured vehicles and Chinook and Puma helicopters.

Not everything went the right way for the special forces. In September 2005, two SAS men were captured by local police during a reconnaissance mission. Special Operations headquarters reacted quickly, knowing that the lives of the SAS men were in danger. They had already been beaten up on capture.

Acting on the hoof and with command structures failing to operate properly, men from A Squadron SAS got on the scene and began to plan an assault. British Army Challenger tanks and Warrior armoured personnel carriers burst into the police station where the men had been held while the SAS focused on a house where they knew the men had been taken. The SAS assaulted the house and the men were rescued.

Crashing armoured vehicles into the police station, which was totally unnecessary as the British knew the men were no longer held there, proved to be an unfortunate symbol of the awkward stand-off between British occupying forces and local Iraqis.

After this, the SAS mission in Iraq became more closely intertwined with the US JSOC headquarters in Balad, which meant greater interoperability and use of resources. At the time, for example, the British did not have access to a Predator UAV and the intelligence from drones had to be provided by the Americans.

CPT HOSTAGE CRISIS, 2006

The Swords of Righteousness Brigade is a terrorist organization that is believed to have links with the Islamic Army in Iraq. Its existence was unknown until it took hostages from the Christian Peacemaker Team (CPT), an organization dedicated to non-violence. On 26 November 2005 four CPT members were on the way to a mosque for a meeting with the Muslim Clerics Association when masked gunmen stopped the car, hauled out the driver and interpreter, and drove away with their hostages. The four CPT members were Tom Fox, an American, James Loney and Harmeet Singh Sooden, both Canadians, and Norman Kember, a Briton. Ironically, the CPT members, who were actively opposed to the US-led occupation of Iraq, were now dependent on US and UK special forces for their rescue.

Major-General Nicolas Matern (right), former commander of Joint Task Force 2 and deputy commander of the Canadian Special Operations Forces Command.

Former hostages Norman Kember (left), James Loney (centre) and Harmeet Singh Sooden (right) from the Christian Peacemaker Team speak to the media at a press conference following their release.

The Swords of Righteousness Brigade demanded that all Iraqi prisoners held by the US and British authorities in Iraq and the United States should be released by 10 December 2005. The Christian Peace Team refused to call for a coercive operation to free the hostages.

On 28 January the Sword of Righteousness Brigade said the US and Britain had one last chance to release the prisoners or the hostages would be killed. On 10 March 2006 the body of one of the hostages, Tom Fox, was found on a garbage dump in Baghdad. He had been shot in the head and chest and Iraqi police speculated that he had been tortured. Tom Fox was an ex US soldier. Due to the imminent danger to the remaining hostages, the case was moved to top priority for armed intervention.

OPERATION LIGHTWATER

At this time UK Special Air Service (SAS) operations in Iraq, named Task Force Knight, were becoming more closely integrated with US Joint Special Operations Command (JSOC). This meant they had greater access to intelligence and also the backing of US aircraft and Intelligence Surveillance and Reconnaissance (ISR) assets. Vehicles used by the SAS included the US M1114 up-armoured HMMWV.

The rescue operation was to be led by Task Force Knight, which consisted of members of B Squadron Special Air Service, and Tier One US special forces. Due to the presence of Canadian hostages, the Canadian Joint Task Force 2 special forces unit was also involved. Elite back-up for the operation would be provided by the British Special Forces Support Group, consisting of members of 1st Battalion Parachute Regiment, with support from the Royal Canadian Mounted Police and Canadian Security Intelligence Service.

Facing page: Iraqis clear rubble from the destroyed Shiite holy al-Hadi Shrine in the northern city of Samarra, February 2006. The bombing of the Golden Mosque began a sectarian civil war that lasted into 2007.

A USAF AC-130A Hercules gunship flies on a mission. The gunship is armed with two 7.62mm GAU-2/A Miniguns, two 20mm (0.3in) M61 Vulcan cannon and two 40mm (1.57in) L/60 Bofors cannon.

Following the bombing of the Golden Mosque in Samarra on 22 February 2006 by terrorists under Abu Musab al-Zarqawi, a civil war broke out across Iraq, with sectarian gangs carrying out abductions and murders. Although this would normally have been the first priority of the SAS, they were under pressure to rescue the UK national Norman Kember and his fellow hostages. The focus and allocation of assets to rescue Kember was given the name Operation Lightwater.

Intelligence services had developed sophisticated techniques for tracking suspects on the basis of mobile phone taps and robust interrogation of suspects on site (called tactical questioning). This enabled security forces to get quick answers from suspects before they had time to think up a cover story. These methods meant that a momentum had built up that hardly gave special forces operators time to draw breath before they were on to another raid, throwing up yet more leads. On one such operation, the SAS found a man called Abu Laith al-Libi, who knew about the location of the captors and hostages. Equipped with this information, the SAS moved swiftly.

At dawn on 24 March 2006 the special forces and their elite support group moved out in taxis and civilian pick-up trucks in order not to attract attention. When they reached the area of their objective, the support forces deployed to secure the area, after which the special forces assaulted the house where the hostages were held.

The special forces cleared each room with ruthless precision; however, such was the reputation of the special forces that, having got wind of the operation, the terrorists had fled the area before the strike. The special forces found the remaining three hostages unharmed and escorted them out to a Bradley infantry fighting vehicle (IFV) before they were driven to the Baghdad Green Zone for immediate medical attention and rehabilitation.

CAPTURE OF ABU ATIYA, 2006

Another successful SAS operation involving B Squadron was the capture of Abu Atiya who was closely associated with al-Zarqawi and attended his training camps. Abu Atiya was a highly dangerous man who was suspected of plotting poison and bomb attacks in Europe.

Abu Atiya's whereabouts were defined by the use of high-tech assets, including satellite tracking of his cell phone. US military satellites were designed to move in space in such a way as to pinpoint the grid reference. The location was a farmhouse and the special forces immediately set about planning their assault.

The SAS would arrive in both Puma HC1 tactical and Lynx AH.9 helicopters. The Lynx helicopters carried SAS snipers who would provide aerial cover from the helicopter platform in case any enemy insurgents tried to escape from the assault zone.

Two USAF C-130 Hercules aircraft were also in the vicinity, one of them acting as a gunship, while far above circled the AC-130 Spectre gunship which could provide devastating firepower if necessary. Back-up was provided by British Parachute

Regiment soldiers and elements from US 1st Battalion, 502nd Infantry Regiment.

The Pumas delivered the SAS team to the location and, after a quick recce, the assault went in. However, a gunman inside the house was ready and waiting, perhaps put on guard by the noise of aircraft, and hit three of the soldiers as they entered the house. The SAS men moved back to check for wounds while another terrorist got on to a roof and lobbed grenades at them.

Having regrouped, the special forces went back into the building where they again ran into gunfire. An insurgent gunman was killed and another ran out of the back of the building. A suicide bomber inside the farm building detonated his vest, wounding an SAS soldier. The suicide bomber outside was killed by gunfire before he could detonate his. The remaining suspects, including Atiya, were handcuffed and taken to a helicopter.

CAPTURE OF QAIS AL-KHAZALI

In 2007 the SAS were involved in an operation against Qais al-Khazali, who ran special groups in

Qais al-Khazali, leader of Iraq's Shi'ite militia Asaib Ahl al-Haq, speaks to supporters during a parade.

Iraq with Iranian backing. They organized a wide range of terrorist activities, including kidnappings, assassinations and arms smuggling. Their most daring and infamous attack was an assault upon the governor's headquarters in Karbala where senior American officers and Iraqi officials had gathered to discuss security for an upcoming ceremony. The highly sophisticated attack involved militants posing as an American security team, wearing US military uniforms and speaking English. The militants then attacked the building, killing some US soldiers and capturing four of them. Driving away with their captives, they were chased by Iraqi police. They then shot the captives and abandoned their vehicles.

On 20 March 2007 the SAS, working with an intelligence picture that had been built up over some time, were able to pinpoint al-Khazali's location and capture him, along with a large amount of valuable information contained in papers and electronic data. Some of the information directly implicated Iran in some of the terrorist operations, including the Karbala raid.

Under the command of General Petraeus, who took command of Multi-National Force-Iraq (MNF-I) on 10 February 2007, Task Force 17 was set up to conduct raids against insurgent groups

acting on behalf of Iran. US Army special forces coordinated efforts with newly formed Iraqi special forces units.

When A Squadron SAS deployed to Iraq in the summer of 2007, they conducted a successful series of missions against al-Qaeda, despite losing three men and suffering other injuries. However well trained the special forces soldiers were, a gunman concealed in a dark room or passageway could all too easily just pull a trigger and either kill or wound.

The British SAS were now working closely with Joint Special Operations Command (JSOC) and benefiting from the flow of joint intelligence. This enabled them and the US special forces to maintain a relentless operational pace that seriously degraded al-Qaeda effectiveness in the region.

The British special forces operation in Iraq finished on 30 May 2009, having killed or captured 3500 insurgents over a six-year period. The much larger US special forces operations during the same period accounted for about 12,000 killed or

A US Black Hawk helicopter sets out on a mission somewhere in Iraq. The Black Hawk is the workhorse of the US military.

captured. The combined effect of American and British special forces upon the security of Iraq against insurgent operations, including murders, suicide bombings and kidnappings, was therefore highly significant.

ABU KAMAL RAID, 2008

US intelligence had revealed that fighters involved in the insurgency against coalition forces in Iraq were using Syria as a base for their incursions. It was alleged that at least 500 fighters had entered Iraq from Syria. It was also claimed that up to 90 Syrian co-ordinators were aiding the insurgency operation.

The location for this insurgency was identified as the village of Abu Kamal, which was not far from the city of Al-Qa'im, on the Syria–Iraq border.

The Syrian-based insurgency was said to have the support of al-Qaeda, whose co-ordinator, Abu Ghadiya, was thought to be present. Abu Ghadiya's original name was Badran Turki Hishan al-Mazidi. He was said to work for the notorious insurgent leader Abu Musab al-Zarqawi and for Abu Ayyub Al-Masri.

Despite being subjected to ground fire, including rocket-propelled grenades (RPGs),

two US Black Hawk helicopters landed near the village and about 24 soldiers from the US Special Operations Forces (SOF) deployed to carry out the raid against a building in the village of As

Sukkaniyah, north of Abu Kamal. Although the details of the raid are confused, the special forces are said to have killed Aby Ghadiya, one of his brothers and two of his cousins.

NORTHERN SYRIA RAID: THE ATTEMPTED RESCUE OF JAMES FOLEY (2014)

James Foley was an American journalist who was abducted by terrorists from the Islamic State of Iraq and the Levant (ISIL) on 22 November 2012. ISIL (also known as ISIS and Islamic State) is a Sunni extremist jihadist group that developed from al-Qaeda in Iraq and which has been branded officially as a terrorist organization by the United Nations. It has also been accused by Amnesty International of ethnic cleansing on an historic scale. ISIL drove Iraqi government forces out of several western cities and in Syria it fought both government and rebel forces.

James Foley had worked as a freelance war correspondent during the Syrian Civil War. Previously, he had written for the military newspaper *Stars and Stripes* in Afghanistan and the *GlobalPost* in Libya, as well as with USAID projects in Iraq. He had previously been captured on another occasion by Gaddafi loyalists in Libya and was released after 44 days in captivity.

Along with the British journalist John Cantile, Foley was captured in Binesh, northwest Syria, on 22 November 2012. He was believed to have been held along with seventeen other hostages in a Syrian Air Force complex in Damascus. Although he was held with various other Westerners, according to fellow hostages who were later released, he was singled out by his captors for particularly severe punishments because he was American. He was subject to frequent beatings and also to mock executions and waterboarding (a form of torture using wet cloths and water, which induces a sense of drowning). He was also forced to stand against a wall and pose as if he had been crucified.

US intelligence agents interviewed some hostages who had been freed through the payment of ransom money. Working on this information, the US National Security Agency (NSA) used satellite surveillance to pinpoint a building in Syria matching the description that had been given to them.

Although they were aware that ISIL might not risk remaining in the same place once some of their hostages had been released, the US Government took the view that they must do their utmost to attempt to save the life of one of their own citizens, along with hostages from other friendly nations.

As a result, a force from 1st Special Forces Operational Detachment-Delta (1st SFOD-D) moved from their base at Fort Bragg, North Carolina, to a secret base in a country bordering Syria, where just after 02:00 on 3 July 2014 several MH-60 Black Hawk helicopters departed the base. Piloted by 160th Special Operations Aviation Regiment, the force included the MH-60K, designed for the insertion and extraction of special forces units, and the MH-60L Direct Action Penetrator (DAP), designed for armed escort missions. The MH-60L DAP is fitted with two 7.62mm (0.3in) M134 Miniguns, an M230 30mm (1.18in) chaingun, M261 FFAR 2.75in (70mm) rocket pods, a GAU 19/A 12.7mm (.50 cal) three-barrelled Gatling gun, AGM-114 Hellfire laser-guided missiles and AIM-92 ATAS (Air To Air Stinger) missiles. The helicopters were joined by two armed MQ-1B Predator drones, armed with two laser-guided AGM-114 Hellfire missiles. The Predator can provide intelligence, surveillance and reconnaissance along with interception of targets. In addition to these aerial assets, other warplanes were on standby in the vicinity to intervene if necessary.

Once they had reached the target area, having run the gauntlet of Syrian air defences on the border, the MH-60K helicopters landed and teams of Delta Force operators quickly jumped out. They immediately found themselves in a firefight with ISIL fighters, at least two of whom were killed. The special forces then moved on to storm the designated ISIL safe house in their search for the hostages. Carrying out a room-to-room clearance, it soon became clear that the ISIL captors and their hostages had moved on. The special forces therefore picked up whatever material they could find that would be useful for forensic examination and fought their way back to the helicopters for extraction.

Operation Jawbreaker (Deployment of CIA teams to northern Afghanistan, 2001)
Operation Bastille (Deployment of Australian forces in Iraq, 2003)

COUNTER-TERRORISM

As can be seen in the previous chapters of this book, military victory was achieved in both Afghanistan in 2001–02 and in Iraq in 2003. In both cases, the major concentrations of enemy armed forces were defeated and key cities were won. The capital cities of both countries were cleared of all traces of enemy administration and arrangements for new governments were put in place. Despite all this, however, both wars refused to go away.

At its high point in 2010, the NATO-led International Security Assistance Force (ISAF) had as many as 130,000 troops stationed in Afghanistan, fighting the Taliban insurgency and al-Qaeda terrorists. In 2010, there were 14,600 improvised explosive device (IED) attacks in Afghanistan, more than double than in 2009, and a record for the war. Of the 711 foreign soldiers killed in 2010, 630 were killed in action. As of August 2014, 3466 NATO forces had been killed in Afghanistan, of which 2234 were US personnel.

The United States was by far the largest force contributor, but despite these sizeable contributions and those from other nations,

Facing page: Soldiers of the Australian SASR face a sandstorm during the opening phase of Operation Bastille, the deployment of Australian forces to Iraq in March 2003.

the security status of both Afghanistan and Iraq was far from stable. In both theatres the constant insurgency and terrorist threat was wearing the regular forces down, and there were serious questions being asked about how long large numbers of conventional and special forces could be kept in the theatres.

If British troops were to come home they would return to a country where the home intelligence service, MI5, had doubled in size since 2001 in order to deal with a wide variety of terrorist threats, each potentially on a cataclysmic scale. One example was made public in late 2006 when British intelligence services thwarted a plot to blow up several airliners in mid-air after leaving British airports.

At the same time, the British government had a policy of primary immigration into Britain that added to the supply of potentially disenchanted Muslim extremists who were being recruited and radicalized by various offshoot organizations of al-Qaeda.

These disenchanted extremists were going to war, as they saw it, both against American, British or other national troops as well as against the civilian populations of the countries in which they lived. Their indoctrination told them that, since Western governments were democratically elected, the people who elected them were also directly responsible for their policies.

193

An Australian SASR soldier scans the desert with night vision goggles (NVGs) during Operation Bastille. He carries an M4 Carbine.

NEW TASKS, NEW STRUCTURES

As long as the ideology was not countered and remained attractive, intelligence services and armed forces would have to deal with the results, which manifested itself in violence on an unprecedented scale. Just as the domestic intelligence services were having to increase their numbers in order to deal with the growing threat, so did the armed forces need to increase the size of the units best equipped to deal with the new threat, namely the special forces. In addition, support forces would be built round the core of special forces in order to maximize the ground, aerial and maritime support for targeted operations. Conventional units would revise their training doctrines in order to be able to adapt to a fast-changing battle environment and to an enemy that never knew when they were beaten.

Even before the events of September 2001, discussion was underway in defence organizations about the need to expand special forces in the future. The reason for this was that the post-Cold War world was already showing a pattern, of which

al-Qaeda would be the most horrific example, of disintegration, ethnic violence and both religious and nationalist extremism. In a world where one superpower had a massive predominance in conventional arms, such disenchanted groups and failed states resorted to asymmetric means of warfare, carrying out disruptive attacks that were designed over the long term to wear down the enemy's morale and will to fight.

To a large extent, countering such threats was the business of intelligence communities, but in its military aspects the forces most likely to succeed against insurgent attacks of this nature were the forces which were trained to think outside the box themselves, namely the special forces.

Special forces would continue to perform duties such as hostage rescue or interdiction of particularly dangerous individuals. Despite the huge advances in reconnaissance technology, including the use of Unmanned Aerial Vehicles (UAVs), the lesson of both of the Gulf wars and in Afghanistan was that there is no adequate replacement for a highly trained pair of eyes and ears on the ground. The real change was that these forces would become more interoperable and integrated with conventional forces. Systems were being developed all the time to make this interface more effective. The ability of special forces to perform 'diplomatic' activities as a flip side to their devastating use of weaponry would also be valued in an environment where the hearts and minds of the local population were an important element of the battle. Special forces faced the continuing challenge of being militarily effective while not cutting themselves off from the people on whose behalf they were fighting.

The USSOCOM Posture Statements of 2000, 2007 and 2011 continued to underline the developing nature of special forces missions including improved interoperability between special operations forces (SOF) and general purpose forces (GPF), improved liaison with foreign special operations forces through the establishment of a Special Operations Liaison Officer (SOLO) and the establishment of a NATO Special Operations Force Headquarters. Foreign Internal Defense (FID) operations were set up to maximize the use of nationals, particularly in Iraq, to provide support to US special operations and to act increasingly on a unilateral basis on counter-insurgency operations. In Afghanistan, special operations training was carried out with the Afghan National Security Forces (ANSF).

What even the authors of this posture statement probably could not have predicted was the sheer scale of the demand for special forces as events

Australian SASR soldiers ready to be deployed from an Australian Defence Force UH-60 Black Hawk helicopter.

developed, and the consequent need for greater interoperability with other units. Special forces were no longer an exotic bolt-on but central to the whole mission. To some extent, however, special forces would also be in danger of becoming the victims of their own success as the increase in demand for their services threatened to undermine the characteristics that make them unique.

The whole point of special forces is that they are formed of men and sometimes women of exceptional calibre and who have passed gruelling tests and lengthy periods of specialist training. By virtue of their personal qualities and the time and money spent in training them, they are extremely valuable human assets and cannot be squandered on tasks that are within the scope of conventional units.

UNCONVENTIONAL WARFARE DOMINANCE

The Joint Special Operations Task Force–North (JSOTF–North) was set up at short notice to carry out operations in Afghanistan during Operation Enduring Freedom. The roots of the new organization could be found in the OSS structures of World War II, and the new task force combined elements of both military special forces and CIA paramilitary forces.

The successes of the 5th Special Forces Group have already been noted, and the achievement was all the greater in view of the fact that 5th SFG was a tactical-level organization which was running a much broader operational campaign than it had originally been designed to cope with.

The 5th SFG had to metamorphose into a joint command and control structure on the move and there have been suggestions with hindsight that, had a larger and more complex unconventional warfare structure already been in place, fewer members of the Taliban and al-Qaeda might have escaped across the borders into Afghanistan and, who knows, Osama bin Laden himself might have been caught.

Questions could therefore be raised: firstly about the organization and structure of the unconventional warfare community, including the relationship between the intelligence services and the military, naval and air force special operations commands; secondly about the relationship between the unconventional warfare community and their national elite and conventional forces; and thirdly the relationship between the US unconventional warfare community and other national special forces such as the British SAS, Australian SASR, New Zealand SAS, French and German special forces and so on. To what extent were the British SAS tuned into US operations at Tora Bora and elsewhere, and how much did they consider they were more effective operating with minimal outside interference.

In Afghanistan the United States effectively got by on a shoestring. Part of the reason for this is that the style of warfare being waged by the Northern Alliance fitted well with the style of special operations forces. Both groups had a tradition of rugged independence, endurance and ingenuity. In view of the nature of the country

DESIRED OPERATIONAL CAPABILITIES

Personnel survivability – improve the survivability of personnel operating in hostile areas.

Counter WMD – improve their ability to perform SOF counter-proliferation missions.

Mobility in denied areas – improve their ability to conduct undetectable ground, air, sea, and (possibly) space mobility operations in areas where conventional forces are denied access.

Recruitment and leader development – improve their ability to recruit, select, assess, train, and retain SOF leaders with strong legal, ethical and moral foundations.

Information avenues – improve the effective use of information technologies across a wide range of SOF capabilities.

Sensory enhancements – improve their ability to augment human sensory systems to provide increased performance.

Organizational design – improve the ability of the SOF organizational structure to integrate, operate, and sustain activities with DoD forces and national and international agencies.

Space and UAV utilization – improve their ability to fully interface and operate within the space surveillance network.

Remote reconnaissance – improve their ability to utilize advances in technology for remote reconnaissance and mission situational awareness.

Versatile weapons – improve multi-role/multi-purpose weapons with target discrimination and broader range of effects.

A soldier of the German **Kommando Spezialkrafte** *(KSK) keeps watch in Afghanistan. He carries a Heckler & Koch G36 assault rifle.*

they were fighting in, this was the ideal form of warfare.

When Iraq was invaded the expectation was fulfilled to some extent that the United States would use overwhelming military power to subdue its adversary. Once again, however, special forces played a key role and, in view of the fact that the United States was prevented from bringing heavy ground forces into northern Iraq, special forces once again proved crucial to success.

To some extent it is barely surprising that the world's only superpower should be able to knock out a Middle Eastern country like Iraq. Soviet-supplied T-55 tanks were no match against American Abrams or British Challenger II main battle tanks. But as has since been seen, however, the key to winning the war was not the initial conflict stage but the post-conflict resolution.

In addition, the United States' propensity for wiping out its foes would not earn it friends in the developing world, no matter how heinous the crimes of the regime in question. If the United States was the only superpower, its best course of action was not to flaunt the fact lest it should set

AUSTRALIAN SPECIAL FORCES IN EAST TIMOR (1999)

Australian special forces were deployed before the intervention of Australian peacekeeping forces in East Timor in 1999. Indonesia had agreed to a United Nations-sponsored referendum for independence after 25 years of rule over the former Portuguese colony. A United Nations Mission in East Timor (UNAMET) was established to oversee the process, which resulted in an overwhelming vote for independence by the local population.

In protest, pro-Indonesian militias started a campaign of violence, looting and arson. Many East Timorese were killed and some hundreds of thousands displaced displaced. A United Nations Security Council resolution authorised the creation of the International Force in East Timor (INTERFET), which began to arrive in September 1999.

The Australian Special Air Service Regiment (SASR) is based on the Australian Z Special Unit and independent commando companies from World War II and was officially established as the Special Air Service Regiment in 1964.

In advance of the movement of the main Australian force, units of the SASR carried out reconnaissance on land while Navy Clearance Diving Teams (CDT) searched Dili harbour for mines and any other traps and obstacles.

The SASR and CDT teams were inserted covertly by submarine and then deployed to the shore to carry out their reconnaissance. The SASR took up covert positions to monitor the movement of nearby Indonesian forces and provided detailed reports on both Indonesian army and local militia movements. The reports were passed directly to the Australian Defence Force (ADF) and to the secret Defence Signals Directorate (DSD).

Once the INTERFET force had arrived, 3 Squadron SASR continued to provide reconnaissance for the INTERFET force. As part of their hearts and minds operations, the SASR also carried out liaison with the FRETILIN guerrilla movement FALINTIL.

off a gang effect in opposition. In this regard special forces had the advantage of presenting a lower profile and a less overtly aggressive one. The United States 9/11 Commission recommended that:

> 'Lead responsibility for directing and executing paramilitary operations, whether clandestine or overt, should shift to the Defense Department [i.e. away from the Central Intelligence Agency (CIA)]. There it should be consolidated with the capabilities for training, direction, and execution of such operations already being developed in the Special Operations Command.'

This recommendation was partly in view of the fact that the CIA did not have a military command structure or forces of its own and therefore had to resort to using 'private armies' to achieve its ends.

In Afghanistan, the CIA deployed agents before the end of September 2001 and these played an important role in helping to bring down the Taliban regime in collaboration with the special forces. Coordination was paramount, following the

9/11 Commission's recommendation that both the Department of Defense and the CIA should reach 'mutual agreement on the tactical and strategic objectives for the region and a clear delineation of operational responsibilities to prevent conflict and duplication of effort'. In Afghanistan, the CIA was responsible for providing supplies directly to the partisan forces of the Northern Alliance. In future, special forces would have the authorization to do this directly themselves.

CIA SPECIAL ACTIVITIES DIVISION (SAD)

The United States Central Intelligence Agency incorporates a National Clandestine Service of which the Special Activities Division (SAD) is a part. The Special Activities Division is divided into two sections – one for covert political action and the other for paramilitary special operations. The Political Action Group within the SAD covers a range of influences, including psychological, economic, political and cyber.

The paramilitary operations are carried out by the Special Operations Group (SOG) incorporated within SAD. The primary mission for the SOG is gathering intelligence in hostile territories in a covert manner and influencing events without overt involvement from the US Government.

Operatives with SOG would not be readily identified as US personnel. Typical involvement for such paramilitaries would be assistance in hunting down high-value targets. SOG operators were responsible for the tracking of Osama bin Laden's courier to the Abbottabad compound, after which they set up a CIA safe house that provided information for the planning of the SEAL Team 6 attack.

SAD and SOG operatives carry on operations in 'denied' areas and have been responsible for capturing a large number of key al-Qaeda operators. SAD/SOG paramilitary forces operated with considerable success in Afghanistan where they set up and ran Counterterrorism Pursuit Teams (CTPTs).

By 2010 there were about 3000 operators in these teams and they were deployed both in known conventional combat areas as well as in remote tribal areas where there was no other official government or military force present. The units also operated across the Pakistan–Afghanistan border, where they targeted al-Qaeda and Taliban personnel.

OPERATION JAWBREAKER

'Jawbreaker' was a codename given to the CIA team that was deployed into northern Afghanistan after the terrorist attacks in New York in 2001. It was also known as the Northern Afghanistan Liaison Team (NALT). The CIA presence was in advance of and to some extent paved the way for the deployment of US special forces in the region, whereupon the collaboration with indigenous Afghan forces would be intensified.

The CIA team set up a base near Barak, armed

A US Navy SEAL aims a SCAR-H battle rifle during a training exercise. The SCAR is the weapon of choice for many US special forces today.

Facing page: A US Marine Corps CH-46E Sea Knight helicopter assigned for special forces duty is marshalled into position as it lands on the flight deck of the USS Harpers Ferry (LSD 49).

with AK-47 automatic rifles, 9mm (0.35in) handguns, satellite communications and several million dollars. The money was given to senior officers in the Northern Alliance so that they could equip their forces with weapons.

The CIA collected intelligence about the possible whereabouts of Osama bin Laden and the location of al-Qaeda training camps and they recce'd the positions of Taliban forces. By 19 October 2001, a detachment from US 5th Special Forces Group was inserted into the area, bringing with it laser target designators to call in air power against the Taliban.

US MARINE CORPS COUNTER-INSURGENCY DOCTRINE

The changes that would place special operations at the forefront of strategic thinking also had a knock-on effect on other commands. As in Great Britain, where elements of elite regiments such as the Parachute Regiment and Royal Marines became tied into a permanent Special Forces Support Group, so did the United States Marine Corps review its basic warfighting concepts.

The Corps planned to meet the challenges of a number of irregular wars often fought in urban environments and against highly adept enemies

US Marines undergo training at Marine Corps Forces Special Operations Command (MARSOC). MARSOC is used to carry out intelligence-gathering and counter-terrorism operations.

that used asymmetric warfare tactics in order to inflict maximum damage to their enemy with the least amount of exposure to themselves. In order to achieve this, the US Marine Corps recognized that it needed to further enhance its integration

A soldier of 1st Battalion 501st Parachute Infantry Regiment (PIR) prepares to move off during Exercise Talisman Sabre in 2005, conducted by US and Australian forces.

and coordination with US Special Operations Command. The key change in thinking was the acceptance that the special operations model was the one to follow rather than expecting conventional forces trained and equipped to fight in major combat engagements against similarly trained and equipped forces to somehow adapt themselves to the very different requirements of irregular warfare.

The sort of concepts outlined elsewhere in this book that have traditionally informed the thinking and action of special forces now had to be absorbed and learned to some extent across the whole spectrum of conventional units and commands but most especially by those with an elite fast deployment capability and tradition, such as marines and air mobile forces.

As has been seen in Iraq, the destruction of the overt military power of a regime does not necessarily end the war. The war against ongoing insurgency and terrorism is a war of ideas as well as military skill. In this respect, special forces have an advantage. Winning hearts and minds has always been an important element of special forces training and an aspect not fully appreciated by the casual observer due to the headline-grabbing nature of some of their more spectacular operations, such as hostage rescue. In the post-World War II era, apart from the Korean War, aspects of the war in Vietnam, the stand-off against the Soviet Union in Western Europe and Operation Desert Storm, many of the wars have been 'small wars' and many of these, as shown in this book, have involved special forces.

What is perhaps new in the twenty-first century is the phenomenon of trans-national extremist ideologies and their ability to foment discontent in both undeveloped as well as developed nations. In undeveloped nations the basis of the discontent might be poverty and corrupt institutions and in developed nations the basis of discontent might be a sense of alienation from the predominant national culture, often exacerbated by Western liberal policies of multiculturalism. The ability to co-opt regional groups and to motivate them and enable them to express their grievances in ways that grab world headlines has demonstrated the relative success of this phenomenon.

Freedom-class littoral combat ship USS Freedom *(LCS 1) returns to Pearl Harbor, Hawaii.*

HOLISTIC APPROACH

In order to counter the disruptive effects of this kind of insurgency and terrorism, the US Marine Corps doctrine takes a more holistic view of its engagement in any conflict scenario. In addition to combat operations, they also identify the following components as required variables in any campaign:
- Training and advising host nation security forces
- Providing essential services
- Promotion of governance
- Economic development
- Information operations

In addition, since counter-insurgency operations are often conducted amidst a civilian population, small, independently active units are best equipped to operate in such an environment.

Small units are also better able to form close relationships with the local population, as opposed to large units that tend to be confined in remote bases. Instead of rigid military structures, new commanders must be trained to survive in a chaotic environment with multiple choices and solutions. The best military solution in the short term might

LITTORAL COMBAT SHIP

Freedom Class LCS-1 (Lockheed Martin)
Independence Class LCS-2 (General Dynamics)
The next-generation Littoral Combat Ship was due to be delivered to the US Navy in 2007. Smaller than the US Navy's guided missile frigates, it is designed for high-speed mobility, easy interoperability with small to medium-sized helicopters and with the potential to provide a platform for a wide range of missions. The ship can also carry out mine countermeasures, interception and a range of other missions.

The competing design to the Lockheed Martin single-hull ship was the General Dynamics catamaran design. The Department of Defense decided to build two of each type of ship in order to properly assess their strengths and weaknesses, and so that an optimum design mixing the best features of both could be agreed upon. It is expected that up to 55 ships in the Littoral Combat Ship class will eventually be built.

not be the best way of resolving the long-term problem. Good intelligence-gathering will also be a key factor here.

The sum total of this well thought out and far sighted programme is that the US Marine Corps will be adopting a model similar to that already successfully employed by special forces throughout the world. This in itself is not surprising as the US Marine Corps trains its own special operations capable forces.

BRITISH SPECIAL FORCES
Special Forces Support Group (SFSG)
In Britain the expansion of the special forces component was manifested in the creation of the Special Forces Support Group on 3 April 2006. This was a purpose-built unit on permanent standby to provide the sort of backup to special forces activity that was seen in the rescue of British soldiers in Sierra Leone (Operation Barras). Whereas before, this backup had been provided on an ad hoc basis, the constant demands on special forces on the ground in the wake of the 9/11 created a requirement for a permanently available force.

The new group is comprised of members of the Parachute Regiment, the Royal Marines and the RAF Regiment, all of whom wear their parent unit insignia as well as the Special Forces Group dagger and lightning badge. Having already passed the P Company Parachute Regiment selection course, the Royal Marines Commando Course or the RAF pre-parachute course,

SFSG members also carry out specialist training from the group's centre in St Athan, near Cardiff in Wales. The Welsh SFSG base is, of course, not a million miles away from the Brecon Beacons, one of the favoured training grounds of the SAS and other specialist units.

As was seen in Operation Barras, what would be required of the SFSG would be fire support and force protection, delivered with the kind of speed and agility that can dovetail with the characteristic

Facing page: British Marines of 45 Royal Marine Commando on patrol in southeast Afghanistan during Operation Condor, May 2002.

lightning-fast strikes of units such as the SAS and SBS. Another advantage of the Special Forces Support Group is that it has allowed the United Kingdom to expand its special forces element without compromising the quality of the core units, namely the SAS and SBS.

Special Reconnaissance Regiment
The Special Reconnaissance Regiment was established at the Royal Military Academy Sandhurst on 6 April 2005 as part of the United Kingdom special forces. The unit is thought to be based near Hereford, which is the base of the SAS.

The idea behind the Special Reconnaissance Regiment is to free other regiments within the special forces group from carrying out the reconnaissance aspect of special forces work, thereby leaving them to carry out offensive action. The unit is known to have been formed from 'existing assets' and these are thought to include members of the Intelligence Corps and the 14th Intelligence Company. As with the Special Forces Support Group, members of the unit will wear both their parent unit badges and the new SAR badge, which consists of a Greek hoplite style helmet, a dagger and the word 'Reconnaissance'.

The skill of reconnaissance personnel lies in keeping out of contact with the enemy, while coming close enough to observe enemy movements and activities. They are normally tasked with covert insertion into a particular location, finding a suitable place to lie up with their advanced optical and communications equipment, passing relevant information back to base and, at the close of the operation, exfiltrating without being seen. SRR members are trained to operate in both urban and field environments.

Although trained to keep out of direct contact with the enemy, SRR personnel have a high level of skill in hand-to-hand combat. They are also highly proficient in escape and evasion and living off the land.

FRANCE
Commandement des Opérations Spéciales (COS)
Like the United States and Great Britain, France has carried out a reorganization of its special forces

COMMANDEMENT DES OPÉRATIONS SPÉCIALES (COS)

1st Ring
Régiment Parachutiste d'Infanterie de Marine (RPIM)
Commandos-Marine (FORFUSCO) *Jaubert, Trepel, De Penfentenyo, De Montfort, Hubert*
Commandos Parachutistes de l'Air N°10 (CPA)
13ème Régiment des Dragons Parachutistes (RDP)
Division des Opérations Spéciales (DAOS)
Antenne CIET
Escadrille des Hélicoptères Spéciaux (EHS)

2nd Ring
Groupement des Commandos Parachutistes (GCP)
URH 27 de la 27e BIM
Groupement de Sécurité et d'Intervention de la Gendarmerie Nationale (GSIGN)

Brigade des Forces Spéciales Terre created for special operations:
1st Régiment Parachutiste d'Infanterie de Marine
13th Régiment de Dragons Parachutists
Détachement Aviation Légère de l'armée de terre des Opérations Spéciales (DAOS)

COS units have been involved in the following deployments:

1992:	Comorros
1992–93:	Somalia
1993:	Adriatic
	Guinea
	Zaire
1994:	Rwanda
1994–present:	Bosnia
	Haiti
	Rwanda, Operation Azalée
1995:	Comorros
	Bulbuzard noir in the Adriatic
	Bangui
1996:	Alamandin 1
	Alamandin 2 with the 8th RPIMa then 2nd REP and 1st RIMa
1996–97:	Bangui
1997:	Pélican 1 and 2 Brazzaville
	Albania
1998:	Bangui Guinea-Bissau
1999:	Kosovo
1999 & 2002:	Côte d'Ivoire
2003:	Congo

in the light of battle experience in the Gulf and the growing terrorist threat. The new organization was modelled on the structure of United Kingdom special forces and brought a range of naval, army and air force units under its umbrella.

It also incorporated the French gendarmerie unit *Groupe d'Intervention Gendarmerie Nationale* (GIGN). The COS force structure is primarily geared towards counter-terrorism operations and other operations such as the arrest of war crimes suspects. They also carry out reconnaissance missions.

RUSSIA
The use of the special forces model in the counter-insurgency battle has spread beyond the borders of the United States and Western Europe and is also now being developed in Russia.

In Chechnya and other republics of the North Caucasus, Russia has also been forced to contend with militant Islamism and to realize that its tactics to date, based on conventional methods and forces, have not been working well.

Like those of the United States, Russian armed forces have been primarily organized for major combat operations against a similarly armed opponent. When trouble arose in Chechnya, major ground and air forces were deployed in both 1994 and 1999, causing up to 100,000 deaths and the displacement of about 400,000 people.

In the light of ongoing failures to draw the line under the Chechen insurrection, in 2006

Facing page: A soldier from the **Régiment Parachutiste d'Infanterie de Marine** *(RPIM)* *trains in southern France.*

the Russian Security Council issued directives to security agencies operating in the Caucasus region to develop special forces capabilities and training with long-term programmes and revised doctrine.

The record of Russian special operations activities in recent years has been troubled by a heavy handed approach that has resulted in many casualties. On several occasions when Chechen rebels have taken hostages to promote their cause, the Russian special forces response has either failed outright or caused numerous casualties. This happened in both 1995 and 1996. In 2003, some 150 civilians were killed by a gas deployed by special forces when attempting to rescue hostages from a theatre. In 2004 there were 300 civilian casualties when Russian special forces stormed a school in Beslan, North Ossetia. Part of the reason for this high casualty rate was lack of coordination between different Federal forces.

New structures

As with the US, British and French special forces commands, the Russians carried out a programme of rationalization for their special forces in order

Russian special forces provide covering fire while an assault is carried out on the school building in Beslan held by Chechen gunmen, September 2004.

to bring them all under one command, known as the *Obedinennaya Gruppirvoka Voysk* (OGV) or Combined Group of Forces. The new structure includes an operational control group for each region in the North Caucasus (*Gruppa Operativnogo Upravleniya* [GROU]). The operations of these regional control groups are now fully coordinated so that more than one agency does not attempt to deal with the same crisis.

The new operational structure showed its effectiveness when in 2005 special forces led an attack against rebels who had taken over the town of Nalchik. The rebels were soon isolated and neutralized with minimal peripheral damage.

Russian special forces also use CAS missions in operations against rebels in mountainous regions, and their improved organization and training is said to be having a marked effect on the rebels using the mountains as their hideouts.

In the light of this success, specialist mountain warfare units were being trained and provided with the latest attack helicopters for close aerial support.

A Russian KA-52 Alligator helicopter performs at the Moscow International Air Show in 2001.

KA-52 ALLIGATOR

A development of the single-seat KA-50 Black Shark helicopter, the KA-52 Alligator is a two-seat multi-role all-weather combat helicopter that allows the pilot and co-pilot to fly the aircraft and handle all systems, including weapons systems. The helicopter is equipped with multi-functional on-board integrated flight, navigation and weapon control systems, and target acquisition is maximized through passive/active observation/search and sighting systems fully operable in either day or night conditions. Both pilots are equipped with helmets with built-in flight and sighting displays. The KA-52 Alligator is armed with a 30mm (1.18in) Shipunov 2A42 cannon and it can carry up to 2000kg (4400lb) of bombs and rockets on the two wing pylons.

In the future, the Russian defence ministry seeks to develop a group of special operations forces large enough to take on the sort of crisis that was presented in Chechynya in both 1994 and 1999. In other words, Russian thinking was identical to that in the West regarding the need to put special forces at the forefront of counter-insurgency operations.

The Russian Ministry of Internal Affairs also carried out a reorganization and rationalization of counter-terrorism assets on a similar basis to the Ministry of Defence. The *Departamenta po Bor'be s Organizovannoi Prestupnost'yu i Terrorizmom* (DBOPiT) or Organized Terrorism and Crime Centre, was set up to include a special forces command. This had responsibility for specialist

A Russian special forces sniper after the operation to rescue about 700 hostages from a Moscow theatre held by Chechen gunmen, October 2002.

police units, special rapid response anti-terrorist squads and also special forces units.

As in the United States, where the defence budget for special forces saw large increases, the Russian defence budget of 2006–2008 also saw generous allocations of financial resources for comprehensive re-equipping and upgrading of special forces equipment and associated aerial assets, including helicopters and ground attack fighters. A major challenge that remained for the Russians, however, was how to change the culture of their armed forces to enable the men on the ground to be more professional and motivated. It would take some time for the conscript culture and the inefficiencies of the Soviet era to be replaced by the kind of professionalism typical of special forces throughout the world.

UNMANNED AERIAL VEHICLES (UAVS)

Part of the reason for the deployment and importance of special forces is their ability to track down, observe and intercept enemy forces without being detected themselves. These aspects of the special forces mission are also being increasingly enhanced by the use of Unmanned Aerial Vehicles (UAVs) that can be deployed to provide additional intelligence on enemy movements and even targeting information.

Since the beginning of the War on Terror in 2001 there have been some 3000 fatalities and 20,000 other casualties among coalition forces. In order to reduce the ongoing attrition rate, the use of UAVs has been expanded and the technology has advanced by leaps and bounds.

The 10th Special Forces Group are known to have made use of UAVs for enemy observation during Operation Iraqi Freedom and their ongoing potential for special forces use is considerable, especially as some of the UAVs are man-portable, not much larger than a toy plane, can be launched by hand and are easily controlled with a joystick.

UAVs can be configured for a variety of operations, ranging across reconnaissance, target acquisition and direct action. The smallest UAV currently in use with the US Army and the one most applicable to army special operations is the Raven.

The Raven has a 1.52m (5ft) wingspan and is only 96.5cm (38in) long. It weighs about 2.04kg (4.5lb). When it is dismantled, the system fits neatly into three boxes that can be easily carried in a special forces Bergen. The airframe can carry three different types of camera: electrical optical,

Soldiers of 101st Military Intelligence Battalion load a RQ-7 Shadow 200 Tactical Unmanned Aerial Vehicle (UAV).

MQ-1 PREDATOR

Power plant: 101hp Rotax 914 four-cylinder engine
Length: 8.22m (27ft)
Height: 2.1m (6.9ft)
Weight: 512kg (1130lb)
Wingspan: 14.8m (48.7ft)
Speed: cruise speed 135kph (84mph); maximum speed 217kph (135mph)
Range: up to 730km (454 miles)

as UAVs designed to remain airborne for up to 12 hours in order to provide long-term observation.

USAF SPECIAL OPERATIONS

US 3rd Special Operations Squadron (SOS), attached to Air Force Special Operations Command (AFSOC), supports theatre commanders with both precision weapons as well as intelligence, surveillance and reconnaissance largely through its fleet of UAVs. In the new special operations environment, 'eyes on' from a UAV has become almost indispensable.

The main tool of the squadron is the MQ-1B Predator. The Predator is not only able to track targets, whether in motion or in fixed positions, but also if necessary to intercept and destroy them with Hellfire missiles. In 2005, the squadron logged 650 combat sorties in Afghanistan and 4243 sorties in Iraq. By 2007 the unit had grown to three times its original size.

infrared and side-mounted infrared. Different cameras are suitable for different missions: the optical camera will work well enough to identify men with weapons on a clear day whereas the IR cameras are better suited to less clear conditions where activity can be identified through hot spots.

US Special Operations Command operate both man-portable systems such as the Raven, as well

A fully armed MQ-9A Reaper taxis down a runway somewhere in Afghanistan, 2007.

MQ-1 Predator

Developed and built by General Atomics Aeronautical Systems, the MQ-1 Predator medium-

altitude, long endurance UAV has been in use since 1995 and seen combat in theatres as varied as Afghanistan, Bosnia, Kosovo, Iraq and Yemen. The system consists of a fixed-wing airframe and a Rotax four-cylinder engine powering a propeller at the rear of the air frame. It can be configured with a satellite data link and typical equipment includes a stabilized gimbal sensor with two colour video cameras and forward-looking infrared (FLIR) camera, and a synthetic aperture radar (SAR). The aircraft also has a multi-spectral targeting system linked to two on-board AGM-114 Hellfire missiles.

Normally the Predator is deployed as a system, as opposed to a single aircraft. This system comprises four aircraft, a ground control station, a Predator Primary Satellite link and about 55 personnel to both fly the aircraft and operate its various on-board systems. Each aircraft has one remote pilot and two sensor operators.

MQ-9A Reaper

US 333rd Special Operations Squadron also operates a system with the sinister name of Reaper. The MQ-9A Reaper carries out a more specific role than the Predator. The Reaper system is tasked with CAS, interdiction and special operations support. It is designed to locate and

An MQ-1 Predator in flight, somewhere over Afghanistan.

intercept fast-moving targets and to destroy them before they have the chance to respond or to find cover. Typical armaments for the MQ-9A Reaper include the GBU-12 laser-guided bomb, GBU-38 Joint Direct Attack Munition (JDAM), four Hellfire missiles and the GPS-plus-laser EGBU-12. The Reaper is four times heavier than the Predator and flies faster at greater altitude with a greater payload.

Fast-developing UAV technology is a new string to the bow of special forces. Either operated by advanced special operations teams on the ground or from remote base stations, UAVs can provide real-time intelligence in the dangerous environment of counter-insurgency as well as direct-attack capabilities, all without risking the lives of pilots and associated personnel.

The latest technology fits neatly into the growing spectrum of special operations capabilities. Far from the days when special forces were regarded as a useful adjunct to conventional forces, they have now become central, and with an influence so great, that conventional forces are to a greater or lesser degree re-modelling themselves in the special forces image.

THE HUNT FOR GADDAFI

During the Libyan civil war of 2011, the unseen face of British and French assistance to the Libyan National Transitional Council (NTC) as it fought against Colonel Gaddafi's loyal troops was the special forces element that helped to train the NTC irregulars and coordinate attacks by them.

Early in the conflict, Britain arranged for the airlift of 150 foreigners, including 20 Britons, from an airstrip in the south of Libya. The landing zone was secured by members of C Squadron, Special Boat Service (SBS), and the RAF C-130 Hercules safely transported the civilians to Malta.

To promote contacts with rebel leaders, the British Secret Intelligence Service (MI6) decided to send some representatives into Libya to meet them. They were accompanied by a highly secret group of special forces from what is known as E Squadron, drawn from both SAS and SBS ranks. This squadron was set up to perform highly delicate tasks in denied territory. Unfortunately the mission was compromised and the delegation was taken captive.

Despite this setback, men from D Squadron SAS were sent to the eastern part of Libya to assist the NTC with techniques such as target acquisition with tactical guidance equipment. The special forces provided real-time intelligence to the rebels through the use of unmanned aerial vehicles (UAVs) and other aerial assets. French special forces from the *Commandement des Opérations Spéciales* were also on the ground performing similar roles.

BENGHAZI ATTACK ON THE US CONSULATE, 2012: DELTA FORCE RESCUE

At about 21:40 on the evening of 11 September 2012, Islamic militants attacked the US diplomatic compound in Benghazi, shouting 'Allahu Akbar'.

Between 120 and 150 gunmen were involved in the assault on the embassy. They carried rocket-propelled grenades (RPG), hand grenades, AK-47 assault rifles and FN 2000 NATO assault rifles, mortars, diesel fuel canisters and heavy machine guns and anti-aircraft artillery mounted on trucks.

Diplomatic Security Service Special Agent (DSSSA) Scott Strickland moved US Ambassador J. Christopher Stevens and information management officer Sean Smith to the safe haven located within the building. Other DSSSAs moved to another building to retrieve M4 carbines but were unable to get back to the main building.

The rebels poured diesel fuel over the floor and furniture and set it alight, forcing Strickland, Stevens and Smith to come out of the safe haven and move to a bathroom with a small window. Strickland climbed out of the window but neither Stevens nor Smith followed him as they were both by now overcome by the smoke.

By 22:05, two ex-Navy SEALs of the CIA security team located in another building had heard of the attack and got into their armoured Toyota Land Cruisers, ready to offer aid. However, they were prevented from moving by an order from a senior CIA official on the site. When the CIA team eventually got to the embassy building, they managed to find Smith's body, but not Stevens'. The CIA agents put Smith's body in the vehicle and drove back towards the CIA building, being fired on as they went by the Islamic militants. They managed to keep the vehicle moving on flat tyres.

A US Army commando unit was at this time on stand-by at Naval Air Station Sigonella in Sicily but was not given the order to deploy. Two Joint Special Operations Command (JSOC) operators of 1st SFOD-D, or Delta Force, commandeered a small jet in Tripoli and flew to Benghazi. They moved to the CIA building at 05:00. Immediately after they arrived, the building came under attack. Two CIA operators were on the roof of the building manning an M46 machine gun. Mortar fire from the insurgents killed both of the CIA operators.

Using intelligence from an unmanned drone overhead, which indicated that insurgent reinforcements were on the way, the two Delta Force operators took urgent steps to evacuate all civilians into the available vehicles and head for the airport. Despite being shot at by the insurgents, they reached the airport safely. Throughout, the JSOC operators demonstrated the calm professionalism that is the hallmark of special forces. They had also shown the ability of special forces operators to take the initiative when assessing urgent developments on the ground.

A US Marine Corps Honor Guard carries the remains of J. Christopher Stevens and three other Americans, 14 September 2012.

CAPTURE OF ABU ANAS AL-LIBI, 2013

Abu Anas al-Libi, whose real name is Nazin Abdul-Hamed al-Ruqai, was high up on the terrorist wanted list for allegedly planning the bombing of US embassies in Nairobi, Dar es Salaam and Tanzania, which killed 224 people and wounded more than 4000. Al-Libi sought asylum in Britain after a conflict with the Gaddafi regime in Libya, but was soon taken in for questioning by London police under suspicion of terrorism. Al-Libi then left Britain, after which the United States placed a reward on his head for US$25 million, later reduced to US$5 million.

Al-Libi is believed to have been one of the founder members of al-Qaeda, and as such ranked as a high-value target for the US. The fact that he was living an apparently normal life in Tripoli, Libya, led to the planning of a sophisticated snatch operation, similar to those carried out by NATO special forces against targets in the Balkan wars.

The Federal Bureau of Investigation (FBI) and the Central Intelligence Agency (CIA) set up surveillance of al-Libi's movements in order to establish patterns of behaviour. This would have involved agents working undercover in vehicles and safe houses. The most regular and predictable part of his routine included regular attendance at morning prayers. This was also a good time for a snatch operation, as it was still relatively dark and there would be comparatively little traffic on the roads.

Having chosen the point at which they would intercept al-Libi, which was right outside his house, the agents and special forces organised a synchronized movement of tail, snatch and blocking vehicles, which would all meet at the same point. Blocking vehicles included those temporarily stopping the flow of civilian traffic into the area of operations.

As scheduled, in the early morning of 5 October 2013, al-Libi came out of his house and got into his car, before setting off towards the mosque. The moment he emerged, surveillance operators informed all other members of the operation of his movements. By the time he came out of the mosque, the tail, snatch and blocking vehicles were all in place and ready to move. As he drove away, a white Mercedes van with blacked-out windows tucked in behind him. In the van was a team of operators from Delta Force.

As al-Libi rounded the corner in front of his house and prepared to park, the white van moved round the left-hand side of his vehicle and pulled in diagonally in front of it, blocking further movement. A block car then arrived head-on from in front of al-Libi's car.

The rear sliding doors and the front passenger door of the van opened and a team of Delta Force soldiers leaped out. One pointed a handgun at al-Libi, another smashed the front window of his car and others whipped round to force open al-Libi's door and prevent him reaching for his personal weapon.

They then hauled him out of the car and bundled him into the back of the van. Once all the Delta Force operators were back in the van, it moved off at high speed, followed by the block cars, including the one blocking civilian traffic unseen

A courtroom sketch shows Ahmed Abu Khattala being arraigned in Washington, DC, on 28 June 2014.

in a road behind. A day after al-Libi was captured, he was in military custody on board the USS *San Antonio* in the Mediterranean Sea.

CAPTURE OF AHMED ABU KHATTALA, 2014

Ahmed Abu Khattala had commanded a small militia during the 2011 uprising against Muammar Gaddafi in Libya in 2011. The militia was called the Obeida Ibn al Jarra. He was suspected of taking part in the 2012 attack against the US diplomatic mission and CIA compound in Benghazi, which resulted in the death of Ambassador J. Christopher Stevens and three other Americans.

The Central Intelligence Agency (CIA) and Federal Bureau of Investigation (FBI) set up covert tracking of Khattala's movements as a prelude to an arrest operation. A meticulously planned operation based on Khattala's predictable and known movements was set up, involving both US Navy SEALs and 24 Delta Force commandos. On 14 June 2014, a day when Khattala had been involved

in militia activities in Benghazi, he then drove alone south from the city towards his home in the dark. He was unaware that he was being tracked by a US unmanned drone and that special forces teams had deployed nearby in unmarked cars and vans. There would have been no reason for him to be suspicious as he saw lights from other vehicles on the road until one of the vehicles got in front of him and forced him to stop, while a vehicle behind boxed him in.

Before he could reach for his gun, masked men ripped open his door and grabbed his weapon. In an instant he was bundled out of the door and a hessian sack was placed over his head. Then he was dragged over to a waiting van and flung into the back, where other strong arms held him down while his hands and legs were tied.

An Australian Special Operations Task Group soldier looks out over the valley during the Shah Wali Kot Offensive, 2010.

He would have lost all sense of direction, time and space as the van moved off at speed, escorted by the other vehicles. Then it came to a halt and he was hauled towards a waiting helicopter at a secret rendezvous in the desert.

Khattala would have had no idea where he was when the helicopter landed on the amphibious ship USS *New York* stationed in the Mediterranean Sea off the coast of Libya. As part of the interrogation process, confusion and bewilderment would have played into the hands of his questioners when the bag was finally taken off his head. He is expected to face trial in a US court for acts of terrorism.

INDEX

Page numbers in *italics* refer to illustrations.

INDEX

PICTURE CREDITS

Alamy: 155 (Jack Sullivan), 216 (EPA)

Australian Department of Defence: 150, 172, 192–195 all, 217

Cody Images: 9–14 all, 16, 19, 21, 32, 38, 40, 41(b), 42/43, 46, 52, 82

Corbis: 18 (David Rubinger), 54 (Liz Gilbert), 63 (Toronto Star), 66 (Peter Turnley), 80 (Reuters), 87 (Leif Skoogfors), 88 (Reuters), 94 (Giordanelli Claudia), 95, 99 (Jeremy Horner), 103 (Reuters), 104 (Herve Collart), 106 (Max Montecinos), 109 (Reuters), 119 (Reuters), 122 (Reuters), 125 (Patrick Robert), 126, 127 (Patrick Robert), 129 (Reuters), 132 (Alistair Wright), 133 (Reuters), 142 (Lynsey Addario), 146 (Reuters), 159 (EPA), 164 (Reuters), 169 (Kate Brooks), 174 (Reuters), 178 (Reuters), 189 (Reuters), 197 (Reuters), 204 (Reuters), 207 (Parrot Pascal), 208 (S. Dal), 210 (Reuters)

EMPICS/PA Photos: 145, 153

Getty Images: 6 (Popperfoto), 8 (Hulton), 58 (Scott Peterson), 76 (Mike Persson), 78 (Anja Niedringhaus), 86 (Gerard Juilen), 90 (Scott Peterson), 96 (Piero Pomponi), 97, 116, 120/121 (Bob Bishop), 128, 184, 186 (Odd Anderson/AFP), 187 (Dia Hamid/AFP), 209 (Oleg Nikishin)

Rex Features: 22 (Sipa Press), 35 (Joe Partridge), 37, 59 (Sipa Press), 92 (Sipa Press)

U.S. Department of Defense: 25, 26, 31, 36, 48, 51, 53, 56, 60, 62, 65, 67–72 all, 79, 85, 90, 100, 107, 110–113 all, 134–140 all, 143, 148, 149, 154, 157, 158, 160, 163, 166, 168, 170, 175, 176/177, 180–182 all, 185, 188, 190, 199–203 all, 211–215 all

U.S.Navy SEALs: 74, 75

All artworks © Amber Books except for:
Art-Tech/DeAgostini: 15, 23, 29, 39
Art-Tech/Aerospace: 50